Programming Win32 Under the API

Pat Villani

CMP Books
Lawrence, Kansas 66046

CMP Books
CMP Media, Inc.
1601 W. 23rd Street, Suite 200
Lawrence, KS 66046
USA
www.cmpbooks.com

Acquisitions Editor:	Berney Williams
Technical Editor:	Mike Wallace
Editor:	Michelle Dowdy
Layout Production:	Kristi McAlister
Cover Art Design:	John Freeman

Distributed in the U.S. and Canada by:
Publishers Group West
1700 Fourth Street
Berkeley, CA 94710
1-800-788-3123
www.pgw.com

ISBN: 1-57820-067-9

R&D Developer Series

To Donna:

for believing in me.

Table of Contents

Preface

Okay, okay, I admit; I'm a computer nerd, a geek. I can't help it. I started playing with computers when I was in high school. But I'm a nerd out of time. High school was Brooklyn Technical High School in the late sixties (1960s for you Y2K fanatics) and early seventies. We wore pocket protectors and slide rules hung off our belts. The computers were old IBM series computers familiar to relatively few people. I remember working with a friend to write a FORTRAN program to generate sin/cos/tan tables for trigonometry. When I went to college, the first programming course I took was in PL/I on an IBM 360. I wrote it on punched cards and submitted it as a batch job. For all my younger readers who are interested in ancient history, this meant handing the deck of cards over to a system operator, who took your deck and stuffed it in with all other decks from other students. The decks each ran sequentially and output was collected up for each deck, collated, and the results stuffed into bins for you to pick up anywhere from a few minutes to several hours later.

A lot has changed since then. The state of computing evolved from large mainframes running batch jobs to mainframes and minicomputers running time-sharing systems to the microcomputer revolution that has evolved to the desktop phenomenon we see today. However, as drastic as the evolution seems, certain aspects remain constant.

Throughout it all, these systems all ran operating systems to coordinate running programs and organizing resources. These operating systems — as radically different as they seem — all had common underlying principles that still exist today. For example, that first computer program required I/O redirection in order to specify where the data would come. I used JCL with a card that contained "//GO SYSIN DD*" to specify system input. Whether we call it SYSIN, STDIN, or CONIN$, the concepts of system input all share certain principles.

By now, you are probably screaming, "Enough with the history lesson!" Well, I am trying to make a point. More than one person has run away from Windows programming intimidated by the graphical programming model. Well, don't be intimidated — there is a whole operating system underneath that graphical layer and the way to get to it is through the Win32 API.

A word of warning: the Win32 API is a rich subject. There are hundreds and hundreds of API functions that span all current Microsoft operating systems, Windows 9X, Windows NT, Windows 2000, and Windows CE, as well as three Linux "Windows Emulators" — wine, twin, and twine. Due to the myriad of functions, attempting to cover this entire API would simply not do justice to either the reader, or the Win32 interface. Therefore, rather than cramming all this into one, unwieldy tome, I decided to cover the API in a different fashion.

This book takes a look at the API, not on a function-by-function basis, but on a more traditional operating system topic-by-topic basis. Rather than group a set of API functions and write about them, I pick a topic such as process or threads and relate how the Win32 API supports this operating system function. I decided to write this book this way because I felt that you, the reader, would prefer a book that is more than just a rehash of Microsoft's reference manuals. This is how I personally learn a new topic. I approach the topic at the concept level and then dive into the implementation.

I also try to peel back the covers and take a look at the underpinnings of the Win32 API. For example, most readers probably feel that the Win32 API is the system call interface for Windows 95, Windows 98, Windows CE, Windows NT, and Windows 2000. This is not the case at all and understanding how Microsoft implemented the Win32 API will help you write better code. Most of all, learning the differences between various Windows operating systems will give you the tools you need to make your code portable to run on all of them flawlessly.

Throughout this book, I present the design of the underlying operating system and show how the API relates to it. I used Microsoft Visual Studio v6.0 to create some examples presented in this book. Using Visual Studio, I present a simple method to perform I/O that bypasses the graphical system so that we can concentrate on the API calls seldom covered by other books. Other examples make use of the Free Software Foundations GNU gcc C compiler, included on the accompanying CD-ROM. I also create a project — our own version of the Windows NT cmd.exe command line interface — to tie it all together. By the time you finish this book, you will have a better understanding of the Win32 operating system interface and how to exploit the API's functionality to develop portable, industrial-strength applications.

Acknowledgments

Writing a book is a challenge. There is no step-by-step process to follow, so each book is a little different, and sometimes difficult to write. This book fell into the category of "somewhat difficult to write," not because the subject matter is difficult, but because it is constantly changing. The changes are a result of Microsoft listening to its customers and constantly fine-tuning their roadmap for Windows. Many of those changes occurred during the time I wrote this book. For example, the release of Windows Millennium Edition changed the ability to enter real mode. I took out some statements regarding real mode booting as a result. Another example is the release where the grand merge of MS-DOS-based and Windows NT-based versions of Windows will occur. It is now planned for the release code named "Whistler." These changes required constant monitoring of Microsoft product announcements, preview of Beta releases, and so on. Sometimes, this meant that I had to re-edit many chapters. But there was one far-reaching change that occurred that drastically changed this book: the dropping of support for the Compaq Computer Corporation Alpha processor. A lot of material discussing portability and comparing the Intel and Alpha versions of Windows NT — as well as examples that ran on Alpha platforms — were scrapped. My goal was to bring you, the reader, the most accurate and up-to-date information as possible. Including such Alpha examples would have served little or no purpose to many of you. The net result is that it took much longer for me to complete this book, but the book is better as a result.

Writing a book is also not a single person effort. Sure, my name appears on the cover and I did write this, but you would not be able to read this book if it wasn't for the efforts of all the people behind the CMP logo. The CMP staff is outstanding and their effort resulted in this high quality book. They also displayed a great deal of patience as the deadline for this book came and went. For that, I want to thank Berney Williams and Michelle Dowdy of CMP for working with me on this project. I also would like to thank Mike Wallace, the co-author with Pete Davis of the book *Windows Undocumented File Formats*. Their book was one of my references and I was delighted when Berney suggested that Mike review my draft. I thank Mike for the valuable technical feedback he provided. Finally, I want to thank Bill

Lanahan who reviews nearly every book and article that I write, and does a fantastic job of technical and grammar review as well as provide readability suggestions that improves the quality of what I write. Without the help of these individuals, there would be no book for you to read.

Pat Villani
`patv@opensourcedepot.com`

Chapter 1

Introduction to Win32

I wrote my first program in 1972. This program was a simple program given as a homework assignment to an engineering college freshman. It was trivial, not much more than the typical "Hello World" program used in introductory C programming textbooks. It was written in PL/1 and was entered into the computer via punched cards. The program was only about five cards thick with one statement per card. It required three more cards wrapped around it to invoke the compiler and identify which cards were program statements and which cards were data. These other cards contained JCL (Job Control Language) statements that were instructions to the operating system. The program was compiled and run in batch mode.

What does all this have to do with Windows and Win32? Actually, nothing other than to illustrate how radical the paradigm shift is between that older generation of computers and those we use today. Today's desktop computers are much faster than the mainframe I worked on as a college student. With that speed, new, more complex application and system software evolved to take advantage of these changes. One of the most radical changes was the window paradigm first introduced by Xerox PARC. This early research found its way into many of the current desktop operating systems such as Apple's MacOS and Microsoft's Windows family.

Along with this complexity in appearance, you can expect complexity in programming. A quick glance at the Microsoft reference manuals may overwhelm you with the sheer numbers of function calls. Microsoft certainly contributes some confusion by the grouping of virtually every DLL — such as the telephony API (TAPI) and more — into the Win32 API set. Lost in all this are the fundamental operating system calls we have come to expect. As a result, many a programmer develops ulcers as well as code. This may be viewed as simply a case of "too much of a good thing," so we will take a look at the basic structure behind the API.

APIs and System Calls

When you start out looking at writing a new application on a new operating system, one of your first tasks is to take a look at the resources available in your application. The questions that first come to mind are:

- How do I access these resources?
- What mechanisms do I use?
- Are there any libraries available that encapsulate the system calls?
- What languages are these libraries for?

Let's do that for the Win32 API and see what we find.

An Exercise: Getting the Scoop on the Win32 API

One way to get a better look at what composes the API is to study its components. Jumping ahead a bit, one file of interest found on a typical Windows 95 system is kernel32.dll. This file contains a good portion of the Win32 API that we will look at later. (We'll see how to determine this in a moment.) First, we create a small file that contains nothing but WinMain(). It is a useless program if you were to try to execute it because it simply loads and exits, but it is the simplest program we can generate to use as a tool for our exploration. This program is in Listing 1.1. As you can see, it consists of nothing more than a single #include of windows.h and WinMain(). It does absolutely nothing. It is, however, an excellent tool for us to use as we dig into the Win32 API.

Listing 1.1 Example Win32 "no op" program.

```
#include <windows.h>

int APIENTRY WinMain(HINSTANCE hInstance,
                     HINSTANCE hPrevInstance,
                     LPSTR     lpCmdLine,
                     int       nCmdShow)
{
    /*
     * Code normally goes here, but all we need is a simple
     * stub for WinMain.
     */

    return 0;
}
```

Since this program is not really executable but a fancy "no op," we obviously need some other tool to assist us in our exploration. To assist us in our detective work, we will use a program contained on the accompanying CD-ROM, objdump. It is a utility that will dump various parameters from any Win32 executable or library. Objdump is quite versatile, and can even be used to disassemble a file. As you can tell, it is a very powerful little utility that few people ever use. A summary of the command line options is in Figure 1.1. It is a command-line-based utility that requires an MS-DOS command line prompt. To use it, open an MS-DOS Prompt window and invoke it as "objdump <file>".

Figure 1.1 `Objdump` **command line syntax.**

```
objdump  [options] objfile …

Options
        [-ahifCdDprRtTxsSlw] [-b bfdname] [-m machine] [-j section-name]
        [--archive-headers] [--target=bfdname] [--debugging] [--disassemble]
        [--disassemble-all] [--disassemble-zeroes] [--file-headers]
        [--section-headers] [--headers]
        [--info] [--section=section-name] [--line-numbers] [--source]
        [--architecture=machine] [--reloc] [--full-contents] [--stabs]
        [--syms] [--all-headers] [--dynamic-syms] [--dynamic-reloc]
        [--wide] [--version] [--help] [--private-headers]
        [--start-address=addr] [--stop-address=addr]
        [--prefix-addresses] [--[no-]show-raw-insn] [--demangle]
        [--adjust-vma=offset] [-EB|-EL] [--endian={big|little}] objfile...

at least one option besides -l (--line-numbers) must be given

supported targets: coff-go32 coff-go32-exe a.out-i386 srec symbolsrec tekhex
binary ihex
```

Now that we are equipped with objdump, a good place to start is with Ex1, our simple example. To start, build the example using make to generate our test executable, ex1.exe. With this binary in hand, we can now start to explore the interface a bit. We begin our exploration by simply running objdump on ex1.exe. We want to generate a disassembled output file of ex1.exe so we can inspect the code generated by the compiler. We do this through the command "objdump–disassemble ex1.exe" in an MS-DOS window. What we get is a full disassembly with all our symbols, e.g., we find our WinMain entry point along with many other symbols. Sometimes a disassembled output can be overwhelming, but in our simple program, there isn't much. This eliminates the traditional logic decoding normally performed when studying a disassembled program — justifying our choice of compiling WinMain by itself. When studying this disassembled output, we see that the code generated for WinMain() consists solely of a C entry and exit code. The compiled code also contains additional code that consists of run time libraries and C start up code. All this is very interesting, but where are the Win32 API calls? This time pedump comes to the rescue. Pedump simply takes one argument, the file name, and outputs its information to the console windows so our command is simply "pedump ex1.exe." We get a list of code entry points that match the Win32 API list published by Microsoft. We also get a reference to both `crtdll.dll` and `kernel32.dll`, as the files needed to satisfy these unresolved external references. Of particular interest to us is `kernel32.dll`. To find where this file is located, we run a simple file find from the Windows "Start" menu. Not very surprising, it shows up in `C:\WINDOWS\SYSTEM`. Further examination of this directory shows us that there are quite a few `*.dll` files in this directory. As it turns out, the Win32 API is a shared library (similar to the UNIX `*.so` files). The Win32 API is the collection of library functions, which act as an intermediary between application program and the underlying operating system. This is a convenient way for Microsoft to create a portable interface. In many ways, this is an old trick. On many UNIX systems, `libc`, the C library, is actually a shared library. Thanks to standardization, it is now the C API for many operating systems including MS-DOS and Windows NT/2000. What Microsoft created for its Win32-based operating systems is an environment where the program loader has the ability to load the binary and dynamically link it to the shared libraries that constitute the API. In Microsoft terms, this shared library is known as a Dynamic Link Library or DLL. In Windows 95/98 and Windows NT/2000, the fundamental Win32 API is contained in three files: `kernel32.dll`, `user32.dll`, and `gdi32.dll`. You can verify this by running `pedump` on these files as well and comparing them to the published Win32 API list. You'll find all those calls contained within those files plus some undocumented entry points. It seems that Microsoft, true to its heritage, has continued its inclusion of undocumented system calls.

Getting back to our `ex1.exe` program, we ran `pedump` to get a list of all imports or unresolved references shown in Table 1.1. In this table, you'll see two columns, one with a function name and another with an ordinal number. The ordinal number is a number assigned to a function used to find the offset of the label in the DLL. According to `pedump`, these are all resolved by `kernel32.dll`. This is very helpful information for us because it allows us to go back to our disassembled output to see what the API calls really looks like. Again, we don't want to get too hung up by the code generated by the compiler, so we choose `CloseHandle` as our test case. It is a simple API entry point that takes a single parameter as an argument, so tracing it will be relatively simple.

Table 1.1 `ex1.exe` **imports.**

Ordinal number	API function
1B	CloseHandle
51	DebugBreak
7D	ExitProcess
AA	FlushFileBuffers
B2	FreeEnvironmentStringsA
B3	FreeEnvironmentStringsW
B9	GetACP
BF	GetCPInfo

Ordinal number	API function
CA	GetCommandLineA
F7	GetCurrentProcess
106	GetEnvironmentStrings
108	GetEnvironmentStringsW
115	GetFileType
11A	GetLastError
124	GetModuleFileNameA
126	GetModuleHandleA
131	GetOEMCP
13E	GetProcAddress
150	GetStartupInfoA
152	GetStdHandle
153	GetStringTypeA
156	GetStringTypeW
174	GetVersion
199	HeapAlloc
19B	HeapCreate
19D	HeapDestroy
19F	HeapFree
1A2	HeapReAlloc
1A7	HeapValidate
1AD	InterlockedDecrement
1B0	InterlockedIncrement
1B5	IsBadReadPtr
1B8	IsBadWritePtr
1BF	LCMapStringA

Ordinal number	API function
1C0	LCMapStringW
1C2	LoadLibraryA
1E4	MultiByteToWideChar
1F5	OutputDebugStringA
22F	RtlUnwind
241	SetConsoleCtrlHandler
26A	SetFilePointer
26D	SetHandleCount
27C	SetStdHandle
29E	TerminateProcess
2AD	UnhandledExceptionFilter
2BB	VirtualAlloc
2BF	VirtualFree
2D2	WideCharToMultiByte
2DF	WriteFile

Next, we use a text editor to open the listing file. We do a text search to find where the call to CloseHandle is located. That code fragment is illustrated in Figure 1.2 (a). Searching again, we find another reference to it in a jump table in Figure 1.2 (b). In both cases, the call is simply a normal call or jump. This doesn't really tell us much because the same would be true of libc linkages, so it becomes necessary to further delve into the code.

When we ran pedump, it specifically referenced kernel32.dll for the DLL to satisfy its imports. This is somewhat different from what programmers working on another operating system may see for a system call. For example, MS-DOS programmers are familiar with the int 21h method of system calls. Under MS-DOS, each system call defines a number of registers that serve various purposes related to that call, and the int 21h acts as a call into the MS-DOS kernel itself, where the system call is serviced. In Win32-based operating systems, the system call is merely an undefined external reference as we saw earlier. This standardized API insulates the developer from the actual operating system "nitty gritties" so we really haven't uncovered anything about the operating system. To better understand the nature of Win32 operating systems, we will examine kernel32.dll.

Figure 1.2   `CloseHandle()` **assembly level calls.**

```
0040B506: E8 C5 F9 FF FF     call      __get_osfhandle
0040B50B: 83 C4 04           add       esp,4
0040B50E: 50                 push      eax
0040B50F: FF 15 FC 51 42 00  call      dword ptr [__imp__CloseHandle@4]
0040B515: 85 C0              test      eax,eax
0040B517: 74 09              je        0040B522


                                       (a)


_SetFilePointer@16:
  0040B710: FF 25 F0 51 42 00  jmp      dword ptr [__imp__SetFilePointer@16]
_SetStdHandle@8:
  0040B716: FF 25 F4 51 42 00  jmp      dword ptr [__imp__SetStdHandle@8]
_FlushFileBuffers@4:
  0040B71C: FF 25 F8 51 42 00  jmp      dword ptr [__imp__FlushFileBuffers@4]
_CloseHandle@4:
  0040B722: FF 25 FC 51 42 00  jmp      dword ptr [__imp__CloseHandle@4]


                                       (b)
```

We begin our search by locating the file. In a Windows 95 system, find locates the file in the Windows home directory, typically C:\WINDOWS\SYSTEM. We can look at it in much the same way as we did our ex1.exe example. We start by looking at the exports as we did earlier. Unlike ex1.exe, kernel32.dll exports many calls, including many undocumented ones, as mentioned earlier. What we want to do next is disassemble it, so that we can see the actual code that services the system call. We run objdump to disassemble kernel32.dll, which produces a very large output. When you search through this output, you find a subroutine call that very much resembles compiled code. (Whether or not this is the case, is only known to few developers who have access to the Windows 95 source code, but this is only of academic concern to us.) What we learned is that Microsoft, in creating the operating system, makes use of shared libraries in order to implement the published API. We will further investigate the relationship between the shared library and the underlying operating system later when we take a close look at the architecture of the various Win32-based operating systems.

If you've been reading along, but you didn't actually put the book down and run objdump and pedump for yourself, you're taking the wrong approach. Familiarization with objdump and the tools that follow are a necessity in peeling back the layers of the OS and really understanding the interactions between the OS and Win32 API. If you've been performing the experiments, then your understanding will continue to grow, and you'll retain more of the knowledge.

Now let's survey more of the tools that we will be using. These tools are all contained on the CD-ROM accompanying this book. They are a collection of various Open Source tools dedicated to Win32 operating systems. The CD-ROM contains both the executables and the source code, when available, allowing you to further study them or change them as you see fit.

Free Development Tools

One of the beauties of the Win32 operating systems is the vast amount of tools available for it. There are many web sites that promote shareware and freeware for Win32 operating systems. There are also quite a few traditional UNIX utilities ported to Win32. Of all of these, the Free Software Foundation GNU (GNU is Not UNIX) development tools were ported to generate code for Win32 operating systems. Included with this book is the mingw (Minimalist GNU for Windows) compiler port. This port includes the C/C++ compiler, Fortran compiler, assembler, linker, librarian, debugger, and other binary utilities. This is an impressive list of development tools and they are distributed under the FSF "copyleft" GNU Public License (GPL). They are distributed in binary form and source form. The mingw-specific changes are distributed as patches to be applied to the basic GNU gcc distribution. The major changes to the compiler suite are modifications to the linker to allow it to generate Win32 PE files and additional tools to assist in generating Win32-specific files such as DLLs.

A GNU gcc Overview

The GNU gcc compiler suite consists of separate compilers for each language. For example, there is a different program that compiles C programs and one that compiles C++ programs. These individual compilers are invoked through the use of a front end. This is a common UNIX design, as opposed to the more traditional Win32 compilers. In this design, for example, the language translation program generates an intermediate assembly file. The intermediate assembly file is later translated to an object file by the assembler to be finally converted to an executable by the linker.

To better understand how this works, we will take a quick tour of the GNU gcc suite. In Figure 1.3, we have an overview of the GNU compiler for the Win32 operating system. It borrows heavily from the traditional UNIX development model. The portion of the compiler that converts the code from a C or C++ source file actually calls three separate programs to accomplish its work. Hence, the command gcc -c file.c to create file.o is actually a wrapper for the preprocessor, language translator, and assembler. To combine the various object files into a singles excutable, gcc invokes ld under the covers. It is through this mechanism that the GNU compiler does its magic. Armed with this knowledge, we will now take a closer look at each part.

Figure 1.3   Win32 GNU compiler overview.

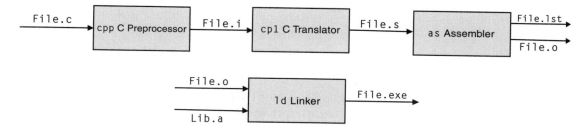

GNU C Compiler

The GNU C compiler is one of the language translator front ends that comes with gcc. The options and command line arguments, listed in Figure 1.4, are easy to remember and understand. It uses these arguments and options to determine which programs to use and the appropriate options for each. It then proceeds to sequentially invoke them. Although there is a small penalty for invoking separate executables for each phase of compilation, the design is solid and much more flexible than the more common Win32 design.

Figure 1.4   gcc command line options.

```
Usage: GCC.EXE [options] file...
Options:
  --help                      Display this information
  (Use '-v --help' to display command line options of sub-processes)
  -dumpspecs                  Display all of the built in spec strings
  -dumpversion                Display the version of the compiler
  -dumpmachine                Display the compiler's target processor
  -print-search-dirs          Display the directories in the compiler's search path
  -print-libgcc-file-name     Display the name of the compiler's companion library
  -print-file-name=<lib>      Display the full path to library <lib>
  -print-prog-name=<prog>     Display the full path to compiler component <prog>
  -print-multi-directory      Display the root directory for versions of libgcc
  -print-multi-lib            Display the mapping between command line options and
                                multiple library search directories
  -Wa,<options>               Pass comma-separated <options> on to the assembler
  -Wp,<options>               Pass comma-separated <options> on to the preprocessor
  -Wl,<options>               Pass comma-separated <options> on to the linker
  -Xlinker <arg>              Pass <arg> on to the linker
  -save-temps                 Do not delete intermediate files
  -pipe                       Use pipes rather than intermediate files
  -specs=<file>               Override builtin specs with the contents of <file>
  -std=<standard>             Assume that the input sources are for <standard>
```

```
-B <directory>        Add <directory> to the compiler's search paths
-b <machine>          Run gcc for target <machine>, if installed
-V <version>          Run gcc version number <version>, if installed
-v                    Display the programs invoked by the compiler
-E                    Preprocess only; do not compile, assemble or link
-S                    Compile only; do not assemble or link
-c                    Compile and assemble, but do not link
-o <file>             Place the output into <file>
-x <language>         Specify the language of the following input files
                          Permissable languages include: c c++ assembler none
                          'none' means revert to the default behaviour of
                          guessing the language based on the file's extension

Options starting with -g, -f, -m, -O or -W are automatically passed on to the various
sub-processes invoked by GCC.EXE.  In order to pass other options on to these processes
the -W<letter> options must be used.

For bug reporting instructions, please see:
<URL:http://www.gnu.org/software/gcc/faq.html#bugreport>.
```

For the GNU C/C++ compiler, the main front end is gcc. It is invoked in a DOS window or other command-line environment through a command line typed by the user. It analyzes the command line and determines which language translator to invoke. It calls the C compiler if you give it a source file ending in .c and calls the C++ compiler for files ending in .cc or .cpp. It also invokes the preprocessor, cpp. It invokes the assembler, as, once the source is translated to assembly language and finally acts as the front end for the linker.

Normally, the GNU C/C++ compiler has a separate utility invoked as cpp for the preprocessor. This is also true for mingw and it may be invoked by the command gcc -E. Gcc can search extra directories for include files using the -I option or the C_INCLUDE_PATH and CPLUS_INCLUDE_PATH environment variables. These environment variables can be set by including SET directives in Windows 95/98 autoexec.bat file, or manually setting the equivalent environment variables in the control panel for Windows NT. These directories will be searched after any directories specified with the -I option, but before the standard system directories.

GNU cpp **Preprocessor**

The preprocessor is the program in the GNU gcc compiler suite that performs text substitutions on your source code based on preprocessor directives as defined in the ANSI standard for the C and C++ languages. Generally speaking, you will not use the preprocessor directly. It is generally called indirectly by gcc for each C and C++ source file before the appropriate language translator is called. You may also invoke it indirectly through the -E option for gcc. The preprocessor is called cpp and may be found in the lib\gcc-lib\i386-mingw32\gcc-* directory.

The options for the preprocessor are listed in Figure 1.5. The command line form is:

```
gcc [options] file...
```

In addition, the preprocessor looks for environment variables C_INCLUDE_PATH and CPLUS_INCLUDE_PATH to determine which directories to search in addition to the -I. This is identical for gcc, as mentioned earlier, because gcc invokes the preprocessor, which in turn looks for these variables.

Figure 1.5   Preprocessor cpp command line options.

```
Usage: CPP.EXE [options] file...
Options:
  --help                    Display this information
  (Use '-v --help' to display command line options of sub-processes)
  -dumpspecs                Display all of the built in spec strings
  -dumpversion              Display the version of the compiler
  -dumpmachine              Display the compiler's target processor
  -print-search-dirs        Display the directories in the compiler's search path
  -print-libgcc-file-name   Display the name of the compiler's companion library
  -print-file-name=<lib>    Display the full path to library <lib>
  -print-prog-name=<prog>   Display the full path to compiler component <prog>
  -print-multi-directory    Display the root directory for versions of libgcc
  -print-multi-lib          Display the mapping between command line options and
                              multiple library search directories
  -Wa,<options>             Pass comma-separated <options> on to the assembler
  -Wp,<options>             Pass comma-separated <options> on to the preprocessor
  -Wl,<options>             Pass comma-separated <options> on to the linker
  -Xlinker <arg>            Pass <arg> on to the linker
  -save-temps               Do not delete intermediate files
  -pipe                     Use pipes rather than intermediate files
  -specs=<file>             Override builtin specs with the contents of <file>
  -std=<standard>           Assume that the input sources are for <standard>
  -B <directory>            Add <directory> to the compiler's search paths
  -b <machine>              Run gcc for target <machine>, if installed
  -V <version>              Run gcc version number <version>, if installed
  -v                        Display the programs invoked by the compiler
  -E                        Preprocess only; do not compile, assemble or link
  -S                        Compile only; do not assemble or link
  -c                        Compile and assemble, but do not link
  -o <file>                 Place the output into <file>
```

```
 -x <language>                  Specify the language of the following input files
                                Permissable languages include: c c++ assembler none
                                'none' means revert to the default behaviour of guessing the
                                language based on the file's extension

Options starting with -g, -f, -m, -O or -W are automatically passed on to the various
sub-processes invoked by CPP.EXE.  In order to pass other options on to these processes
the -W<letter> options must be used.

For bug reporting instructions, please see:
<URL:http://www.gnu.org/software/gcc/faq.html#bugreport>.
```

GNU as **Assembler**

Included as part of the GNU C/C++ package is the as assembler. It is an integral part of the package since the gcc front end invokes it during compilation. Thanks to its UNIX heritage, it is similar in command to the UNIX as assembler. It has extensions over the more traditional UNIX assembler in that it will generate listings, typically not done under UNIX. This is due to its development as a generic language translation package that includes support for embedded and cross-platform development. The command line options for as are in Figure 1.6. The command line form is:

```
as [option...] [asmfile...]
```

One word of warning to the user: as only works with the Free Software Foundation assembler mnemonics. This differs significantly from the familiar Intel mnemonics and more closely resembles the AT&T UNIX assembler mnemonics. The most notable change from the Intel mnemonics format is that the order of operands is reversed from the familiar Intel notation. Other changes include slight differences in the mnemonics and PE/COFF unique segments as opposed to the Intel user-definable sections.

Figure 1.6 as **command line options.**

```
Usage: C:\GCC-29~1.2\BIN\AS.EXE [option...] [asmfile...]
Options:
  -a[sub-option...]    turn on listings
    Sub-options [default hls]:
    c   omit false conditionals
    d   omit debugging directives
    h   include high-level source
    l   include assembly
    m   include macro expansions
```

```
     n    omit forms processing
     s    include symbols
     =file set listing file name (must be last sub-option)
    -D                        produce assembler debugging messages
    --defsym SYM=VAL          define symbol SYM to given value
    -f                        skip whitespace and comment preprocessing
    --gstabs                  generate stabs debugging information
    --help                    show this message and exit
    -I DIR                    add DIR to search list for .include directives
    -J                        don't warn about signed overflow
    -K                        warn when differences altered for long displacements
    -L,--keep-locals          keep local symbols (e.g. starting with `L')
    -M,--mri                  assemble in MRI compatibility mode
    --MD FILE                 write dependency information in FILE (default none)
    -nocpp                    ignored
    -o OBJFILE                name the object-file output OBJFILE (default a.out)
    -R                        fold data section into text section
    --statistics              print various measured statistics from execution
    --strip-local-absolute    strip local absolute symbols
    --traditional-format      Use same format as native assembler when possible
    --version                 print assembler version number and exit
    -W                        suppress warnings
    --itbl INSTTBL            extend instruction set to include instructions
                              matching the specifications defined in file INSTTBL
    -w                        ignored
    -X                        ignored
    -Z                        generate object file even after errors
    --listing-lhs-width       set the width in words of the output data column of
                              the listing
    --listing-lhs-width2      set the width in words of the continuation lines
                              of the output data column; ignored if smaller than
                              the width of the first line
    --listing-rhs-width       set the max width in characters of the lines from
                              the source file
    --listing-cont-lines      set the maximum number of continuation lines used
                              for the output data column of the listing
    -m                        do long jump

Report bugs to bug-gnu-utils@gnu.org
```

GNU ld **Linker**

In the GNU C/C++ compiler suite, the linker is called ld. The command line options for use with ld are in Figure 1.7. The command line for ld is:

```
ld [options] file...
```

Unlike the Microsoft link linker, ld possesses much more capabilities — allowing for development of executables other than those for Win32. It can create stand-alone executables for other environments, such as embedded, and other operating systems as well as Win32 Operating Systems. For most Win32 program development, you will probably never need to run ld by itself. Typically, the gcc front end discussed earlier is the mechanism used to link a program to create a Win32 executable. This is accomplished by specifying .o files instead of .c or .cpp files in the command file. For example, to create WinHello.exe from WinHello.o and WinOther.o, the command line you'd use would be:

```
gcc -o WinHello.exe WinHello.o WinOther.o
```

The advantage to using gcc instead of ld is that gcc invokes ld as part of its operation and possesses enough knowledge to know what start-up and language support libraries to include. Having a powerful linker available for your use is an advantage that quickly justifies learning about ld.

In addition to simple object files, ld will also search libraries. In the GNU C/C++ compiler suite, libraries are denoted by an .a suffix. This, again, follows the UNIX standard for filenaming thanks to its UNIX heritage. For example, if our previous example required a library, libhello.a, the above command would simply become

```
gcc -o WinHello.exe WinHello.o WinOther.o libhello.a
```

In this example, the linker would search the libhello.a library for components that satisfy any unresolved references resulting from the previous .o files and include them into Win-Hello.exe. This is a handy tool for virtually any project.

You can also tell gcc to use libhello.a through the use of a command line switch, -l. In this example, you would specify -lhello in the command line, which then expands the file specification to libhello.a internal to ld. This is also valuable because when used in combination with the -L option, it allows you to place common libraries in a single directory that can later be shared by multiple components of a project.

Order is important with both ld and gcc. Both check libraries in the order they appear and will only resolve references to symbols in libraries based on files preceding it. For example, specifying libhello.a first in our previous example would have caused the link to fail. Also, this forces you to take care in dividing functions between libraries. For example, if the file libhello.a has a dependency in libgoodbye.a, libhello.a must precede libgoodbye.a and the link would successfully complete. However, if libgoodbye.a also had dependencies in libhello.a, the link would fail.

As with the C preprocessor, both ld and gcc look for the environment variable LIBRARY_PATH to identify directories to find libraries. This environment variable can be set by including SET directives in Windows 95/98 autoexec.bat file, or manually setting the equivalent environment variables in the control panel for Windows NT.

Figure 1.7 Linker ld command line options.

```
Usage: C:\GCC-29~1.2\BIN\LD.EXE [options] file...
Options:
  -a KEYWORD                 Shared library control for HP/UX compatibility
  -A ARCH, --architecture ARCH
                             Set architecture
  -b TARGET, --format TARGET  Specify target for following input files
  -c FILE, --mri-script FILE  Read MRI format linker script
  -d, -dc, -dp               Force common symbols to be defined
  -e ADDRESS, --entry ADDRESS  Set start address
  -E, --export-dynamic       Export all dynamic symbols
  -f SHLIB, --auxiliary SHLIB  Auxiliary filter for shared object symbol table
  -F SHLIB, --filter SHLIB   Filter for shared object symbol table
  -g                         Ignored
  --gc-sections              Remove unused sections on certain targets
  --no-gc-sections           (Don't) Remove unused sections on certain targets
  -G SIZE, --gpsize SIZE     Small data size (if no size, same as --shared)
  -h FILENAME, -soname FILENAME
                             Set internal name of shared library
  -l LIBNAME, --library LIBNAME
                             Search for library LIBNAME
  -L DIRECTORY, --library-path DIRECTORY
                             Add DIRECTORY to library search path
  -m EMULATION               Set emulation
  -M, --print-map            Print map file on standard output
  -n, --nmagic               Do not page align data
  -N, --omagic               Do not page align data, do not make text readonly
  -o FILE, --output FILE     Set output file name
  -O                         Ignored
  -r, -i, --relocateable     Generate relocateable output
  -R FILE, --just-symbols FILE
                             Just link symbols (if directory, same as --rpath)
  -s, --strip-all            Strip all symbols
  -S, --strip-debug          Strip debugging symbols
  -t, --trace                Trace file opens
  -T FILE, --script FILE     Read linker script
  -u SYMBOL, --undefined SYMBOL
                             Start with undefined reference to SYMBOL
  -v, --version              Print version information
  -V                         Print version and emulation information
  -x, --discard-all          Discard all local symbols
```

```
-X, --discard-locals          Discard temporary local symbols
-y SYMBOL, --trace-symbol SYMBOL
                              Trace mentions of SYMBOL
-Y PATH                       Default search path for Solaris compatibility
-z KEYWORD                    Ignored for Solaris compatibility
-(, --start-group             Start a group
-), --end-group               End a group
-assert KEYWORD               Ignored for SunOS compatibility
-Bdynamic, -dy, -call_shared
                              Link against shared libraries
-Bstatic, -dn, -non_shared, -static
                              Do not link against shared libraries
-Bsymbolic                    Bind global references locally
--cref                        Output cross reference table
--defsym SYMBOL=EXPRESSION    Define a symbol
--dynamic-linker PROGRAM      Set the dynamic linker to use
-EB                           Link big-endian objects
-EL                           Link little-endian objects
--embedded-relocs             Generate embedded relocs
--force-exe-suffix            Force generation of file with .exe suffix
--help                        Print option help
-Map FILE                     Write a map file
--no-keep-memory              Use less memory and more disk I/O
--no-warn-mismatch            Don't warn about mismatched input files
--no-whole-archive            Turn off --whole-archive
--noinhibit-exec              Create an output file even if errors occur
--oformat TARGET              Specify target of output file
-qmagic                       Ignored for Linux compatibility
-Qy                           Ignored for SVR4 compatibility
--relax                       Relax branches on certain targets
--retain-symbols-file FILE    Keep only symbols listed in FILE
-rpath PATH                   Set runtime shared library search path
-rpath-link PATH              Set link time shared library search path
-shared, -Bshareable          Create a shared library
--sort-common                 Sort common symbols by size
--split-by-file               Split output sections for each file
--split-by-reloc COUNT        Split output sections every COUNT relocs
--stats                       Print memory usage statistics
--task-link SYMBOL            Do task level linking
--traditional-format          Use same format as native linker
-Tbss ADDRESS                 Set address of .bss section
-Tdata ADDRESS                Set address of .data section
```

```
         -Ttext ADDRESS              Set address of .text section
         -Ur                         Build global constructor/destructor tables
         --verbose                   Output lots of information during link
         --version-script FILE       Read version information script
         --version-exports-section SYMBOL
                                     Take export symbols list from .exports, using SYMBOL as
                                     the version.
         --warn-common               Warn about duplicate common symbols
         --warn-constructors         Warn if global constructors/destructors are seen
         --warn-multiple-gp          Warn if the multiple GP values are used
         --warn-once                 Warn only once per undefined symbol
         --warn-section-align        Warn if start of section changes due to alignment
         --whole-archive             Include all objects from following archives
         --wrap SYMBOL               Use wrapper functions for SYMBOL
C:\GCC-29~1.2\BIN\LD.EXE: supported targets: pe-i386 pei-i386 srec symbolsrec tekhex
binary ihex
C:\GCC-29~1.2\BIN\LD.EXE: supported emulations: i386pe
C:\GCC-29~1.2\BIN\LD.EXE: emulation specific options:
i386pe:
   --base_file <basefile>         Generate a base file for relocatable DLLs
   --dll                          Set image base to the default for DLLs
   --file-alignment <size>        Set file alignment
   --heap <size>                  Set initial size of the heap
   --image-base <address>         Set start address of the executable
   --major-image-version <number>    Set version number of the executable
   --major-os-version <number>       Set minimum required OS version
   --major-subsystem-version <number> Set minimum required OS subsystem version
   --minor-image-version <number>    Set revision number of the executable
   --minor-os-version <number>       Set minimum required OS revision
   --minor-subsystem-version <number> Set minimum required OS subsystem revision
   --section-alignment <size>     Set section alignment
   --stack <size>                 Set size of the initial stack
   --subsystem <name>[:<version>]    Set required OS subsystem [& version]
   --support-old-code             Support interworking with old code

Report bugs to bug-gnu-utils@gnu.org
```

GNU ar **Librarian**

The GNU ar librarian allows you to collect a set of object files, .o, into a single file. The resulting file is the library file, typically ending with .a, that the linker scans. This allows you to group related files and better manage your project.

The librarian options are listed in Figure 1.8. Each main option listed performs a simple function, such as delete or add. The option may then be followed with a command modifier to further refine the function. The command line form is:

```
ar [-]{dmpqrstx}[abcilosSuvV] [member-name] archive-file file...
ar -M [<mri-script]
```

Figure 1.8 Egcs ar **librarian**.

```
Usage: C:\GCC-29~1.2\BIN\AR.EXE [-]{dmpqrstx}[abcilosSuvV] [member-name] archive-file
file...
        C:\GCC-29~1.2\BIN\AR.EXE -M [<mri-script]
commands:
 d              - delete file(s) from the archive
 m[ab]          - move file(s) in the archive
 p              - print file(s) found in the archive
 q[f]           - quick append file(s) to the archive
 r[ab][f][u]    - replace existing or insert new file(s) into the archive
 t              - display contents of archive
 x[o]           - extract file(s) from the archive
command specific modifiers:
 [a]            - put file(s) after [member-name]
 [b]            - put file(s) before [member-name] (same as [i])
 [f]            - truncate inserted file names
 [o]            - preserve original dates
 [u]            - only replace files that are newer than current archive contents
generic modifiers:
 [c]            - do not warn if the library had to be created
 [s]            - create an archive index (cf. ranlib)
 [S]            - do not build a symbol table
 [v]            - be verbose
 [V]            - display the version number

Report bugs to bug-gnu-utils@gnu.org
```

GNU gbd **Debugger**

The GNU gdb debugger is a powerful source level debugger for the mingw32 GNU C/C++ compiler suite. It can single step, break, watch variables, etc. The gdb command line options are listed in Figure 1.9. The command line form is:

```
gdb [options] [executable-file [core-file or process-id]]
```

However, it is not simply a command line program that is invoked, performs its function, and then exits. It is an interactive, interpreted program that accepts command line directives to perform typical debugging functions.

The best way to understand how to use gdb is to begin using it. We will walk through a gdb session so that we can see how it works. Upon start up, gdb outputs an introductory screen as seen in Figure 1.10.

Gdb is a text-based, interactive debugger that is very powerful. In order to use it, you must build your executable using the -g option on gcc. We can build our example with the command line

```
gcc -g -o ex1.exe ex1.c
```

which turns on debugging and creates the executable ex1.exe. With debugging turned on, we can proceed with our debugging session using ex1.exe.

Figure 1.9 gdb **command line options.**

```
This is the GNU debugger.  Usage:


    gdb [options] [executable-file [core-file or process-id]]


Options:

   -b BAUDRATE        Set serial port baud rate used for remote debugging.
   --batch            Exit after processing options.
   --cd=DIR           Change current directory to DIR.
   --command=FILE     Execute GDB commands from FILE.
   --core=COREFILE    Analyze the core dump COREFILE.
   --dbx              DBX compatibility mode.
   --directory=DIR    Search for source files in DIR.
   --epoch            Output information used by epoch emacs-GDB interface.
   --exec=EXECFILE    Use EXECFILE as the executable.
   --fullname         Output information used by emacs-GDB interface.
   --help             Print this message.
   --mapped           Use mapped symbol files if supported on this system.
   --nw               Do not use a window interface.
   --nx               Do not read .gdbinit file.
   --quiet            Do not print version number on startup.
   --readnow          Fully read symbol files on first access.
   --se=FILE          Use FILE as symbol file and executable file.
   --symbols=SYMFILE  Read symbols from SYMFILE.
   --tty=TTY          Use TTY for input/output by the program being debugged.
   --version          Print version information and then exit.
   -w                 Use a window interface.
```

```
--write              Set writing into executable and core files.
--xdb                XDB compatibility mode.


For more information, type "help" from within GDB, or consult the GDB manual (available
as on-line info or a printed manual).
Report bugs to "bug-gdb@prep.ai.mit.edu".
```

Figure 1.10 gdb introductory screen.

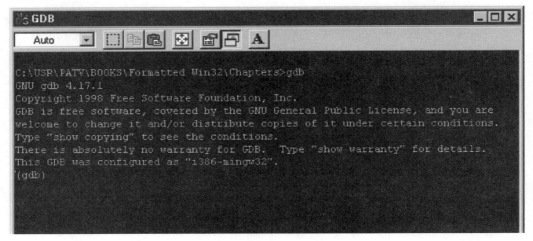

The first command we want to try is the list command, abbreviated 1. Simply typing "1" at the gdb prompt followed by Enter yields the screen in Figure 1.11. As you can see, gdb is completely a source level debugger and our listing shows exactly the first ten lines of our source file. You can additionally specify the address of the listing by adding the line number as in "list 15." Naturally, we want to run the program, but we'd like to stop it as soon as it enters WinMain. This is usually a convenient breakpoint as it is initially past the C initialization code, but before execution of our first line of code. To do this, type "break WinMain" then "r." The program starts and stops at the first line of code in WinMain (line 17 for this example). If you've been following along, you should now have a display similar to Figure 1.12. Unfortunately, there isn't much more we can do with this example but when we get to other, more complex examples, you'll be able to single step, trace through call frames, etc. If you're interested in finding out about more commands, type "help" and follow the instructions for getting more detailed help about any command. For now, just type the letter "q" to quit.

Figure 1.11 gdb **list.**

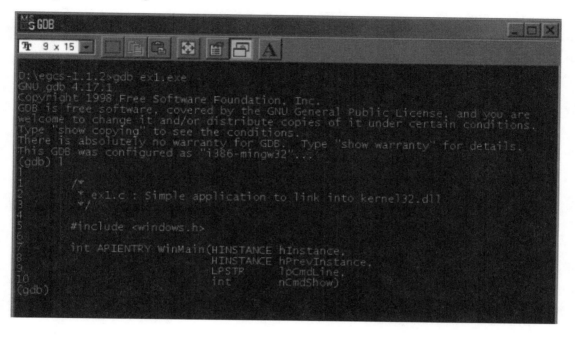

Figure 1.12 gdb **breakpoint example.**

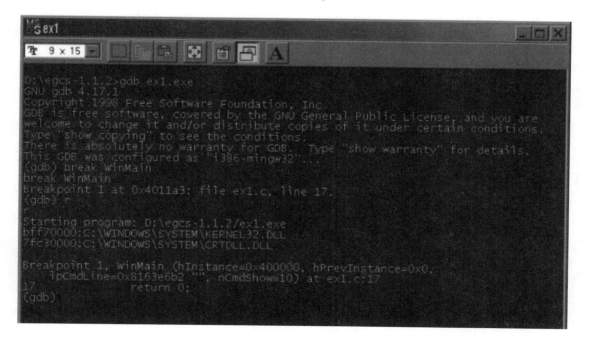

Where to Get More Information

The CD-ROM that accompanies this book contains full documentation for the GNU Compiler Suite. This information is contained in the \gcc\doc directory and is in html form. You can use your favorite browser to view this documentation. Simply point your browser to the appropriate index.html file. For example, to view the gcc documentation, point your browser to \gcc\doc\gcc\index.html. This documentation is much more detailed than the simple overview presented here. The disk also contains the source code for these tools allowing you to examine or modify any or all of the tools. Examine the \gcc\src directory for instructions on how to rebuild these tools, license, etc. Although not as fancy as commercial development tools, it is an excellent, low cost way to develop Win32 programs.

Disassemblers

If you're like me, the last heading you expected to see was "Disassemblers." In my mind, this immediately conjures up the image of some disheveled geek in a back room or basement studying reams of disassembled listings to uncover the internals of a commercial package. Frankly, I don't think I fit that description so I avoided using them. I also read, with some trepidation, various license agreements that warned me about stiff penalties for reverse engineering their product. Naturally, I didn't want any sort of civil action taken against me so I avoided these tools like a plague. Well, it really isn't all that bad.

I've included a disassembler in \dsassm02 directory written by Sang Cho of ChongJu University in South Korea. Sang Cho has written an open source disassembler that he distributes under the terms of the GNU Public License (GPL). This disassembler is a straightforward tool that is capable of disassembling any Win32 operating system executable, including many of the components of the operating system themselves. It is powerful and, when used properly, will help you uncover quite a bit of the hidden details of your Win32 executables.

Before you embark on attacking your Win32 operating system with a disassembler, I want to give you a word of warning. There are many local laws that cover reverse engineering and intellectual property. These laws vary drastically from municipality to municipality and more so when crossing international borders. Policies governing software are relatively new to many governments so these laws are still in flux. You should become familiar with your local laws. Reverse engineering any licensed product may also break any existing licensing agreements between you and the software owner, so check your license agreement also before applying any disassembler to a product. However, reverse engineering programs that you write to get a better understanding of what your tools produce usually is allowed and I find it good practice. Whenever I do look at a compiled program that I wrote, I gain insights into the inner workings of the environment. I find this especially true when working with Win32 operating systems.

Microsoft is notorious for hiding information. Many of their products take advantage of undocumented APIs and features. As a result, they've spawned "undocumented" books and articles throughout the computer industry press. Typically, these undocumented features give Microsoft applications an edge over their competitors. This has been, and continues to be, the subject of legal actions between Microsoft, their competitors, and local governments all over the world. From my own personal vantage point, I have never been content with simple answers. I have always had a need to know more about the things I work on. It was the driving force behind becoming an engineer. However, when working on a Win32 operating system, I find it more necessity than nicety. So I use disassemblers in "self-defense" against the information-hiding techniques used by Microsoft.

We will look at how to use a disassembler to our advantage. Let's go back to our ex1.c example we examined earlier. To disassemble that program, we simply run dsassm02 ex1.exe >ex1.lst at an MS-DOS prompt window. The program runs with minimal output and generates the disassembled listing ex1.lst. Next, look at the output with your favorite editor. You'll find that dsassm02 first analyzes the executable and prints pertinent statistics. This, by itself, is valuable information similar to what we obtained earlier from Microsoft's dumbin utility as seen in Figure 1.13. However, further perusal down the file shows us the more or less expected disassembled output. Unfortunately, it is missing any symbols. A better disassembly is one obtained through objdump as seen in Figure 1.14. Although it is in AT&T assembler format, much more information is present in the form of symbols. Both tools, when used properly, yield tremendous insight into the Win32 nitty gritties.

Figure 1.13 Disassembler module import listing.

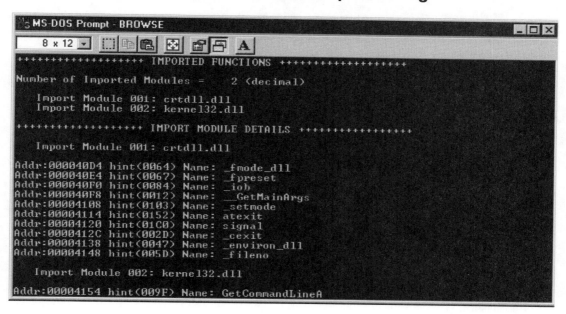

Figure 1.14 Disassembler code output.

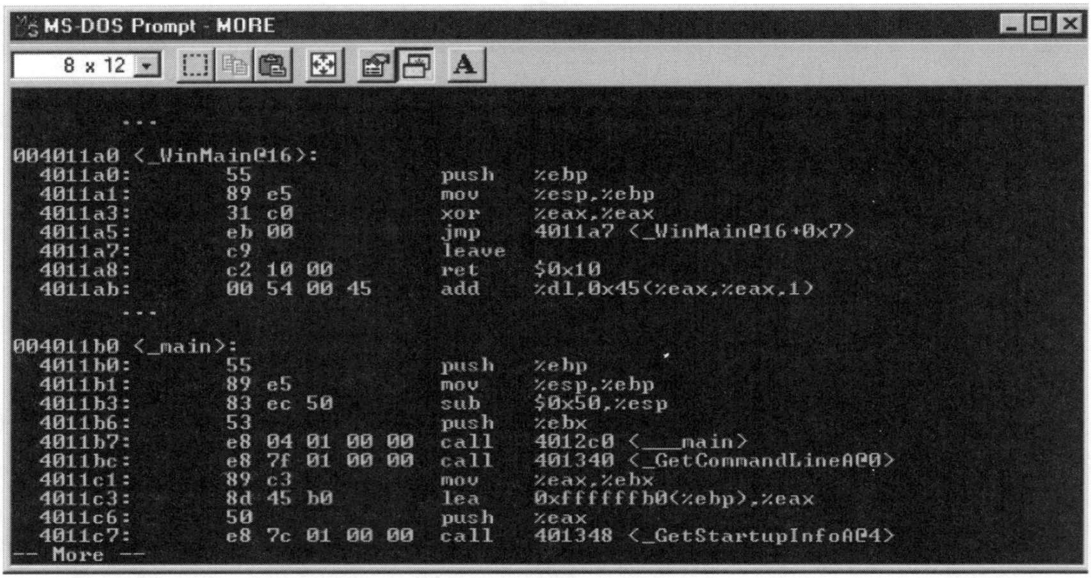

Commercial Development Tools

Of course, if you have funding, you may want to consider commercial development tools. There are compilers available from companies such as Inprise/Borland and Microsoft. These tools are very powerful and include features that allow you to quickly develop graphic screens and generate programs by simply hooking in small bits of code into code generated by the tools. This is commonly known as "Rapid Application Development" and should be considered whenever you have a pure application that needs to be delivered on a tight schedule. By their very nature, they shield the programmer from the underpinnings of the Win32 operating system. At first examination, this would seem to be against what we are trying to accomplish. However, offering such automated code generation doesn't rule them out.

Take for example Microsoft's Visual C++. This is an example of such a product. However, you don't need to use the code generation portions of it if you have a need to get deep into the Win32 aspects of C programming. You can simply use it as a simpler IDE for the C/C++ compiler. The same is true for other commercial development packages. I suggest you surf the web and visit the web sites for Inprise/Borland, Symantec, and Microsoft for more information on these tools.

Where Do We Go from Here?

With this discussion, we now have some tools to use with our Win32 operating systems. You have a choice of using either a commercial compiler or the free ones included with this book. In addition, we began looking under the covers of Win32 programming to get a peek at the Win32 interface. Armed with this, we will now proceed to dig deeper into the Microsoft Win32 operating system to truly understand what they are all about.

2

Chapter 2

Win32 Overview

In the last chapter, we looked at the user side of the API. As a developer, your primary interest is what the API looks like and how to make the best use of it. After all, your employer or customer hired you to write an application, not Windows itself, unless your employer happens to be Microsoft. Yet, many developers face the daily challenge of writing an application to work across Microsoft platforms such as Windows 9X, Windows CE, Windows NT, and Windows 2000. They are a set of drastically different operating systems that share a common user side. It is the common interface presented through the API that makes applications portable across the entire family of Microsoft operating systems.

There are two sides to that API. The first is the one that interfaces that application. This defines the Win32 API. The other side is the one that interfaces the operating system itself. It is radically different between Win32 operating systems. For example, the Windows 9X operating systems have not changed much over the years and are still 16-bit operating systems that can manage 32-bit process space while Windows NT is a true 32-bit operating system. The system call interface is radically different between the two. As we saw earlier, the API is what gives us a layer of standardization that allows such portability.

We will now take a look "under the hood" and get a better understanding of the various implementations. We will examine recent Microsoft implementations of Windows NT and Windows 9X to better understand the operating systems themselves. This will clarify differences in schedulers and resource allocations that can readily break portable applications.

High-Level Win32 Architecture

As we start to look at the basic Win32 operating system, we see that there is a common architecture for all Win32 operating systems. This is illustrated in Figure 2.1. In this family of operating systems, much of the published system functionality is contained in an Application Programming Interface or API contained in the uppermost layer of the operating system. This layer is actually a set of shared libraries, known as Dynamic Load Libraries or DLLs, that each have a common set of calls collectively known as the Win32 API.

Figure 2.1   Windows NT 3.51 architecture.

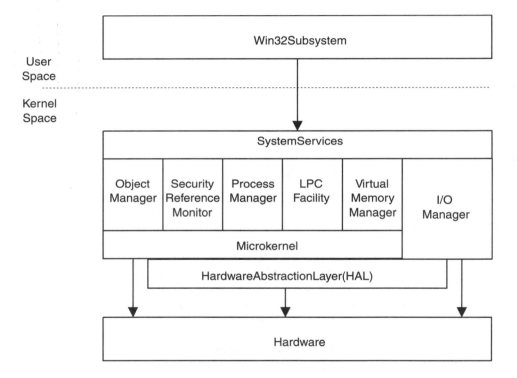

This is not uncommon. In UNIX, for example, the familiar C library is typically contained in a shared library libc.so. This library typically contains the common C library calls such as fread() and fwrite(). These calls provide a common interface that a C programmer can rely on regardless of which flavor of UNIX the application is compiled to run on. In the Win32 operating systems, similar sets of calls are defined and contained in user space. The actual kernel level calls are shielded by these DLLs and allow Microsoft to create dramatically different operating systems that share applications. We will now take a look at two of these — Windows NT and Windows 9X — to better understand how the Win32 operating systems work.

Starting at the Bottom

As we just discovered, looking down into a Win32 operating system from the application layer we don't really see any differences between any of the Microsoft operating systems. Yet, we know that these are different operating systems with different goals. Since the differences do not appear in the high-level DLLs, we need to drill down to the lowest level, the kernel itself, so that we may better understand the differences between the operating systems. We will look at the kernels for Windows NT and Windows 9X so we may better understand them.

Windows NT

Microsoft's Windows NT represents their first attempt at designing a Windows-based operating system of workstation or server class. Unlike earlier operating systems, Windows NT contained true multitasking, security, and other features that differentiated it from the MS-DOS/Windows PC operating system. Windows NT is not, however, the first operating system marketed by Microsoft for server class machines. They did, for a short time, sell XENIX, an AT&T UNIX-based operating system. It was popular and sold on platforms such as Intel 80386 and Motorola 68000 platforms. This was not a Microsoft design but rather a simple porting effort and it looked very much like every day UNIX. Many copies were sold and it was even the operating system delivered on a series of Tandy computers targeted for business applications. SCO eventually bought XENIX and later dropped it in favor of a new UNIX source stream obtained from Novell, derived from the original AT&T version.

Prior to Windows NT, Microsoft designed OS/2 for IBM. OS/2 was designed to take advantage of the Intel 80286 — a processor that featured true memory management and two modes of operation, a real mode and a protected mode. The 80286 real mode operation is virtually identical to the prior 8086/8088 processor and allowed MS-DOS to simply run without modifications. The 80286 protected mode sports a memory management scheme that modifies the processor behavior in a way that memory access is very different from real mode. Any access to memory utilizes the contents of descriptors, in place of segment registers, to look up a new base address and add it to the offset address. The descriptor plus offset scheme expanded memory capacity from 1 Mb in the earlier 8086/8088 to 16 Mb in the 80286.

To make OS/2 attractive to MS-DOS developers, virtual devices and API entries similar in functionality to BIOS calls were added. This eliminated the need for INT XX style real mode BIOS calls prevalent in MS-DOS applications, while retaining the functionality familiar to developers. With API calls defined in C, OS/2 encouraged greater developer productivity through use of high-level languages. OS/2 also sported a windows-like graphical interface known as Presentation Manager. When combined with a powerful operating system, this was a remarkable, advanced environment that should have taken the industry by storm. However, it was only available for IBM platforms and simply never caught on because of restrictive marketing.

Concurrent with OS/2, Microsoft designed a new GUI environment, Windows, which was layered on top of MS-DOS. Windows acted very much as a DOS extender, allowing protected mode programs to run within the Windows environment. Windows also provided a DOS Protected Mode Interface (DPMI) server. Through necessity, Windows hooked the underlying MS-DOS operating system. The reason behind this is the symbiotic relationship shared by MS-DOS and Windows. Although operating from protected mode, Windows programs still made use of the underlying MS-DOS operating system for program and file services. For version 3.3 and all subsequent releases, MS-DOS and Windows became more tightly coupled so that both could cooperatively take advantage of 80386+ processors. The newer processors featured improved memory management, linear addressing, and a V86 mode. The V86 mode allowed real mode programs to function while taking advantage of operating system services for process protection and multitasking. Through it all, MS-DOS remained the foundation for 80x86 desktop computing. Microsoft has announced plans to phase out this type of operating system after the release of Windows ME (Millennium Edition) with the release of "Whistler," the operating system that will merge the two code streams so that Windows NT-based operating systems will become the standard.

Some time in 1988, and at about the same time as the Windows/MS-DOS 16-bit operating systems were released, the IBM-Microsoft agreement came to an end. According to *Barbarians Led by Bill Gates: Microsoft from the Inside* by Jennifer Edstrom and Marlin Eller, what was originally slated as being the next OS/2 design became the basis for a new operating system, Windows NT. This design also took advantage of the 80386+ features but was designed as a true operating system, not a protected mode DOS extender that 16-bit Windows represented. Microsoft also went out and hired Dave Cutler from Digital Equipment Corporation's VMS development team to act as chief architect for the new operating system. With Microsoft's previous learning experiences with OS/2 and talent from the outside that was familiar with operating systems designed for business, Windows NT showed the most promise for expanding Microsoft's market share.

Windows NT went through an extended development cycle. It was first demonstrated in August 1991 at the Microsoft Windows Developers Conference. Windows NT then went through an extended beta period in which many developers participated and Microsoft eventually released it in July 1993 as "Version 3.1" to match the revision level of their Windows 3.1 graphical interface for MS-DOS. They based this choice on functionality and appearance of Windows NT to its 16-bit sibling. Of particular interest is that it was the first appearance of the Win32 interface. Another interesting point to note was that Windows NT supports not only Intel processors but RISC processors such as PowerPC and Alpha, as well. Eventually, new versions of Windows NT were released, with v3.51 in June 1995, v4.0 in July 1996, and with the Windows 2000 release in March 2000. Other processor support also came and went and today Windows 2000, originally Windows NT v5.0, is available only for Intel IA-32 processors (80x86 and Pentium series). Throughout it all, the Win32 interface remains the staple of the API for this operating system.

Windows NT Executive Architecture

Windows NT is a modular operating system that is comprised of many modules split between user and kernel space. Microsoft differentiates between these modules as protected subsystems that reside in user space and the Windows NT Executive for subsystems and components of the operating system that execute in the microprocessor's kernel space. These conceptual "spaces" are differentiated by whether the module runs in *application mode* (user space) or *privileged mode* (kernel space). Many processors, including Intel's IA-32 processors, incorporate some form of privilege level that differentiates these spaces. Typically, kernel mode may operate with a different set of stacks that may be controlled by the processor such as in the Motorola 68000 series and will only run certain instructions that may deal with port access and other privileged operations in certain privilege levels. With Windows NT, only two levels are used although some processors have more, such as the Intel processor's four privilege levels known as *rings*.

The construction of the Windows NT Executive is a combination of layered and parallel modules. Figure 2.1 illustrates the Windows NT Executive for v3.51. As you can see, there are three layers: the Hardware Abstraction Layer (HAL), the microkernel, and servers for various Windows NT services such as security, file servers, etc. To better understand the functionality contained within the kernel, we will examine each layer from the bottom up.

The bottom most layer of the Windows NT Executive is the Hardware Abstraction Layer (HAL). This layer provides a common software abstraction over such hardware devices as clocks, cache and memory controllers, peripheral adapters, symmetric multiprocessing functions, and system buses. This abstraction allows Windows NT to provide support for a wide range of hardware designs within a given microprocessor family.

The next layer in the NT design is the *microkernel*. In many ways, the microkernel is the core of the operating system because it provides critical operating system functions such as first-level interrupt handling, deferred procedure call, thread scheduling, and synchronization primitives. An important design concept of a microkernel is that large portions of the operating system that traditionally run entirely in the kernel or privileged mode of the microprocessor can now be executed in user or application mode. In much of the microkernel branch of operating system research, many of the functions provided by monolithic kernels are contained within servers that execute in user space.

One very good example of this is the Carnegie Melon University Mach microkernel. In Mach, the functions provided by the microkernel fall strictly within process, thread, memory management and low level interprocess communications, i.e., ports. File system management, system call interfaces, program loading and execution, etc., is all contained in the servers. In this type of design, it is conceivable to have multiple execution environments for different programs. For example, one program could be running within a UNIX environment while another may be running within an MS-DOS environment on the same computer using the same processor.

To the operating system designer, this represents a truly modular operating system. For the OS designer, a microkernel provides modularity, encapsulation, and data hiding. It provides a set of well-defined functions that are available systemwide. Other higher levels of the operating system access this set of function through a well-defined interface. This lends itself to a cleaner design where typically there is no duplication of functionality and no "back doors" to critical data structures. Thanks to the microkernel, all access to system data structures is through software interfaces. Also, software maintenance costs are typically lower because it possible to upgrade or replace entire modules within the operating system kernel without disturbing the remainder.

Operating systems such as Windows NT, however, make use of microkernel designs but don't strictly adhere to them. This is similar to the Open Software Foundation (now The Open Group) OSF/1 operating system. Microsoft defines an operating system that follows this design a "pure" microkernel operating system. Windows NT does not provide a separate microkernel as in Mach but rather provides only modularity and strong encapsulation within their kernel. They refer to this as modified microkernel or "macrokernel" operating systems. There are advantages to this design. For example, the pure microkernel design is too procedurally expensive, i.e., it suffers from the overhead of entering the microkernel through exceptions or call gates whereas in the macrokernel the services are simply function calls.

Microsoft claims that there are insufficient benefits from running core portions of the operating system in user mode to make up for resulting losses in performance. In my opinion, this macrokernel design is really the traditional monolithic kernel design, only better designed.

This isn't a bad design, it just isn't a microkernel. The design permits Windows NT to be very flexible. An example given by Microsoft is that the Windows NT operating system does not depend on a particular size for the processor's virtual memory page. It is determined dynamically at boot time by the HAL. Once booted, all operating system code — including the memory manager itself — uses the page size determined by the HAL as the operating system booted. This allows them to easily port Windows NT between processors featuring different page sizes with no consequence to the code. This lowers Microsoft's software maintenance costs by spreading a great deal of the operating system code across multiple architectures.

The final layer provides the remainder of the system services. These are the parts of the kernel that give it its "personality," and contained in the upper level. This layer now provides the benefits of the microkernel design. For example, this layer provides POSIX functionality through a POSIX subsystem as well as the Win32 functionality in a Win32 subsystem. You could add another piece of functionality, such as VMS, to the Windows NT operating system without disturbing the other subsystems. In fact, this layer provides the graphics interface as well. This is similar to UNIX and X Windows, where the graphics server is entirely within user space.

Figure 2.2   Windows NT 4.0 architecture.

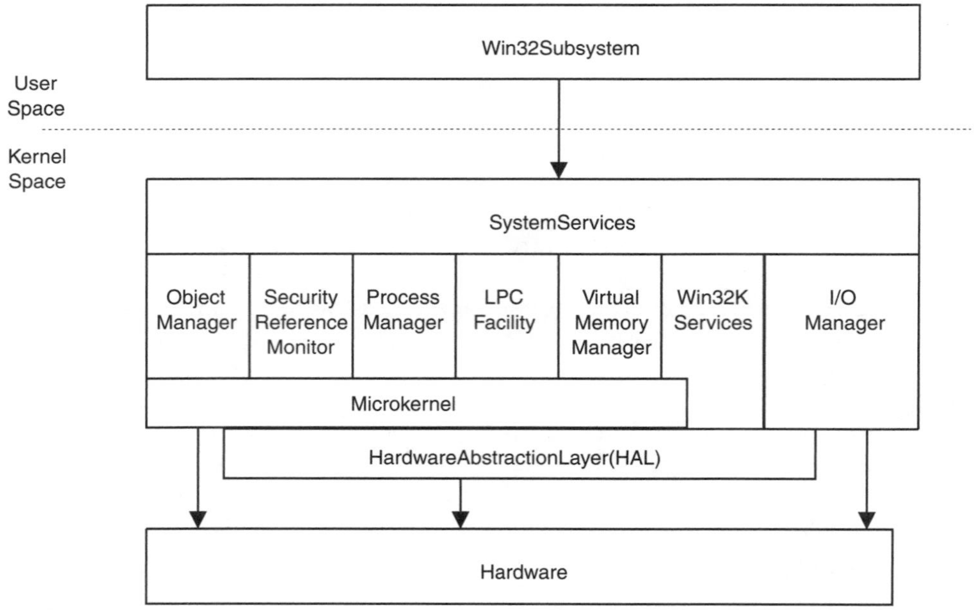

Figure 2.2 illustrates the architecture for Windows NT 4.0. As you can see, there are very minimal differences between v3.51 and v4.0. In fact, from the executive point of view, the

only difference is the addition of Win32K Window Manager, graphics drivers, and GDI. Microsoft made this change for the sake of performance. V3.51 was comparatively slow from a graphics standpoint and moving the graphics into the executive resulted in significant performance improvement.

One interesting sidenote is that we see that the Win32 personality is actually outside the kernel space. This tells us that Windows NT, the operating system that introduced the Win32 interface, is not a Win32 operating system. In fact, the Win32 personality resides side-by-side with POSIX and OS/2 personalities. This little bit of computer schizophrenia should give the user a better insight into the extent that Win32 API is a translation layer and library very much like the `libc` calls normally found on UNIX and variants such as Linux. It is this basic fact that fuels such Windows emulation tools as `WINE` and `twin` for Linux and commercial packages such as Bristol Technology, Inc. Wind/U Win32 API library. Each of these packages takes advantage of the portable Win32 API to allow programs written for the Microsoft family of operating systems to run under UNIX.

Windows 9X

Some Windows 9X Background

To better understand the operations of the Windows 9X family of operating systems, you really should inspect its lineage. Windows began in the early 1980s as a simple multitasker riding on top of MS-DOS. Its sole purpose was to allow users to switch between running programs in individual windows that represented the "virtual" environment for that program. It ran on an 8088, which meant that all this code was crammed into the 640K of memory then available in that architecture. Since there was no memory protection or address translation schemes available for the processor and hence the underlying operating system, there was little value added to the computer. In fact, using Windows placed the user at a major disadvantage because it consumed quite a bit of the user's resources, namely memory and processor time. It was also crude in design because the multitasking was "cooperative," meaning that a program had to give up its use of the processor in order to allow another program to run. In essence, the multiprogramming capability was nothing more than marketing hype.

Now fast forward to the 1990s. Windows has undergone a few evolutionary stages at the consumer's expense. For example, it became aware of 80286-protected 16-bit modes in Windows 2.0 along with some virtual machine capability to run MS-DOS programs in a window. By the time it was re-released as Windows 3.0, it was fully capable of running on 80386 processors by allowing multiple virtual 8086 machines to run MS-DOS in multiple windows. However, it is still limited to only 16-bit programs where the 80386 is capable of 32-bit operation. Buggy at best, Windows 3.0 shows more marketing polish than technical innovation through prettier user interfaces.

Stopping temporarily in 1993, Microsoft prepared to release MS-DOS v6.0. By this time, Windows 3.1 had been released and MS-DOS was facing competition in the retail channels from Digital Research whose DR-DOS 5.0 was running many of the applications designed for MS-DOS. Reports of "incompatibilities" resulting from code buried within Windows scared users to switch from DR-DOS to MS-DOS although it worked equally well on both. Microsoft then released MS-DOS 6.0 which, when combined with Windows for Workgroups began to translate the duo into an "operating system." You may notice that I've placed quotes around operating system in the last sentence because in and by itself, Windows cannot operate. It requires the underlying MS-DOS operating system to operate properly. Even further, Windows is aware of the operating system and to properly operate, must tie into special hooks for all versions of MS-DOS after 4.0 and patch versions of 3.x. MS-DOS is also Windows-aware with special multiplex interrupt (int 02fh) hooks used from both the device drivers (io.sys) and the kernel itself (msdos.sys). The programming interface has not changed very much. In fact, the new tact taken on by Microsoft is to add additional shared libraries in the form of DLL files and begin calling them APIs. One enhancement, however, is the evolution of a particular type of shared library known as the Virtual Device Driver or VxD. This is a trusted shared library that normally runs within Ring 0 of the 80x86 processor allowing full use of processor resources. We now begin to see more use of 32-bit features through these VxDs as well as the virtual 8086 machine (vm86) handled through one and 32-bit disk drivers to speed up the operating system.

Fast forward again. Through an advanced marketing campaign that generated more fanfare than the lunar landing in 1969, Microsoft released its long awaited Windows 95. Quite a bit of speculation followed regarding its release based on early "Chicago" beta releases. It hit the market in August 1995 after being touted by Microsoft as being a 100% redesign, but was it really? Now is a good time to begin to make use of disassemblers and trace system calls down into the kernels to gain better understanding about what Windows 9X is really all about.

Windows 9X Architecture

Probably the most common of the Win32 operating systems are the Windows 9X family. These operating systems have stronger roots in the older MS-DOS/Windows design than all of the Win32 operating systems. This should come of little surprise when you consider the evolution of the Windows 9X family. It is interesting that while the path taken to Windows 9X was evolutionary, a great deal of significant advances were made during that time.

Windows 9X and VxDs

Figure 2.3 shows an architectural view of the typical Windows 9X operating system. You will notice is that there are quite a few components to the kernel portion of the operating system. Each of these components are commonly referred to as a VxD. The term VxD comes from the original concept of Virtual Device Drivers for Windows — derived from the convention used for naming the device driver. For example, the device driver that controls the Programmable Interrupt Controller, or PIC, is named VPICD. Hence, the general term for a virtual device driver became known as a VxD where the "x" refers to the device name. However, the VxD takes on much more responsibility than simple device drivers, so it is now a term for a generic, protected mode executable that follows certain conventions. Within the Windows 9X family of Win32 operating systems, the collection of VxDs form a protected mode kernel around which Microsoft wraps the familiar Win32 interface. In essence, this collection of kernel modules forms a protected mode kernel similar to the Windows NT protected mode kernel. In comparison, the Windows 9X kernel is a much more robust design allowing the operating system to be highly configurable — adapted to the underlying hardware during the installation of the operating system.

Figure 2.3   Windows 9X architecture.

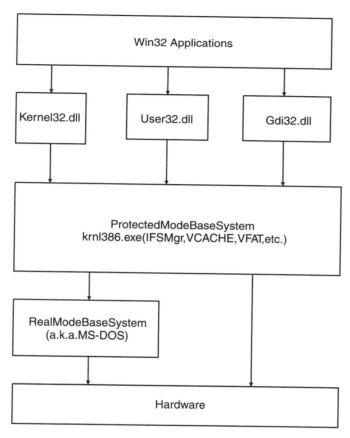

Now that we've identified that VxDs make up the Win9X kernel, the question is: what is a VxD? It is a special binary executable designed to operate in both 16-bit real mode and 32-bit flat mode. This unusual feature gives the VxD the extraordinary ability to switch between both real and protected mode. This allows for the Windows 9X kernel to inter-operate between the 32-bit Win32 applications and 16-bit MS-DOS services and device drivers.

The ability to straddle 16-bit and 32-bit modes places more complexity on the binary than a normal executable. For example, the file must be organized in segments, each containing a code segment and a data segment. These segments are:

- real mode initialization
- protected mode initialization
- pageable
- locked
- static
- debug

If you think about the environment in which these code modules run, the reason for the segments is simple. A VxD is a kernel module, so it must control which pieces of code go where. Why? Well, there are conditions that kernel modules must meet that a normal application normally does not deal with. For example, certain pieces of code, such as an interrupt handler, must always be resident. This code must reside in a locked segment. If the code is not always necessary, it may go into a pageable segment. Other pieces of code are only necessary for system start up and can be later discarded. These sections go into real mode or protected mode initialization sections. Notice that there are two sections. This is the only part of the VxD that may have real mode code in it.

Now we will take a closer look at a VxD so that we can better understand its structure. A VxD provides services to other VxDs as well as to the Win32 layer. It contains an in memory data structure known as a *Device Descriptor Block* that contains pointers to a service table, a V86 API procedure, and a protected mode API procedure. As you can see, the basic structure of a VxD is significantly more complex than a typical Win32 application, but with reason.

The Win32 kernel is assembled from a collection of VxDs performing functions ranging from thread and virtual machine to device and file system drivers. These files are found in the \windows\system directory. The fundamental kernel is in the file vmm32.vxd and other *.vxd files contained in that directory perform other services. The vmm32.vxd file is of special interest. It is built at installation time and is actually a collection of VxDs. This significantly improves load time during boot by loading a single file as opposed to individual file open and seeks individual VxDs. Other VxD files contained in \windows\system may be loaded at boot time depending on hardware configuration. When combined, they form the fundamental Windows 9X kernel.

There is one area in Figure 2.3 that we haven't discussed and that is the VM86 box containing MS-DOS. There is a VxD that is part of the kernel that manages the VM86 virtual machine. In this virtual machine, Windows 9X places the fundamental MS-DOS or real mode Windows 9X kernel. This facilitates process management because a Win32 process data structure contains a real mode component, typically the PSP. This allows the process to use real mode services and device drivers by providing a virtual environment to fool the real mode code to think it is in full control of computer. This is very different from the Windows NT kernel where a VM86 process is only for MS-DOS windows. The real mode kernel is exposed to the world in this architecture and it is a weakness in the Windows 9X design that frequently results in Windows 9X crashes. However, it is a design trade-off that allowed for the migration of millions of pre-Windows 95 systems into the 32-bit world while retaining old device driver compatibility. If Microsoft had not taken this approach, an upgrade from Windows 3.X to Windows 95 could have resulted in many unhappy customers as disk drives or other devices failed after the upgrade.

Moving Up a Level

So far, our discussions have focused primarily on how the kernels for Windows 9X and Windows NT are designed. These two drastically different designs both offer the Win32 API despite these differences. Now we need to figure out how the Win32 API, i.e., kernel32.dll, communicates with the underlying kernel.

For Windows 9X, the method of communication isn't really a means of communication at all. It seems that the Win32 API, knowing a bit about the internals of the VxD "microkernel" goes in and "tickles" it. What I mean is that the DLLs seem to have fundamental knowledge of the underlying VxD layer and either make direct calls to what appears to be a jump table, or directly access variables contained within the VxD layer. This fuzzy communication method is not very clean from an architectural standpoint and again points to one of the weaknesses of the Windows 9X design.

For Windows NT/2000, the picture gets much clearer. When we earlier examined this design, we saw a clear delineation between the kernel and the DLLs that form the Win32 API. In fact, it is that delineation that allows other subsystems to exist, e.g., POSIX and OS/2. Given such a clean delineation, you expect a better-defined method for the Win32 API DLLs to communicate with the kernel and in this case, you would be correct.

In the Windows NT/2000 arena, there exists a native API. This API, although only documented recently by Microsoft, is a key part of the Windows NT/2000 kernel. It is this native API that forms the common foundation for all the Windows NT/2000 subsystems. The best way to see how this API interacts with the Win32 API is to take a look at one of the Win32 system calls and trace it into the Windows NT/2000 kernel.

If we were to disassemble `kernel32.dll` for Windows NT 4.0, we would find an entry point for the Win32 API call `CloseHandle`. When we first look at it, we see a number of tests performed on the parameters of this call. As we look down further, we see that some of these tests are meant to separate out calls to close a console handle as opposed to everything else. The console call is marshaled to `CloseConsoleHandle` while all others conditions make direct calls to `NtClose`. The same is true for `CreateFile`. Any call we make within a C program to `CreateFile` usually ends up being a call to `CreateFileA`, which is the ASCII version of `CreateFile`. When we look inside the kernel, we see that the call `CreateFileA` eventually calls `CreateFileW`, the Unicode or "wide" version. This is a lot of code within `CreateFileW` — again separating console calls from all others and handling them differently. It makes other internal function calls until eventually, the code makes a call to `NtCreateFile`. In the form that `kernel32.dll` takes on disk, this is a typical external reference. However, if we look at it through a debugger, we find that the call takes on form of "`int 0x2e`" as seen in Figure 2.4. The Windows NT/2000 kernel intercepts all `int 2eh` calls and internally dispatches these calls in a manner somewhat similar to the way that MS-DOS dispatched `int 21h` system calls. Internal to the Windows NT/2000 kernel, the dispatcher is a function called `KiSystemService` and uses a table `KiSystemServiceTable` to get the address of the function represented by a number in the `eax` register. It is interesting to note that the majority of the `int 2eh` exceptions are handled internal to the Windows NT/2000 kernel, but some are handled by table supplied by the `WIN32K.SYS` graphics subsystem. You may remember this as being the performance improvement introduced in Windows NT 4.0. The improvement comes in the form of integrating graphics subsystem calls with the Windows NT/2000 internal API.

Figure 2.4   **Resolved** `NtCreateFile` **call.**

```
NtCreateFile:

               mov    eax, 0x0000001A
               lea    edx, [esp+04]
               int    0x2E
               ret    0x2C
```

The steps involved in discovering how the Windows NT/2000 kernel and the Win32 API DLLs communicate are not trivial by any stretch of the imagination. It involves a lot of investigative work, disassembly, debugging sessions, and so forth but the results produce a much better understanding of how the Windows NT/2000 kernel works.

Now What?

By now, we've got a better understanding of what the Windows 9X and Windows NT/2000 kernels look like and how they do their work. We also know that the Win32 API is handled by a set of DLLs that give these two drastically different architectures a common facade. Now it is time to look at some of the standardized file types such as the PE executable file to see how they interact with Win32 API.

Chapter 3

Win32 File Formats

Win32 File Formats is an extremely rich topic deserving of a book by itself. There are many, varied file formats for both the OS and applications, but we will concentrate on the file formats that are operating system related. In this chapter, I take apart the PE file format to show you how the various sections of the file relate to the in-memory process. If you are in a hurry, you can easily skip this chapter. However, if you want to really understand how the operating system makes use of the code, this is the chapter to read. I will also describe the Intel IA-32 architecture and relate how the Microsoft operating systems make use of the processor architecture to provide virtual memory services.

File System Overview

If there's one thing about Win32 operating systems, it's that they rely on a wide variety of file formats. As a result, it is to your advantage to better understand how these file formats work within the Win32 operating system. Before we get into such details, we need to understand the terms used to describe how the disk stores data and how it actually works. Figure 3.1 is a view of a generic disk. This disk has one or more physical *platters* that hold the data. Each platter allows data to be read and written from either one or both surfaces due to a coating capable of being magnetized. This coating is similar to that used on Mylar tapes used to store data or audio. Data is stored by magnetizing a portion of this surface as the surface moves beneath a read/write head. Unlike a tape, where the tape is spooled from one reel to another, a disk rotates so that the same physical location is available once per revolution so data can be written and repeatedly accessed by waiting for the next revolution. This stripe of recorded data is called a *track*. Within the track, data is grouped together to allow blocks of data to be read and written instead of transferring an entire track of data. These groups of data are called *sectors*. Since a disk may have more than one platter, a group of the tracks at the same head position across all platters is known as a *cylinder*. The individual side of a platter within this cylinder is referred to as a *side*.

Figure 3.1 Diagram of a generic disk architecture.

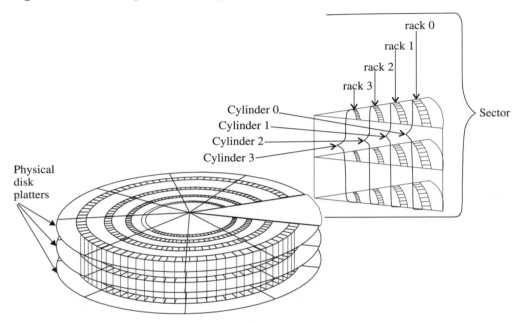

Reading and writing data to a physical location on a disk is crude. It is difficult to keep this data straight and the last thing a programmer or user wants to do is say they need to write data at cylinder 7, side 3, sector 12. So, we organize this data into a logical entity called a *file* and refer to it by assigning it a name. The underlying operating system then imposes a data structure on this disk in order to convert "myfile.dat" to cylinder 7, side 3, sector 12. This level of abstraction makes the data access much more civilized for both the user and the developer. Further levels of abstractions, such as hierarchical directories, may be applied to the disk to make it even easier for users and programmers.

However, it does not stop here. Data within each file takes on different structures in order to fulfill a certain function. For example, the data that makes up the file for this chapter has information within it that represents all the sentences and paragraphs I wrote, along with hidden data used by the word processor to format it. There are other files that contain executable data or information used by the Win32 operating system. Depending on the file content, the programmer accesses this data using different API calls, or possibly programs, outside the Win32 operating system.

This is the "50,000 foot view" of a generic operating system file system. We need to take a closer look at each of these components of the file system and file format. This will help you, the software developer, to develop better applications.

Physical Disks and File Systems

Raw Disk Drives

An area of mystery for many developers is the location where sectors are physically stored on a disk. Unless you've developed disk drivers, you've probably never seen this. Even if you did write a disk driver, odds are that you've never looked at the physical file system organization before. We'll look at both the physical and logical organization of the various file systems so that the mystery will finally be cleared up.

Generic Disk Organization

Disk drives are ubiquitous. Nearly every desktop computer, workstation, server, and mainframe has at least one. They are the preferred secondary storage for computers. Typically, their size is many times the primary RAM and ROM storage contained within the computer itself. They're also taken for granted. Why? Because storing data onto the disk is done without regard to either physical or logical organization. Just pause for one moment — when was the last time you thought about the file you just created and which sectors it occupies?

At this point, you may ask what is a sector? How does it fit onto a disk? Possibly, you may even be asking, "what is a disk?" Thanks to modern programming technology and methodology, there is no need for you to think of the internals of secondary storage. So asking these questions is by no means a reflection of your programming knowledge or education. So let's take a brief tour of our hardware and the particulars of a disk drive.

If you were to take apart your computer, you probably won't find anything that resembles a true disk. There won't be anything flat and round sitting anywhere inside. There will be, however, a set of boxes interconnected with the main board by some cables, some of which are round, others flat. These boxes are the disks. Inside the box, there are small, plate-like disks that spin (Figure 3.1). Above each spinning disk, but not touching, are arms that move across the disk. These arms have small electronic circuitry, known as a head, which is used to store and retrieve data from the spinning disk. As the data is written to the disk, it is written in concentric rings. These rings are known as *tracks*.

This track contains all the data. We desire to access this data much the same way we access internal memory — we want to be able to modify it at random intervals. In order to facilitate this, the track is broken down into sectors that have prerecorded markers (laid down by a formatting program) that identify where a sector is physically located on the track. By prior agreement, this sector is defined as a fixed number of bytes designed to fit within the physical space between the prerecorded markers. With a fixed number of bytes contained within each sector, we can store a number of bytes equal to the size of the sector times the number of sectors recorded on each track.

There is more than one track per disk. In fact, there are two directions in which we can distribute the tracks: (a) on different surfaces of the platter and (b) across the surface. Typically, a disk has, at least, more than one surface. It may have only one, but usually two surfaces and multiple platters. By placing a read/write head in close proximity of each surface, as mentioned earlier, we can access this data by simply electrically switching heads and reading or writing data on this surface. This organization is known as a cylinder because you can visualize the track as physically extending through each platter forming a three dimensional cylinder of data (Figure 3.2). We can now store the number of bytes in each track times the number of tracks in each cylinder worth of data. By moving the heads, we can take advantage of the surface area by forming concentric rings or tracks on each surface and concentric cylinders across the platters. With this additional dimension of storage, we can store the number of bytes in each cylinder times the number of cylinders worth of data on each disk drive.

File Systems

The current file systems used by all the Win32 Operating Systems evolved from the basic MS-DOS FAT operating system. This naturally followed the development of the Windows 9X operating systems themselves. As a result, it is best to examine the file system design by beginning with the basic FAT file system common to all Microsoft operating systems. The Windows NT/2000 operating system also supports NTFS, a file system that dramatically departs from the FAT design. We won't cover NTFS, but will review the design of the FAT file system and its variations.

FAT File System

The FAT file system is the fundamental Microsoft file system. Its name comes from the "file allocation table" structure used to track sectors on the disk and it dates back to the original MS-DOS 1.0 design. It has evolved, much like the operating system itself, over time as newer, larger disk drives added additional demands. Today, with the FAT-32 file system, the file system can now be used to exponentially store more than the original FAT-12, but it is still closely related. We'll begin by looking at how the FAT-12 file system was used on floppy disks, then examine the changes made to the FAT file system design as it was modified to encompass larger and larger disks.

Floppy Disk Drives

To better understand how the FAT file system organization relates to the physical disk, we need to select a specific disk type to study. Hard drives vary in architecture from vendor to vendor. Floppy disks are much more standard and easier to study. We'll look at a 360K floppy disk.

Like the generic disk, the data organization on a floppy disk is broken into sectors, tracks, and cylinders. The platter on a floppy disk is made from Mylar as opposed to aluminum or some other alloy. Since Mylar is very flexible as compared to the metal platter, the term "floppy" was applied to it. There is only a single platter with one or two surfaces, so a maximum of two tracks composes a cylinder. The number of cylinders varies, but most common is 40 and 80.

For a 360K floppy, the organization is nine sectors per track, two tracks per cylinder, and forty cylinders per disk. Other architectures are possible and that is how 720K and 1.44M floppy disks are also encompassed. These disks also have different physical sizes, typically

5.25" and 3.5", but other sizes such as 8" and 3" existed in the past. For Microsoft operating systems, the sector size is typically 512 bytes.

Logical vs. Physical

MS-DOS and Win32 operating systems internally reference the disk drive as an array of fixed-size blocks of data. Each block of data in this array is sequentially numbered from zero to one less than the maximum size of the disk (in sectors). They impose a structure upon this array of sectors in order to easily access data and organize files. The logical file system organization is shown in Figure 3.2. The FAT file system format places a boot sector at the first sector (sector 0) on the disk because this is the only sector guaranteed to be on the disk. As a result, the boot sector acts as an "anchor," fixing the file system location. The boot sector contains the bootstrap code to load the operating system and a data structure that contains all the pertinent variables that define the disk geometry. For a 360K floppy disk, the next sector is a reserved sector and it's followed by two FAT areas, each two sectors long. The last area reserved by the file system is the root directory and it's 7 sectors long. The remainder of the disk is dedicated to data and subdirectories.

Figure 3.2   Logical FAT file system.

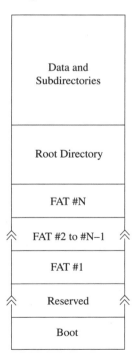

As I mentioned earlier, the operating system prefers to work with a more general, logical organization. This logical view virtualizes the disk by eliminating the disk geometry. Mapping this logical structure into the physical disk requires some thought. In order to map the disk, we need to standardize how the logical sector numbers map into the physical sector, cylinder, and track numbering. For Microsoft operating systems, the first block is mapped into sector 1 of cylinder 0, track 1. The track number increases for every nine sectors on a 360K floppy, followed by increasing cylinder number. This mapping is illustrated in Figure 3.3. The file system structure does not take up a full cylinder and is spread out over two tracks.

Figure 3.3   Logical to physical mapping.

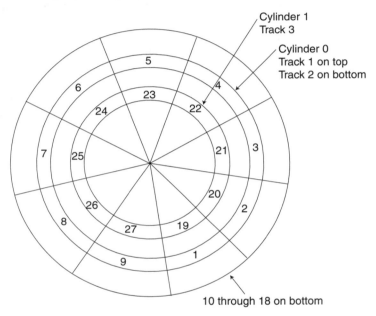

Although not immediately apparent, this organization allows for most rapid access when reading files sequentially. Each sequential sector can be accessed immediately upon reading the previous sector. When reading or writing the last sector on the track (sector 9 for a 360K disk), the first sector on the next track can be immediately accessed on the start of the next rotation. Once all sectors for every track in the cylinder are read (two tracks for a 360K disk), the next cylinder is read by physically moving the heads. This is important because there is a time penalty of several milliseconds for stepping the disk. It's also important that the sectors follow each other so that you don't incur a penalty of unnecessary rotation of the disk before reading the next sector. This delay can also be several milliseconds. Although the sectors are sequential on a floppy disk, some early hardware was not fast enough, so the sectors may be interlaced in a way that the sequential disk reads are completed in a minimum number of rotations. This is known as *sector interlace* and was necessary on hard drives contained in old XT type systems. For example, an 18 sector may be formatted with sectors 0, 9, 1, 10, 2, 11, etc., instead of 0, 1, 2, 3, 4, 5, etc. Reading or writing sectors 0 and 1 in the first number scheme allows the hardware to read or write sector 0, then gives the hardware the time it takes for sector 9 to pass under the head before starting again for sector 1. With this scheme, all sectors on the track may be operated on in two rotations of the disk.

In summary, *rotational speed* is the limiting factor for access to a given sector in a cylinder and *head movement* for access to a given cylinder. Great care must be taken in mapping the physical disk geometry to the logical one supported by the operating system. If you don't plan well, you'll suffer from poor performance of the operating system.

FAT File Format

Both the Windows NT/2000 and Windows 9X operating systems supply applications with a number of services through the Win32 API. These services provide process management, memory management, file management, and other services. Virtually all the services pertaining to disk and process management are provided by `kernel32.dll`. In this section, we'll explore the fundamental FAT file system and examine key details and data structures. We will expand on this later and show the relationship between the FAT file system and other FAT-based file systems.

Floppy Disk Architecture

The original MS-DOS mission was to manage small, 160Kb floppy disks. Fixed disks with gigabyte storage capacities on a desktop computer and multi-megabyte memory were unheard of. Back then, MS-DOS designers faced space restrictions both on disk and in memory. They also faced high rotational and head positioning latency times inherent to the 5.25" floppy disk drives. This forced MS-DOS designers to be creative in both disk layout and system call functionality. This creativity will be apparent as we closely examine the FAT file system.

We begin our examination of the FAT file system by studying a simple DOS floppy disk. This floppy disk contains only a root file system and is representative of a freshly formatted floppy disk. Its structure is flexible enough to be compatible with almost any removable media, regardless of size. In MS-DOS, a logical disk is a sequential set of 512 byte sectors. The disk consists of a boot sector, followed by zero or more reserved sectors and the file system. The boot and reserved sectors are for disk booting and disk maintenance — although the boot sector also carries file system information.

Following the boot-related area is one or more File Allocation Table, or FAT, areas. Each FAT consists of one or more sequential sectors where each entry has a forward pointer in a linked list of pointers. Values of zero indicate free space, while other values indicate bad sectors, disk size, and disk type. There are typically two FAT tables, for sake of redundancy. The need for more than one FAT is the MS-DOS FAT file system's greatest weakness. If a program crash destroyed one of the FAT areas, no other information anywhere within the file system allows you to recover your files. Becasue disks are the components in a computer with the lowest reliability (next to power supplies), redundant FAT areas improve the file system reliability when compared to a single FAT.

Immediately following the FAT(s) is the root directory. In early MS-DOS days, the root directory was the only disk directory, similar to its CP/M cousin. All data relating to filename, location, creation date, file size, and file protection were contained within an entry in the directory. Starting with MS-DOS 2.0, the file system became a hierarchical file system with other directories that extend from the root directory. However, there are differences between a root directory and other disk directories. The first significant difference is that the root directory does not contain an entry for "." (itself) or ".." (its parent) directories. This choice allowed for backwards compatibility with systems running pre-2.0 versions. Another significant difference is that the root directory is fixed in length, while a subdirectory can be expanded. Again, compatibility with pre-2.0 versions forced this limitation.

Hard Disk Architecture

Hard disks are very similar to the floppy disk in design. The biggest difference is that hard disks can support multiple disk images, which in turn can support more than one operating system (Figure 3.4). This concept borrows the idea of multiple volumes from other operating system designs. It improves on the concept, however, by placing the multiple volume concept *outside* the operating system and in control of the boot code. Each volume is called a *partition* and shares a single master boot record.

Figure 3.4 Hard disk partition layout.

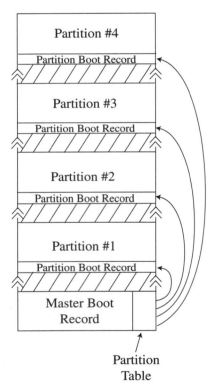

As with floppy disks, when an X86 system boots, it loads the first sector into memory. The difference between the floppy and hard disk is in the functionality of the boot code contained in this sector. The master boot record contains code that examines a partition table also contained in this sector. It determines the active partition and proceeds to load the first sector of this partition into memory. The remainder of the boot process is exactly the same as for a floppy diskette. By using this design, the file system remains identical for both floppy disks and hard disks.

However, some on-disk data structure changes are necessary when certain physical sizes exceed particular structure member sizes. This occurs on drives when the physical size begins to exceed a 12-bit encoding limit in the FAT and a 16-bit limit on the device drivers. These limits challenged MS-DOS, but its designers were smart enough to extend to 16-bit FAT entries and 32-bit block addressing to overcome these hurdles.

So far, we have reviewed the principal FAT file system architecture. There are other file systems supported by Microsoft operating systems, such as the CD-ROM file system, but we will not cover them here. However, we will further examine each of the file system components in detail so that we can better understand the fundamental FAT file system.

Boot Area

The first area of the disk, as seen earlier, is the *boot area*. This area consists of the boot sector plus zero or more reserved sectors. This sector executes first in order to start the operating system loaders — every disk has one, whether or not it is bootable. The reason for this is that typically, the Win32 boot sector has code that searches for the files it needs and gracefully recovers if they are not present. We've all seen the message when we try to boot up with a non-bootable floppy in drive A. Let's take a closer look at the structure of this sector and how the Win32 operating system knows how to access a given sector on different disk geometries.

Figure 3.5 shows a pictorial view of the boot sector. There are three areas shown, although this varies for Master Boot Record. Every disk boot must contain these three areas. The first area, called *boot sector*, contains an important disk structure that contains all information about the disk's architecture. The second area is the body of the executable boot code. The final area is a signature word, 0x55AA, used to identify this sector as a valid boot sector. The variation for the Master Boot Record is that the partition table precedes the signature, which has a pointer to the start of each partition and in turn the Partition Boot Record.

Figure 3.5 Boot sector map.

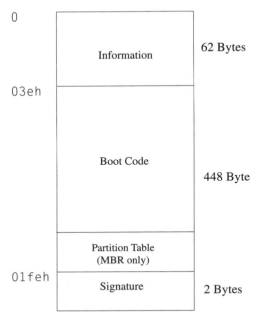

By convention, the ROM BIOS loads the boot sector into location 0:7C00h and transfers control to this address. The bootsector data structure, shown in Figure 3.6, makes this possible. The first entry into this table is an area called bsJump. This is a reserved entry that contains an Intel 3 byte jump, either E9 XX XX absolute jump or EB XX 90 relative jump. Unfortunately, the ugliness of the Microsoft design for Intel processors rears its head with this entry. The sequences are actually Intel opcode for an absolute jump or a relative jump followed by a no-op instruction. This unfortunate limitation forces Windows NT/2000 system designers to work around this for architectures such as IA-64. It does, however, explain how the disk information (in the boot sector area) placed ahead of the boot code does not interfere with the booting process because this entry points to the actual boot code entry address.

The remainder of the data structure is much of what you'd expect from the boot area. The next entry, bsOemName, is 8 bytes allocated to an OEM name and version. This entry identifies who formatted the disk, not which operating system is currently running. It is on the disk for informational purposes only and serves no other purpose.

Starting with the next entry, the boot sector duplicates the MS-DOS BIOS parameter block (BPB). The first BPB entry, bsBytesPerSec, is a 16-bit entry that specifies how many bytes are in a sector. This is typically 512, but can be different.

Figure 3.6   Boot sector data record.

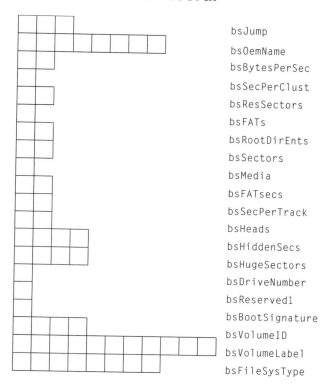

The next area, `bsSecPerClust`, indicates how many sectors are in a cluster. Although we have not discussed the cluster yet, this is where we first encounter it. A *cluster* is a group of sectors used as a fundamental unit of storage allocation. This serves two purposes. First, it places a level of indirection between the operating system and the physical disk media format. This allows changes in disk and operating system technology to be mutually exclusive. Second, it allows disk sizes to grow much larger than would be possible with just a sector allocation scheme. An example of this is a typical hard disk allocation scheme. These disks typically use 4096 byte clusters, allocating 8 sectors per cluster. If our addressing limit is 16 bits, our limit is 33Mb of storage using sector allocation but increases to 268Mb using an 8Kb cluster allocation scheme. With 32 bits, sector allocation yields approximately 2200Gb and 17600Gb respectively.

The entry `bsResSectors` specifies how many reserved sectors are on the drive or diskette, including the boot sector. This entry is useful for both the operating system and the boot program. As we'll see later, the operating system uses this entry in computing the location of key disk data structures. Boot can use this entry to compute how many additional sectors to load into memory for more complex booting schemes. An example of such a scheme may be booting multiple operating systems. It is possible for boot to load a secondary, more complex boot program that would then proceed to present a menu and load the selected operating system. Other schemes are also possible, limited only by the developer's imagination.

Jumping ahead, `bsMedia` is the media descriptor. This scheme was an early attempt at automated identification of the media type present in a drive. Originally, this entry switched a drive from low to high density. It is, however, an incomplete scheme where the same byte appears to specify more than one type of media for some earlier media types supported by MS-DOS. However, it is perfectly safe for Win32 operating systems because these older media types are not supported and hence the ambiguous mapping disappears.

The entries `bsFATs`, `bsRootDirEnts`, `bsFATsecs`, `bsSecPerTrack`, and `bsHeads` — when combined with `bsResSector` — are used to translate a logical sector number to a physical sector location. For example, to get to the primary FAT disk logical sector, start at logical sector `bsResSector` (logical sectors start at 0). To get to the secondary FAT logical sector, start at `bsResSector` + `bsFATsecs`. An interesting note: more than two FATs are permitted on any disk, implied by `bsFATs`. So, if we want to get to the *n*th FAT, start at

```
bsResSector + (n * bsFATsecs)
```

— resulting in the generalized FAT algorithm.

From Figure 3.2, we saw that the root directory followed the FAT areas. We can compute the start of the root directory with the following algorithm.

```
bsResSector + (bsFATs* bsFATsecs).
```

Finally, any data sector we need to find starts at the logical sector:

```
bsResSector + (bsFATs * bsFATsecs)
 + (32 * bsRootDirEnts / bsBytesPerSec).
```

Concerning logical sectors, we'll see later that this is the method the Win32 operating system uses to convey a desired sector to the device driver. The de facto convention for physical translation is the *sequential cylinder model*, where each cylinder is composed of a number of tracks and cylinders increase with logical sector numbering. To translate a logical sector to a physical cylinder, track, and sector model, the cylinder number is computed as the integral computation:

```
LogSector / (bsSecPerTrack * bsHeads).
```

`LogSector` is used to compute the track number.

```
mod (bsSecPerTrack * bsHeads) / bsSecPerTrack.
```

Finally, the physical sector number is

```
(LogSector mod (bsSecPerTrack * bsHeads)) * mod bsSecPerTrack + 1.
```

(Physical sector numbering starts at 1).

There are only two other key entries, `bsSectors` and `bsHugeSectors`. These entries are used for error checking by the device driver. If a logical sector number is greater than or equal to `bsSectors` or `bsHugeSectors`, then there exists an error condition. The reason for two separate entries is historical. Originally, `bsSectors` was the only entry governing disk size. It is limited to 16 bits, which is insufficient for larger hard disk drives. During its evolution, MS-DOS and Windows gained a second entry to handle these larger drives, `bsHugeSectors`. The method used to decide which entry to use is a simple algorithm: look at `bsSectors`. If it is zero, use `bsHugeSectors`; instead, use `bsSectors`.

The remaining entries, bsDriveNumber, bsReserved1, bsBootSignature, bsVolumeID, bsVolumeLabel, and bsFileSysType deal with either disk volume identification or are internal data structure members. Although we will see bsBootSignature used in other calls, all of these remaining calls are informational only.

FAT Area

All files contained on the basic DOS file system are composed of three distinct parts: a directory entry, a linked list in a File Allocation Table (FAT), and a collection of disk sectors that contain the information in the file. We'll discuss the directory entry later, but for our purposes in this section, the directory entry contains the means by which the Win32 operating system identifies the file by name and a number used as an index into the FAT array. As an example, when Windows 2000 opens a file for read access, it finds the file by matching the filename and retrieves the starting FAT index. In essence, this is the only action necessary to open a file, although there are other internal data structures Windows 2000 maintains that are also updated.

The FAT and the data area have a one-to-one relationship. This relationship allows the Win32 operating system to keep track of the data clusters in an efficient manner. By definition, each FAT entry corresponds to its equivalent sequential cluster. For example, any reference to cluster number 3 also refers to FAT entry number 3. The FAT functions as a single link linked list. If we want to find the cluster that follows cluster number 3, we look at the FAT entry number 3 and get its content. This number now gives us the next data cluster number. Figure 3.7 illustrates how this works.

Figure 3.7 Win32 FAT read example.

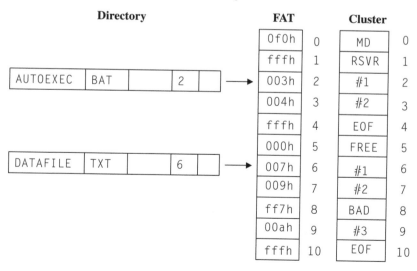

In our example, we see two files. The first file, AUTOEXEC.BAT, is probably very close to one you may have on your boot disk if you are running a Windows 9X operating system that uses either an MS-DOS device driver or TSR. When the Win32 operating system opens the file, it first goes to the directory and begins a linear search for the filename AUTOEXEC.BAT by looking for a string match. When it finds it, it performs some internal file table updates and picks up the entry for the starting disk cluster, in this case, 2. An interesting note about this entry: all clusters on a disk begin with cluster number 2, with zero reserved as a free cluster indicator and 1 reserved for the operating system.

If we now instruct the Win32 operating system to read the file sequentially, we'll read all sectors in cluster number 2 first. Utilizing the underlying virtual memory inherent in the operating system, the Win32 operating system reads a sector from the cluster into a buffer contained in a page and transfers the requested number of bytes to memory. The disk operation may be deferred if the requested sector is already contained in a page buffer. This operation may be repeated until all data from the cluster has been transferred. When the operating system begins to read the next cluster, it needs to find its physical location on disk. It does this by looking at the FAT in the entry corresponding to the current cluster number. The number it reads corresponds to the next entry to be read. In this fashion, each FAT entry corresponding to a physical cluster forms a forward link for the corresponding file data area. This process continues until the Win32 operating system encounters an end of file marker. Our example shows this for the third cluster of AUTOEXEC.BAT. The sequence of clusters, is 2, 3, and 4. FAT entry 4 contains an FFF, which signals MS-DOS that this is the last cluster of the file (by definition, any entry in the range of FF8 through FFF indicates the end of file). Table 3.1 lists all possible values contained in a FAT entry and their meaning.

NOTE: This discussion used 12-bit values, which correspond to the type of FAT typically found on floppy disks and small hard disks. You quickly run out of range on larger hard disks, so there also exists a 16-bit FAT and 32-bit FAT for these. The discussion holds true for both of these FATs, just sign extend the reserved, bad, and last cluster numbers.

Table 3.1   FAT entry values and meanings.

Value	Meaning
(0)000h	Free Cluster
(0)001h	Not Used
(0)002h - (f)fefh	Data cluster indices
(f)ff0h - (f)ff6h	Reserved
(f)ff7h	Bad Cluster
(f)ff8h - (f)ffffh	Last Cluster

For a write, the operation is somewhat more complex since file position plays a big part in how write works. However, we can examine some fundamental FAT principals for write with a simple sequential file create and write example. Figure 3.8 illustrates this example.

Figure 3.8 FAT write example.

Before create operation

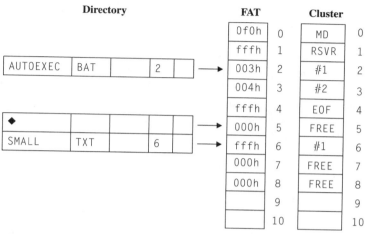

◆ = 00h or 0E5h in first filename byte.

After create, write, and close

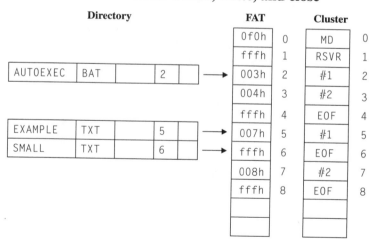

We started by creating EXAMPLE.TXT, our example file. The Win32 operating system starts searching for a free directory entry to begin its allocation. It does this by searching for either a 00h or 0E5h for the first character of the entry (we'll discuss their meaning in our next section). When it's found, internal file data structures are updated and the operation is complete. We can now begin our write operation and this is when the FAT fun starts. As soon as we do a write, the very first cluster allocation occurs. In our example, cluster 5 is the first available cluster and is allocated to our example file. When we have written exactly one cluster size plus one byte, the next cluster is allocated. In our example, a cluster belonging to SMALL.TXT occupies cluster 6, so the search returns cluster 7. The FAT forward link entry for cluster 5 now contains 7 and the writing continues. This operation continues until we finally close the file. In our example, this occurs somewhere in the third cluster. The Win32 operating system updates its data structures and places an EOF indicator in the FAT forward link entry, relative cluster 3, or physical cluster 8.

I've been very careful in discussing the write operation by avoiding all references to time in my discussion. This is because disk buffers may be flushed to disk at times that are not necessarily under the application's control. What we described, in very high-level terms, was the Win32 API function WriteFile. Jumping ahead, the WriteFile function typically writes data to an internal buffer that the operating system writes to disk on a regular basis. The Win32 operating system provides another API function, FlushFileBuffers, to write all of the buffered information for the specified file to disk.

Directory Area and Directories

The last part of the FAT file system discussion is the *directory area*. We've already covered both data area cluster mapping and the FAT forward link and have shown how a file on a FAT file system is composed of three components. The directory is the glue that holds the file together. For FAT file systems, there are two types of directories: the root directory and subdirectories. I draw this distinction because there are some subtle differences between them.

The first distinction is that every disk must have a root directory. The root directory is the starting point for all directories and files. Beginning a search from the root directory is guaranteed to get you to the exact file or directory.

Another difference is in the contents of the root directory. A root directory contains entries not only for files and subdirectories; it contains the volume label as well. It is also the reason that there exists a volume label limit of 11 characters because it must fit into the space normally reserved for filename (8) and extension (3). Additionally, it does not contain an entry for "." (self) and ".." (parent) while all subdirectories must always contain these entries.

The final distinction between the root directory and subdirectories is the location and size. The root directory consists of a sequential set of sectors starting at a fixed location on the disk, where a subdirectory is actually a special FAT file that can only be accessed by the Win32 operating system itself for both read and write. The size of the root directory is fixed by an entry in the boot area and subdirectories can grow in much the same way as a file can.

Having noted these critical differences, we can now state what is common in all types of directories. Any FAT file system directory is stored as a linear array of directory entries. The rules for use of a directory entry are common for all file types. Figure 3.9 illustrates a directory entry structure.

Figure 3.9   FAT directory structure.

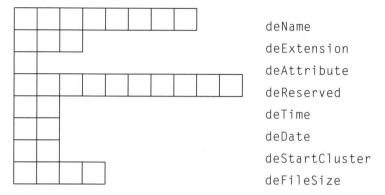

deName
deExtension
deAttribute
deReserved
deTime
deDate
deStartCluster
deFileSize

There aren't very many directory entry fields, reflecting the simple fact that a directory entry performs within the FAT file system. There are four functions that the directory entry performs: name the file, specify access rights, hold timestamps, and specify the file location and size.

When it comes to filenames, the Win32 operating system, through its MS-DOS evolution, borrows from its CP/M heritage by using the filename and file extension method. FAT file system drivers limit the filename to an eight byte entry and the extension to a three byte entry. Each entry is left justified and space-filled. Hence the file abc is stored as ABC, the file B.C is BC, and the file FileName.Txt is FILENAMETXT. Note: there are no typographical errors in the previous example; all filenames and extensions are converted to uppercase by the file system driver, further simplifying filename match algorithms. One final point: an unused field is denoted by a 00h in the first location of deName and a 0E5h denotes a deleted file. The data is still there and may be accessed by some clever tools, although this is not the way that the Win32 implements the "Recycle Bin."

Restricting file access is accomplished through the deAttribute entry. In this field, a set bit indicates that an attribute is active. Table 3.2 lists these attributes. One interesting note: the ATTR_ARCHIVE bit is actually a "modified" bit set whenever the Win32 operating system does a write operation to the file. In this way, a file that has this bit set needs to be archived. There's one entry, ATTR_LFNENTRY, that consists of more than a single bit. We'll see this used later in our discussion of VFAT.

Table 3.2 FAT attribute bits

Mnemonic	Value	Meaning
ATTR_READONLY	01h	A read-only file
ATTR_HIDDEN	02h	Hidden (can't be deleted)
ATTR_SYSTEM	04h	System (can't be deleted)
ATTR_VOLUME	08h	Volume label (not a file)
ATTR_DIRECTORY	10h	Directory
ATTR_ARCHIVE	20h	Modified file
ATTR_LFNENTRY	0fh	Part of a LFN record

Timestamping is another function of the directory entry. In timestamping, the Win32 operating system uses the last file access that modified the file to generate the date and time fields. Unlike UNIX, where the timestamp is seconds from an epoch, the FAT timestamp consists of both date and time. Like UNIX, the FAT timestamp is 32-bits wide, broken into a 16-bit date field and a 16-bit time field. The choice of encoding method, to have it one way or the other, was the preference of the operating system architect. These two fields are further broken down into bit fields composed of the logical parts of the element, such as hours:minutes:seconds and year:month:day. Figure 3.10 shows this pictorially. Timestamps are a critical data item to update for the Win32 operating system.

Figure 3.10 FAT time encoding.

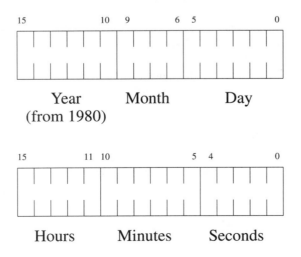

NOTE: Logical word format shown.

The final tie, and probably the most important, is the file location links. These fields link the FAT and data clusters to the directory entry. The field deStartCluster is the FAT link to the first FAT entry. This is, in essence, the anchor for the file. The entry deFileSize completes the file description by specifying the size of the file in bytes. With this entry, the file becomes independent of file system architecture or cluster size. It does, however, limit physical file sizes to 4.3Gb.

The design of the directory is pivotal in any program that manipulates a FAT disk. There are design tradeoffs concerning the timing of directory updates that will affect file system robustness. There are also design issues regarding when to switch between 16-bit and 32-bit FAT tables, etc.

VFAT File Format

One improvement that the Win32 operating systems introduced was the VFAT file system. In this file system, the size of filenames was increased, allowing you to drop cryptic names such as "CH3.DOC" and replace it with "Chapter 3.doc" instead. By the way, there's not a typographical error in that last sentence; VFAT allows embedded spaces as well. What is even more amazing is that this file system is fully compatible with both FAT-12 and FAT-16 as well. How does Microsoft accomplish this little bit of magic? By adding a new data structure to the directory entry.

In the VFAT file system, the directory entry is a new structure as shown in Figure 3.11. The original directory entry still exists, but now takes on the role of an *"alias."* The original filename contained in the alias is an algorithmically-generated name derived from the real filename to allow removable media, i.e., floppy disks, zip drives, etc., to still be usable by non-Win32 operating systems such as MS-DOS. This is great for reading, but what happens if the non-Win32 operating system modifies the volume by creating a file, deleting a file, renaming a file, etc.? The new directory entry contains a checksum of the alias. Should the alias checksum not match the stored checksum, the new directory entry is assumed to be invalid and discarded. The name in the remaining aliases that do not have a directory entry associated with them become the name used by the Win32 operating system. There are other new entries in this new directory structure and a closer examination will help us better understand how it all fits together.

Figure 3.11 VFAT long directory structure.

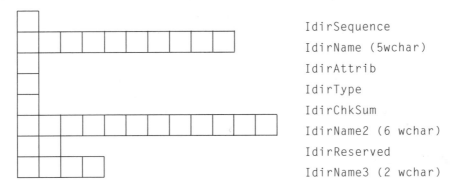

```
IdirSequence
IdirName (5wchar)
IdirAttrib
IdirType
IdirChkSum
IdirName2 (6 wchar)
IdirReserved
IdirName3 (2 wchar)
```

The first new data entry is the `1dirSequence` field. In order to accomplish long filenames, more than one directory entry must be used. This field contains the sequence number in the lower 6 bits. To identify the last entry used, this field is or'ed with a `40h`. The next field is the `1dirAttrib` field. In order to remain compatible with older FAT systems, the size of the directory entry is the same as the alias. So, the search algorithm looks for a `0fh` in this field. As it turns out, older non-Win32 operating systems ignore these entries thanks to the `0fh`. The directory entry also contains the `1dirChksum` which is a checksum of the alias.

A sequence of entries stores the new name. Each one can hold 13 Unicode characters spread across the fields `1dirName`, `1dirName2`, and `1dirName3`. The Win32 operating system allows filenames to be up to 255 characters long, necessitating up to 20 entries. Although the file system can support up to 64 entries, allowing filenames to be 832 characters long, the Win32 operating system enforces a 255 character limit.

FAT-32 Disk Format

Naturally, disk sizes continue to increase with time. As a result, the 4Gb limitation resulting from FAT-16 needed to be resolved. So Microsoft introduced a FAT-32 file system. Basically, this new file system type changes the sizes of some of the words used to address disk blocks or sectors to 32 bits. This increases the upper limit of the file system to 2Tb. This file system type was introduced with the Windows 95 OEM service release 2.

In order to do so, the `BPB`, `DPB`, `DEVICEPARAMS` structures and the FAT were updated to accommodate the new 32-bit file pointers. These new structure sizes allow Microsoft to improve system features as well by eliminating the restrictions mentioned earlier of having a special root directory. Starting with FAT-32, the root directory is now the same as any other subdirectory. This means that the root directory also contains "." and ".." entries is well. The FAT-32 file system also improves efficiency by reducing the cluster size to 4096, eliminating some wasted space on small files.

There is some additional overhead however. The new file system format reserves a greater number of reserved sectors than either FAT-16 or FAT-12. The boot block is now larger than a single sector, and another sector is now dedicated to file system overhead functions such as the number of free sectors and recently allocated clusters; overall, a small price for such a dramatic increase in storage capacity.

The remainder of the file system structures remain similar enough to the VFAT versions of FAT-16 and FAT-12 that all other functionality remains virtually identical. So, all of our earlier descriptions still hold true, thanks to FAT-32's heritage.

Executable File Formats

COM File Format

A COM file is an exact binary image of the program as it initially appears in memory. The image must reserve the first 100h bytes for the PSP and use the tiny or small programming model. This file type can only be executed by a VM86 session, as the image contains no information usable by the other virtual machines. In addition, the COM file is not allowed for architectures other than IA-32 except when running IA-32 emulators in Windows NT/2000 running on non-IA-32 targets.

EXE File Format

MS-DOS had only two executable file types, disregarding the batch file. The first was the COM file we just examined. The other method is an EXE file that is composed of a header, image, and an optional relocation table. The exe_header data structure is the mechanism used to tie the program together (Listing 3.1).

Listing 3.1 C Version of .EXE file header.

```c
typedef struct
{
        UWORD exSignature;
        UWORD exExtraBytes;
        UWORD exPages;
        UWORD exRelocItems;
        UWORD exHeaderSize;
        UWORD exMinAlloc;
        UWORD exMaxAlloc;
        UWORD exInitSS;
        UWORD exInitSP;
        UWORD exCheckSum;
        UWORD exInitIP;
        UWORD exInitCS;
        UWORD exRelocTable;
        UWORD exOverlay;
} exe_header;
```

The first entry in the EXE structure is `exSignature`. This entry is the ASCII characters "MZ." This signature identifies an EXE file. It is in this entry that MS-DOS and Win32 operating systems differentiate between the two real mode executables: COM and EXE files. It is also present in other protected mode executables, as we will see later, but it takes on a different function at that time.

One of the key elements in any executable file is the size or sizes of the section of the executable. In an EXE file, there is only a single section, but there is no single member that indicates the file size. This must be computed, and is done so with the help of the two members: `exExtraBytes` and `exExtraBytes`. The size is stored as a count of 512 byte pages, and another that indicates the remainder of bytes necessary to complete the file size. The first of these two is `exExtraBytes`. This member indicates the number of bytes in the last partial page. It is followed by `exPages` that contains the number of whole pages in the file. Member `exRelocItems` is a count of the number of relocation entries in the relocation table. Each entry is four bytes long and is stored in 8086 segment:offset fashion. The final member that determines EXE file size is `exHeaderSize`. This is the size of the header in 16-byte paragraphs.

Like the COM file format, this executable file format contains only information useful to VM86 virtual machines and is limited to IA-32 architectures or IA-32 emulators in Windows NT/2000 running on non-IA-32 targets.

PE File Format

In order to encompass all the requirements of the Win32 operating system, Microsoft decided to invent a new executable file format. Although other file formats existed that were capable of 32-bit operation, primarily from their work with OS/2, Microsoft decided to introduce the Portable Executable (PE) file format. It is based on the COFF (Common Object File Format) specification common to UNIX operating systems. However, to remain compatible with previous versions of the MS-DOS and Windows operating systems, the PE file format also retains the familiar EXE header from MS-DOS.

A great deal of the information that defines the PE executable file format comes from a file included in the Win32 Software Development Kit (SDK), `WINNT.H`. It is, however, incomplete. You may, however, find the additional information necessary in a sample application contained on both the MSDN CD-ROMs and the Microsoft web site. These structures are defined in `PEFILE.H`, included in the `PEFile` sample application available on these resources. Unfortunately, much of the Win32 information is scattered in this way and requires you, the developer, to hunt through the Microsoft documentation to accomplish your task. However, I have collected this information and will present it in the following section, so you won't have to.

Structure of PE Files

The PE file format is shown in Figure 3.12. The PE file format begins with an MS-DOS header, a real-mode program stub, and a PE file signature. The reason for this is simple. MS-DOS lacks the necessary logic to limit its execution to COM and EXE files. MS-DOS, in its attempt to support the COM file, assumes that any file lacking in the 'MZ' signature is a COM file. That means that should you try to execute a file that doesn't begin with this signature, MS-DOS will load it as an image and simply jump to it. This could have disastrous results. In an attempt to prevent this and allow for backward compatibility, Microsoft always prepends the non-MS-DOS executable file with a small EXE executable stub. You can see this stub in action by using a Windows 9X system, shutting down to MS-DOS mode, and running a Win32 executable. Typically, you will see an error message saying that the file cannot run in this mode and requires another operating system to run.

Figure 3.12 Structure of a PE file image.

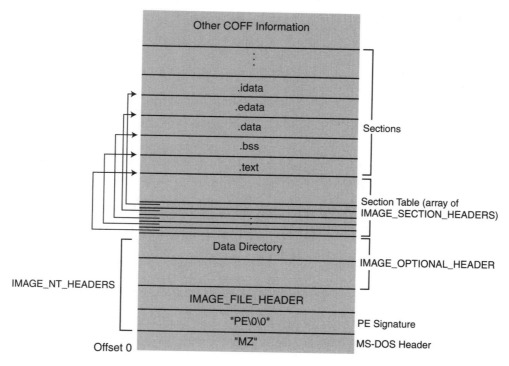

Again, referring to Figure 3.12, immediately following the EXE stub is the PE file header, optional header, section headers, and section bodies. The section bodies typically contain the various code images such as text, data, and BSS. At the end of the PE file is miscellaneous information that may include relocation information, symbol table information, line number information, and string table data.

MS-DOS/Real-Mode Header

The first component in the PE file format is the MS-DOS header. As mentioned earlier, this structure at the beginning of the PE file format is actually a small stub program. When you attempt to load a PE file created for a Win32 operating system on Windows v3.1 or earlier, or MS-DOS version 2.0 or later, the operating system can read the file and run the stub. The stub usually prints that it is not compatible and exits. In Figure 3.12, we see that there are some additional fields not described earlier. That is because these fields only appear in Win32 file formats such as the PE format.

The MS-DOS header occupies the first 64 bytes of the PE file. Two entries, exReserved1 and exReserved2, are spacers that force field alignment within the 64-byte header. Fields exOemID and exOemInfo contain some OEM-specific information regarding the file. However, the most important field in these EXE header extensions is exHdrOffset — used to point to the offset within the file where we can find the PE/COFF header. By placing this pointer sufficiently ahead of the EXE header, we provide room for the stub code.

Real-Mode Stub Program

The real-mode stub program is the program run by MS-DOS when the executable is loaded. This code is the only code loaded by MS-DOS as instructed by the EXE header. All the following data within the file is ignored. For other operating systems, such as Windows, OS/2, and the Win32 family of operating systems, this code is an MS-DOS stub program that typically does no more than output a line of text and terminate, protecting the unsuspecting user from strange behavior. This stub code is common, but other code may be placed here, such as a loader as used in earlier Windows 3.X operating systems. This is accomplished by overriding the default linker behavior by substituting your own valid MS-DOS-based program in place of WINSTUB.EXE. This is a very powerful but seldom used mechanism. In the vast majority of applications, WINSTUB.EXE is used.

PE File Header and Signature

As mentioned earlier, the PE file header is located by indexing the exHdrOffset field of the MS-DOS header. To find the start of the PE header, simply add the contents of the exHdrOffset field to the offset of the start of the file, typically 0 for traditional file access and the base address of the file in memory for memory mapped files. Note that this is a pointer to the signature, not the header itself. The Win32 operating systems use this feature to further refine their logic to identify the exact type of file, such as Win16, that may also be executed by the operating system.

Notice that instead of retrieving the offset of the PE file header, this macro retrieves the location of the PE file signature. Starting with Windows and OS/2 executables, .exe files were given file signatures to specify the intended target operating system. Table 3.3 lists the various file types, operating system, and associated signatures. It also identifies a standard Windows macro associated with each. Note that there is no difference between Windows executables and OS/2 executables. The only difference between the two is system version specification contained within the header. This allows both operating systems to share the same executable file structure. For the PE file format used in Win32 operating systems, the signature occurs immediately before the PE file header structure. In versions of Windows and OS/2, the signature is the first word of the file header. In Win32 operating systems, the PE file format uses a DWORD for the signature.

Table 3.3 Executable file types and signature.

Macro	Type	Operating System	Hex signature
IMAGE_DOS_SIGNATURE	MZ	MS-DOS	0x5A4D
IMAGE_OS2_SIGNATURE	NE	OS/2, Windows	0x454E
IMAGE_OS2_SIGNATURE_LE	LE	OS/2, Windows	0x454C
IMAGE_NT_SIGNATURE	PE	Window NT/2000, Windows 9X	0x00004550

Immediately following the signature is the PE File Header (refer to Figure 3.12 on page 59). Listing 3.2 shows an excerpt from WINNT.H that is used to describe this header. We will examine the version supplied with GNU gcc. Versions available in the Microsoft platform SDK and Visual C++ are different, but the definitions themselves are identical.

Listing 3.2 PE file header.

```
    .
    .

#define IMAGE_SIZEOF_FILE_HEADER        20

    .
    .
    .

typedef struct _IMAGE_FILE_HEADER {
        WORD Machine;
        WORD NumberOfSections;
        DWORD TimeDateStamp;
        DWORD PointerToSymbolTable;
        DWORD NumberOfSymbols;
        WORD SizeOfOptionalHeader;
        WORD Characteristics;
} IMAGE_FILE_HEADER, *PIMAGE_FILE_HEADER;

    .
    .
    .
```

The first piece of information regarding the File Header we encounter is the IMAGE_SIZEOF_FILE_HEADER. This allows us to use a predetermined constant. Alternately, you could use the C/C++ sizeof operator to get this information. You must be careful to make certain that the compiler does not pad the structure for alignment. This is also true if you are memory mapping the file.

The first field, Machine, indicates the type of machine for which the executable was built. Since Windows NT/2000 has been available on a number of platforms, such as the Compaq Alpha, MIPS R4000, PowerPC, Intel IA-32, and Intel IA-64 processors, this field helps further refine the validity of the executable. The Win32 operating system uses this information whether or not the files are valid by examining it before going any further into the rest of the file.

The Characteristics field identifies specific characteristics about the file. This field is essentially a bit field and is also identified in WINNT.H. The field contains data about:

• the presence of relocation information	(IMAGE_FILE_RELOCS_STRIPPED)
• debug information	(IMAGE_FILE_DEBUG_STRIPPED, IMAGE_FILE_LINE_NUMS_STRIPPED, IMAGE__FILE_LOCAL_SYMS_STRIPPED, and IMAGE_FILE_BYTES_REVERSED_LO)
• machine information	(IMAGE_FILE_32BIT_MACHINE, IMAGE_FILE_BYTES_REVERSED_LO, and IMAGE_FILE_BYTES_REVERSED_HI)
• system information	(IMAGE_FILE_REMOVABLE_RUN_FROM_SWAP, IMAGE_FILE_NET_RUN_FROM_SWAP, IMAGE_FILE_SYSTEM, IMAGE_FILE_DLL, and IMAGE_FILE_UP_SYSTEM_ONLY)

The file also contains a timestamp in the TimeDateStamp that may be used to identify when the file was generated.

In order to support debugging, the file contains two fields that help the debugger locate debug information. The first field, PointerToSymbolTable, contains an offset into the file at the start of the symbol table. The other field, NumberOfSymbols, contains a count of the number of symbols included in the file.

Again, referring back to Figure 3.12, we see that the file contains a number of sections such as text, bss, and so on. The entry NumberOfSections indicates how many section headers and section bodies are in the file. This allows the Win32 operating system to extract the information easily. Each section header and section body is laid out sequentially in the file, so the number of sections is necessary to determine where the section headers and bodies end.

PE Optional Header

The next section in the PE file is the PE Optional Header, a misnomer because the entry is not optional. This section is quite long, 224 bytes in length, and contains many fields. The PE Optional Header contains vital information about the executable image, such as initial stack size, program entry point location, preferred base address, operating system version, section alignment information, etc. Listing 3.3 contains the structure definition for this header. We will examine some of the fields and discuss their function with respect to the file. Note that these fields are those common to the Common Object File Format (COFF), which most UNIX executable files use. Although the fields retain the names defined in COFF, the Win32 operating systems actually use some of them for purposes other than those defined in the COFF standard. For example, note that the structure is divided into "Standard fields" and "NT additional fields." This is a common Microsoft technique that forces the developer to constantly be on the lookout. Just be careful that the field name does not confuse you with its actual purpose.

Listing 3.3 PE optional header fields.

```
typedef struct _IMAGE_OPTIONAL_HEADER {
        WORD Magic;
        BYTE MajorLinkerVersion;
        BYTE MinorLinkerVersion;
        DWORD SizeOfCode;
        DWORD SizeOfInitializedData;
        DWORD SizeOfUninitializedData;
        DWORD AddressOfEntryPoint;
        DWORD BaseOfCode;
        DWORD BaseOfData;
        DWORD ImageBase;
        DWORD SectionAlignment;
        DWORD FileAlignment;
        WORD MajorOperatingSystemVersion;
        WORD MinorOperatingSystemVersion;
        WORD MajorImageVersion;
        WORD MinorImageVersion;
        WORD MajorSubsystemVersion;
        WORD MinorSubsystemVersion;
        DWORD Win32VersionValue;
        DWORD SizeOfImage;
        DWORD SizeOfHeaders;
        DWORD CheckSum;
        WORD Subsystem;
        WORD DllCharacteristics;
        DWORD SizeOfStackReserve;
        DWORD SizeOfStackCommit;
        DWORD SizeOfHeapReserve;
        DWORD SizeOfHeapCommit;
        DWORD LoaderFlags;
```

```
        DWORD NumberOfRvaAndSizes;
        IMAGE_DATA_DIRECTORY
DataDirectory[IMAGE_NUMBEROF_DIRECTORY_ENTRIES];
} IMAGE_OPTIONAL_HEADER,*PIMAGE_OPTIONAL_HEADER;
```

The following is a description of the fields of the PE Optional Header:

Magic	Another signature used to identify the optional header.
MajorLinkerVersion, MinorLinkerVersion	Indicates version of the linker that linked this image. Note that the versions may not be unique because different vendor linkers may have been used to link this file and the version numbers will not bear any relationship to each other.
SizeOfCode	Size of code section, or their sum if multiple code sections.
SizeOfInitializedData	Size of initialized data section, or their sum if multiple code sections.
SizeOfUninitializedData	Size of uninitialized data section, or their sum if multiple code sections.
AddressOfEntryPoint	Indicates the location of the entry point for the application.
BaseOfCode	Offset, relative to image base, of code or .text section, in loaded image.
BaseOfData	Offset, relative to image base, of uninitialized data or .bss section in loaded image.

The following fields, not present in the standard COFF file, were added by Microsoft to the PE file format to provide loader support for much of the Win32-specific process behavior.

ImageBase	Preferred base address in the address space of a process to map the executable image.
SectionAlignment	Each section is loaded into the address space of a process sequentially, beginning at ImageBase. SectionAlignment dictates the minimum amount of space a section can occupy when loaded. All sections are aligned on SectionAlignment boundaries. Section alignment can be no less than the page size and must be a multiple of the page size as dictated by the behavior of the Win32 operating system virtual memory manager.
FileAlignment	Minimum granularity of chunks of information within the image file prior to loading. For example, the linker zero-pads a section body (raw data for a section) up to the nearest FileAlignment boundary in the file. This value is constrained to be a power of 2 between 512 and 65,536.

`MajorOperatingSystemVersion`	Indicates the major version of the Win32 operating system.
`MinorOperatingSystemVersion`	Indicates the minor version of the Win32 operating system.
`MajorImageVersion`	Used to indicate the major version number of the application.
`MinorImageVersion`	Used to indicate the minor version number of the application.
`MajorSubsystemVersion`	Indicates the Win32 subsystem major version number.
`MinorSubsystemVersion`	Indicates the Win32 subsystem minor version number.
`Win32VersionValue`	Reserved
`SizeOfImage`	Indicates the amount of address space needed to reserve the loaded executable image, including all headers. This number must be a multiple of `SectionAlignment`.
`SizeOfHeaders`	This field indicates how much space in the file is used for representing all the file headers, starting from the beginning of the file. The section bodies begin at this location.
`CheckSum`	A checksum value used to validate the executable file at load time.
`Subsystem`	Field used to identify the target subsystem for this executable. These include: • `IMAGE_SUBSYSTEM_UNKNOWN`: Unknown subsystem. • `IMAGE_SUBSYSTEM_NATIVE`: Used for device drivers and native Windows NT processes. • `IMAGE_SUBSYSTEM_WINDOWS_GUI`: Image runs in the Windows graphical user interface (GUI) subsystem. • `IMAGE_SUBSYSTEM_WINDOWS_CUI`: Image runs in the Windows character subsystem. • `IMAGE_SUBSYSTEM_POSIX_CUI`: POSIX Character cell User Interface (Windows NT/2000 only). • `IMAGE_SUBSYSTEM_WINDOWS_CE_GUI`: Image runs in Windows CE. • `IMAGE_SUBSYSTEM_EFI_APPLICATION`: Image is an EFI application. • `IMAGE_SUBSYSTEM_EFI_BOOT_SERVICE_DRIVER`: Image is an EFI driver that provides boot services. • `IMAGE_SUBSYSTEM_EFI_RUNTIME_DRIVER`: Image is an EFI driver that provides runtime services.

`DllCharacteristics`	Flags used to indicate if a DLL image includes entry points for process and thread initialization and termination. The following are valid entries: • `IMAGE_DLLCHARACTERISTICS_NO_BIND`: Do not bind image. • `IMAGE_DLLCHARACTERISTICS_WDM_DRIVER`: Driver is a WDM Driver. • `IMAGE_DLLCHARACTERISTICS_TERMINAL_SERVER_AWARE`: Image is Terminal Server aware.

`SizeOfStackReserve,`
`SizeOfStackCommit,`
`SizeOfHeapReserve,`
`SizeOfHeapCommit`
	These fields control the amount of address space to reserve and commit for the stack and local heap. Both the stack and heap have default values of 1 page committed and 16 pages reserved.

`LoaderFlags`	Tells the loader whether to break on load, debug on load, or the default, which is to let things run normally.
`NumberOfRvaAndSizes`	This field identifies the length of the `DataDirectory` array that follows. Note that this field is used to identify the size of the array, not the number of valid entries in the array.
`DataDirectory`	Indicates where to find other important components of executable information in the file. It is an array of `IMAGE_DATA_DIRECTORY` structures that are located at the end of the optional header structure.

Data Directories

Each data directory is a structure defined as an `IMAGE_DATA_DIRECTORY`. Although data directory entries themselves are the same, each directory type is entirely unique. Each data directory entry specifies the size and relative virtual address of the directory. To locate a particular directory, you determine the relative address from the data directory array in the optional header. Next, you use the virtual address to determine which section the directory is in. Once you determine which section contains the directory, the section header is then used to find the exact file offset location of the data directory — not straightforward, but easily done via macros and functions.

PE File Sections

Within the PE file, sections contain the parts of the file, code, data, resources, and other executable information, that directly relates to your source code. Each section has a header and a body, which is the raw data for that section. Although section headers are well defined, section bodies consist only of variable data generated by the code translator used to generate the file, e.g., compiler, assembler, linker, etc. There is no predefined order in which these sections can appear because all the information necessary to decipher this random data is contained within the header.

Section Headers

Section headers are defined in the structure illustrated in Listing 3.4. Located directly after the optional header are one or more section headers. Each section header is 40 bytes long and ends on a byte boundary. Because there is no positional information associated with the section headers, each section and section header is identified by name.

Listing 3.4 Section header structure.

```
typedef struct _IMAGE_SECTION_HEADER {
        BYTE Name[IMAGE_SIZEOF_SHORT_NAME];
        union {
                DWORD PhysicalAddress;
                DWORD VirtualSize;
        } Misc;
        DWORD VirtualAddress;
        DWORD SizeOfRawData;
        DWORD PointerToRawData;
        DWORD PointerToRelocations;
        DWORD PointerToLinenumbers;
        WORD NumberOfRelocations;
        WORD NumberOfLinenumbers;
        DWORD Characteristics;
} IMAGE_SECTION_HEADER,*PIMAGE_SECTION_HEADER;
```

Section Header Fields

Name	Each section header has a name field up to eight characters long. By definition, the first character of the string must be a period.
PhysicalAddress or VirtualSize	• PhysicalAddress: Specifies the file address. • VirtualSize: Total size of the section when loaded into memory. If this value is greater than SizeOfRawData, the section is filled with zeros.
VirtualAddress	Identifies the virtual address in the process's address space in which to load the section. The logical address is created by adding the value of this field to the ImageBase virtual address in the optional header structure. If this image file represents a DLL, the actual ImageBase value should be verified programmatically using GetModuleHandle in order to correctly compute the logical address.

SizeOfRawData	The size of the section body, which must be a multiple of FileAlignment, less than or equal to a multiple of FileAlignment in the file. Once the image is loaded into a process's address space, the size of the section body becomes less than or equal to a multiple of SectionAlignment. If this values is less than VirtualSize, the remainder of the section is filled with zeros.
PointerToRawData	Offset to the location of the section body in the file.
PointerToRelocations	File pointer to beginning of relocation entries for the section. Set to 0 for executable images or if there are no relocations.
PointerToLinenumbers	File pointer to beginning of line-number entries for the section. Set to 0 if there are no COFF line numbers.
NumberOfRelocations	Number of relocation entries for the section. Set to 0 for executable images.
NumberOfLinenumbers	Number of line-number entries for the section.
Characteristics	Defines the section characteristics. This is illustrated in Table 3.4.

Table 3.4 Section characteristics bit field definition.

Value	Definition
0x80000000	Section can be written to.
0x40000000	Section can be read.
0x20000000	Section can be executed as code.
0x10000000	Section can be shared in memory.
0x08000000	Section is not pageable.
0x04000000	Section cannot be cached.
0x02000000	Section can be discarded as needed.
0x01000000	Section contains extended relocations.
0x00E00000	Align data on a 8192-byte boundary.
0x00D00000	Align data on a 4096-byte boundary.
0x00C00000	Align data on a 2048-byte boundary.
0x00B00000	Align data on a 1024-byte boundary.

Value	Definition
0x00A00000	Align data on a 512-byte boundary.
0x00900000	Align data on a 256-byte boundary.
0x00800000	Align data on a 128-byte boundary.
0x00700000	Align data on a 64-byte boundary.
0x00600000	Align data on a 32-byte boundary.
0x00500000	Align data on a 16-byte boundary.
0x00400000	Align data on a 8-byte boundary.
0x00300000	Align data on a 4-byte boundary.
0x00200000	Align data on a 2-byte boundary.
0x00100000	Align data on a 1-byte boundary.
0x00001000	Section contains COMDAT data.
0x00000800	Section will not become part of the image.
0x00000200	Section contains comments or other information. The .drectve section has this type.
0x00000080	Section contains uninitialized data.
0x00000040	Section contains initialized data.
0x00000020	Section contains executable code.
0x00000008	Section should not be padded to next boundary. This is obsolete and replaced by IMAGE_SCN_ALIGN_1BYTES.

Predefined Sections

A Win32 application typically has the nine predefined sections named .text, .bss, .rdata, .data, .rsrc, .edata, .idata, .pdata, and .debug. Not all of these sections are necessary and depend on the application, if compiled with debug options, etc. However, some applications may define more sections to suit their needs. This is similar to code and data segments in MS-DOS and Windows v3.1. Let us now take a look at sections common to typical Win32 PE files.

Executable Code Section, .text

Unlike earlier Windows v3.X, all code segments are contained in a single section called .text in Win32. Because all Win32 operating systems use a page-based virtual memory management system, there is no advantage to separating code into distinct code segments. As a result, one large code section is easier to manage for both the operating system and the application developer.

The .text section also contains the entry point mentioned earlier. You also find the IAT in the .text section immediately before the module entry point. The IAT's presence in the .text section makes sense because the table is really a series of jump instructions, the fixed-up address being the specific location to jump to. When Win32 executable images are loaded into a process's address space, the IAT is fixed up with the location of each imported function's physical address. The loader finds the IAT in the .text section by locating the module entry point and relies on the fact that the IAT occurs immediately before the entry point. Because each entry is the same size, it is easy to "walk" backward in the table to find its beginning.

Data Sections, .bss, .rdata, .data

There are three data sections commonly found in a Win32 PE file. The .bss section corresponds to uninitialized data for the application, including all variables declared as static within a function or source module. The .rdata section represents read-only data, such as literal strings, constants, and debug directory information. All other variables are stored in the .data section.

Resources section, .rsrc

The .rsrc section is not found in the standard COFF definition and is unique to Win32 operating systems. That is due to the fact that a traditional Windows executable requires file space to carry what Microsoft calls the "file resource." That is where you will find information such as the icon for the file, string tables, etc. The .rsrc section begins with a resource directory structure similar to other sections, but data for this section is further structured into a resource tree. Listing 3.5 illustrates the structure IMAGE_RESOURCE_DIRECTORY that forms the root and nodes of the tree.

Listing 3.5 Image resource directory structure.

```
typedef struct _IMAGE_RESOURCE_DIRECTORY {
        DWORD Characteristics;
        DWORD TimeDateStamp;
        WORD MajorVersion;
        WORD MinorVersion;
        WORD NumberOfNamedEntries;
        WORD NumberOfIdEntries;
} IMAGE_RESOURCE_DIRECTORY,*PIMAGE_RESOURCE_DIRECTORY;
```

If we look at Listing 3.5, we find the data structure that constitutes the directory for the .rsrc section. This header uses two entries, NumberOfNamedEntries and NumberOfIdEntries, to determine the size of the following entries. Each of the following entries takes on the form shown in Listing 3.6, and is of fixed length. These entries are sorted with named entries first in alphabetical order, followed by the numbered entries in ascending numerical order. Each entry in the directory may point either to another directory entry or a leaf. The resources form a tree structure that allows nesting. Of all the PE file constructs, it is probably the most complex.

Listing 3.6 Resource directory entry.

```
typedef struct _IMAGE_RESOURCE_DIRECTORY_ENTRY {
    union {
        struct {
            DWORD NameOffset:31;
            DWORD NameIsString:1;
        }DUMMYSTRUCTNAME;
        DWORD Name;
        WORD Id;
    } DUMMYUNIONNAME;
    union {
        DWORD OffsetToData;
        struct {
            DWORD OffsetToDirectory:31;
            DWORD DataIsDirectory:1;
        } DUMMYSTRUCTNAME2;
    } DUMMYUNIONNAME2;
} IMAGE_RESOURCE_DIRECTORY_ENTRY,*PIMAGE_RESOURCE_DIRECTORY_ENTRY;
```

Export Section, .edata

The .edata section is the part of the file that gives us our exports. It is this section that holds the information we obtained when using the objdump program in Chapter 1. You can see its structure in Listing 3.7. As with the other sections, the fields are composed of the following:

Characteristics	Reserved (always 0).
TimeDateStamp	Indicates when this file was created.
MajorVersion, MinorVersion	Reserved (always 0).
Name	Identifies the name of the executable module.
Base	Starting ordinal number for exported functions.
NumberOfFunctions, NumberOfNames	Indicates how many functions and function names are being exported from the module.
AddressOfFunctions	Offset to a list of exported function entry points.

AddressOfNames	Offset to the beginning of a null-separated list of exported function names.
AddressOfNameOrdinals	Offset to a list of ordinal values (each 2 bytes long) for the same exported functions.

Listing 3.7 Export section directory structure.

```
typedef struct _IMAGE_EXPORT_DIRECTORY {
        DWORD Characteristics;
        DWORD TimeDateStamp;
        WORD MajorVersion;
        WORD MinorVersion;
        DWORD Name;
        DWORD Base;
        DWORD NumberOfFunctions;
        DWORD NumberOfNames;
        PDWORD *AddressOfFunctions;
        PDWORD *AddressOfNames;
        PWORD *AddressOfNameOrdinals;
} IMAGE_EXPORT_DIRECTORY,*PIMAGE_EXPORT_DIRECTORY;
```

Import section, .idata

The .idata section imports data, such as the information we saw in our output from objdump in Chapter 1. It includes the import directory and import address name table. From the data in this section, you can retrieve the names of modules and all functions in each module imported by an executable.

Debug section, .debug

Debug information for the PE file is in the .debug section but the debug directories are contained in the .rdata section. Each of those directories reference debug information in the .debug section. The structure is in Listing 3.8. It is this data that Win32 debuggers use for identifying the function entry points, variable names, etc.

Listing 3.8 Debug section entry.

```
typedef struct _IMAGE_DEBUG_DIRECTORY {
        DWORD Characteristics;
        DWORD TimeDateStamp;
        WORD MajorVersion;
        WORD MinorVersion;
        DWORD Type;
        DWORD SizeOfData;
        DWORD AddressOfRawData;
        DWORD PointerToRawData;
} IMAGE_DEBUG_DIRECTORY,*PIMAGE_DEBUG_DIRECTORY;
```

This section is optional — it may be stripped from the file into a separate debug file. When this is done, a flag is specified in the PE file header to indicate that the debug data has been stripped. More often than not, the executable files you will deliver will be stripped.

OK, Had Enough?

If there's one thing the Win32 operating system is not shy on, it's file types. Frankly, we've only scratched the surface. There are special file types for VxD files, the registry, etc., but that's way too much to cover in a single chapter. In fact, there are books that concentrate on nothing other than Win32 file types. What we've done in this chapter is cover the basic executable file types so that we can better understand what we're looking at when we need to analyze an executable or DLL. With these basics under our belts, we'll now move on to studying the Win32 API function calls.

4

Chapter 4

Win32 Console Mode

When someone mentions Windows, usually you think of the graphical user interface that you can see. After all, why wouldn't you? It is "windows" isn't it? The fact of the matter is the graphical user interface made this operating system popular. When the more simple MS-DOS dominated Intel-based systems, there were many people who wouldn't touch a computer. They were intimidated, nearly frightened, by the mere thought of memorizing arcane key sequences — rightfully so. Remember such classics as WordStar? The keystroke sequence control-Q-R for moving to the start of the document and control-Q-C to move to the end were far from intuitive. It's no wonder that people became computer-phobic. Copying the Xerox PARC and Apple OS graphical user interface was a good move on the part of Microsoft. However, the graphical interface brings with it a complexity that transfers that intimidation from the user to the programmer.

Why do I make such a statement? Well, for one thing, there are a vast amount of books written for Windows programming that cover graphical programming, libraries that encapsulate the API to make it easier, and so on. For another, I speak from experience. My observation is that the graphical user interface changes the mode that programmers work in. User interfaces such as Windows introduce event-driven programming — changing the frame of reference from one where the *program* determines the execution, to one where *external events*, such as keystrokes and mouse movements, determine what will execute.

There is, however, a console mode that allows you to write non-graphical applications. This is the Win32 console mode and the API is presented in Table 4.1. As with all other Win32 APIs, there are quite a few calls and we'll examine at them in this chapter.

Table 4.1   Win32 console functions.

Function	Description
AllocConsole	Allocates a new console for the calling process.
CreateConsoleScreenBuffer	Creates a console screen buffer and returns a handle to it.
FillConsoleOutputAttribute	Sets the text and background color attributes for a specified number of character cells, beginning at the specified coordinates in a screen buffer.
FillConsoleOutputCharacter	Writes a character to the screen buffer a specified number of times, beginning at the specified coordinates.
FlushConsoleInputBuffer	Flushes the console input buffer. All input records currently in the input buffer are discarded.
FreeConsole	Detaches the calling process from its console.
GenerateConsoleCtrlEvent	Sends a specified signal to a console process group that shares the console associated with the calling process.
GetConsoleCP	Returns the identity of the input code page used by the console associated with the calling process.
GetConsoleCursorInfo	Retrieves information about the size and visibility of the cursor for the specified console screen buffer.
GetConsoleMode	Reports the current input mode of a console's input buffer or the current output mode of a console screen buffer.
GetConsoleOutputCP	Returns the identity of the output code page used by the console associated with the calling process.
GetConsoleScreenBufferInfo	Retrieves information about the specified console screen buffer.
GetConsoleTitle	Retrieves the title bar string for the current console window.
GetLargestConsoleWindowSize	Returns the size of the largest possible console window, based on the current font and the size of the display.
GetNumberOfConsoleInputEvents	Retrieves the number of unread input records in the console's input buffer.
GetNumberOfConsoleMouseButtons	Retrieves the number of buttons on the mouse used by the current console.

Function	Description
GetStdHandle	Returns a handle for the standard input, standard output, or standard error device.
PeekConsoleInput	Reads data from the specified console input buffer without removing it from the buffer.
ReadConsole	Reads character input from the console input buffer and removes it from the buffer.
ReadConsoleInput	Reads data from a console input buffer and removes it from the buffer.
ReadConsoleOutput	Reads character and color attribute data from a rectangular block of character cells in a console screen buffer, and writes the data to a rectangular block at a specified location in the destination buffer.
ReadConsoleOutputAttribute	Copies a specified number of foreground and background color attributes from consecutive cells of a console screen buffer, beginning at a specified location.
ReadConsoleOutputCharacter	Copies a number of characters from consecutive cells of a console screen buffer, beginning at a specified location.
ScrollConsoleScreenBuffer	Moves a block of data in a screen buffer.
SetConsoleActiveScreenBuffer	Sets the specified screen buffer to be the currently displayed console screen buffer.
SetConsoleCP	Sets the input code page used by the console associated with the calling process.
SetConsoleCtrlHandler	Adds or removes an application-defined HandlerRoutine function from the list of handler functions for the calling process.
SetConsoleCursorInfo	Sets the size and visibility of the cursor for the specified console screen buffer.
SetConsoleCursorPosition	Sets the cursor position in the specified console screen buffer.
SetConsoleMode	Sets the input mode of a console's input buffer or the output mode of a console screen buffer.
SetConsoleOutputCP	Sets the output code page used by the console associated with the calling process.

Function	Description
SetConsoleScreenBufferSize	Changes the size of the specified console screen buffer.
SetConsoleTextAttribute	Sets the text and background color attributes of characters written to the screen buffer by the WriteFile or WriteConsole function, or echoed by the ReadFile or ReadConsole function.
SetConsoleTitle	Sets the title bar string for the current console window.
SetConsoleWindowInfo	Sets the current size and position of a console screen buffer's window.
SetStdHandle	Sets the handle for the standard input, standard output, or standard error device.
WriteConsole	Writes a character string to a console screen buffer beginning at the current cursor location.
WriteConsoleInput	Writes data directly to the console input buffer.
WriteConsoleOutput	Writes character and color attribute data to a specified rectangular block of character cells in a console screen buffer.
WriteConsoleOutputAttribute	Copies a number of foreground and background color attributes to consecutive cells of a console screen buffer, beginning at a specified location.
WriteConsoleOutputCharacter	Copies a number of characters to consecutive cells of a console screen buffer, beginning at a specified location.

A Graphical "Hello World"

In order to better understand what this type of programming looks like, let's examine a simple "Hello World" program that uses the graphical mode APIs from USER32.DLL and GDI32.DLL. I used Microsoft's Visual Studio v6.0 to generate the program in Listing 4.1. This Microsoft application includes "wizards" that can generate skeletal programs for different types of applications. In order to help illustrate my point, I used the "generate Hello World" selection to quickly generate the application. Then I took a quick look to see what the wizard generated. (Discourse continues on page 83.)

Listing 4.1 Graphical Hello World program.

```cpp
// FirstConsole.cpp : Defines the entry point for the application.
//

#include "stdafx.h"
#include "resource.h"

#define MAX_LOADSTRING 100


// Global Variables:
HINSTANCE hInst;                                    // current instance
TCHAR szTitle[MAX_LOADSTRING];                      // The title bar text
TCHAR szWindowClass[MAX_LOADSTRING];                // The title bar text


// Foward declarations of functions included in this code module:
ATOM                MyRegisterClass(HINSTANCE hInstance);
BOOL                InitInstance(HINSTANCE, int);
LRESULT CALLBACK    WndProc(HWND, UINT, WPARAM, LPARAM);
LRESULT CALLBACK    About(HWND, UINT, WPARAM, LPARAM);

int APIENTRY WinMain(HINSTANCE hInstance,
                     HINSTANCE hPrevInstance,
                     LPSTR     lpCmdLine,
                     int       nCmdShow)
{
    // TODO: Place code here.
    MSG msg;
    HACCEL hAccelTable;

    // Initialize global strings
    LoadString(hInstance, IDS_APP_TITLE, szTitle, MAX_LOADSTRING);
    LoadString(hInstance, IDC_FIRSTCONSOLE, szWindowClass, MAX_LOADSTRING);
    MyRegisterClass(hInstance);

    // Perform application initialization:
    if (!InitInstance (hInstance, nCmdShow))
    {
        return FALSE;
    }
```

```
        hAccelTable = LoadAccelerators(hInstance, (LPCTSTR)IDC_FIRSTCONSOLE);


    // Main message loop:
     while (GetMessage(&msg, NULL, 0, 0))
     {
            if (!TranslateAccelerator(msg.hwnd, hAccelTable, &msg))
            {
                    TranslateMessage(&msg);
                    DispatchMessage(&msg);
            }
     }


    return msg.wParam;
}




//
//  FUNCTION: MyRegisterClass()
//
//  PURPOSE: Registers the window class.
//
//  COMMENTS:
//
//    This function and its usage is only necessary if you want this code
//    to be compatible with Win32 systems prior to the 'RegisterClassEx'
//    function that was added to Windows 95. It is important to call this function
//    so that the application will get 'well formed' small icons associated
//    with it.
//
ATOM MyRegisterClass(HINSTANCE hInstance)
{
    WNDCLASSEX wcex;

    wcex.cbSize = sizeof(WNDCLASSEX);

    wcex.style              = CS_HREDRAW | CS_VREDRAW;
    wcex.lpfnWndProc        = (WNDPROC)WndProc;
    wcex.cbClsExtra         = 0;
    wcex.cbWndExtra         = 0;
    wcex.hInstance          = hInstance;
    wcex.hIcon              = LoadIcon(hInstance, (LPCTSTR)IDI_FIRSTCONSOLE);
    wcex.hCursor            = LoadCursor(NULL, IDC_ARROW);
```

```
        wcex.hbrBackground          = (HBRUSH)(COLOR_WINDOW+1);
        wcex.lpszMenuName           = (LPCSTR)IDC_FIRSTCONSOLE;
        wcex.lpszClassName          = szWindowClass;
        wcex.hIconSm                = LoadIcon(wcex.hInstance, (LPCTSTR)IDI_SMALL);

        return RegisterClassEx(&wcex);
}


//
//   FUNCTION: InitInstance(HANDLE, int)
//
//   PURPOSE: Saves instance handle and creates main window
//
//   COMMENTS:
//
//       In this function, we save the instance handle in a global variable and
//       create and display the main program window.
//
BOOL InitInstance(HINSTANCE hInstance, int nCmdShow)
{
   HWND hWnd;

   hInst = hInstance; // Store instance handle in our global variable

   hWnd = CreateWindow(szWindowClass, szTitle, WS_OVERLAPPEDWINDOW,
      CW_USEDEFAULT, 0, CW_USEDEFAULT, 0, NULL, NULL, hInstance, NULL);

   if (!hWnd)
   {
      return FALSE;
   }

   ShowWindow(hWnd, nCmdShow);
   UpdateWindow(hWnd);

   return TRUE;
}


//
// FUNCTION: WndProc(HWND, unsigned, WORD, LONG)
//
```

```
//   PURPOSE:  Processes messages for the main window.
//
//   WM_COMMAND- process the application menu
//   WM_PAINT- Paint the main window
//   WM_DESTROY- post a quit message and return
//
//
LRESULT CALLBACK WndProc(HWND hWnd, UINT message, WPARAM wParam, LPARAM lParam)
{
      int wmId, wmEvent;
      PAINTSTRUCT ps;
      HDC hdc;
      TCHAR szHello[MAX_LOADSTRING];
      LoadString(hInst, IDS_HELLO, szHello, MAX_LOADSTRING);

      switch (message)
      {
          case WM_COMMAND:
              wmId    = LOWORD(wParam);
              wmEvent = HIWORD(wParam);
              // Parse the menu selections:
              switch (wmId)
              {
                  case IDM_ABOUT:
                      DialogBox(hInst, (LPCTSTR)IDD_ABOUTBOX, hWnd,
                          (DLGPROC)About);
                      break;
                  case IDM_EXIT:
                      DestroyWindow(hWnd);
                      break;
                  default:
                      return DefWindowProc(hWnd, message, wParam, lParam);
              }
              break;
          case WM_PAINT:
              hdc = BeginPaint(hWnd, &ps);
              // TODO: Add any drawing code here...
              RECT rt;
              GetClientRect(hWnd, &rt);
              DrawText(hdc, szHello, strlen(szHello), &rt, DT_CENTER);
              EndPaint(hWnd, &ps);
```

```
                    break;
              case WM_DESTROY:
                    PostQuitMessage(0);
                    break;
              default:
                    return DefWindowProc(hWnd, message, wParam, lParam);
        }
    return 0;
}


// Mesage handler for about box.
LRESULT CALLBACK About(HWND hDlg, UINT message, WPARAM wParam, LPARAM lParam)
{
        switch (message)
        {
              case WM_INITDIALOG:
                        return TRUE;

              case WM_COMMAND:
                    if (LOWORD(wParam) == IDOK || LOWORD(wParam) == IDCANCEL)
                    {
                            EndDialog(hDlg, LOWORD(wParam));
                            return TRUE;
                    }
                    break;
        }
    return FALSE;
}
```

What I found was a very typical Windows Win32 program that has not changed much since its 16-bit predecessor reigned supreme. It starts, as do all other Win32 programs, at the entry point WinMain(). This is actually convention rather than necessity because the underlying operating system starts the program at an address within the code segment of the processor that is actually contained in the C startup code. This startup code initializes variables and makes the WinMain arguments accessible from the user program. It also handles program termination gracefully so that the user program terminates properly.

WinMain begins by allocating some local variables and then moves on to load strings used within the program from the resources area. This is accomplished by successive calls to Load-String(). It then completes its initialization by a call to MyRegisterClass() which we will examine later. It moves on to calling the function InitInstance() that creates the window through the function CreateWindow(), and then causes the underlying Win32 operating system to display the window through ShowWindow() and UpdateWindow(). If InitInstance() fails to create the window, it returns FALSE.

Next, `WinMain()` loads all keyboard accelerators from the resources area through a call to `LoadAccelerators()`. In much the same way the strings were loaded earlier, the accelerator key bindings such as Alt-F4 are stored within the resources area of the program file. It is bound to the application during the linking phase of the compilation. This mechanism allows for simple internationalization by placing all strings and other potential customizations in a single file that can be linked in when initially building the application or modified in the final binary with a resource editor. We saw how this was possible in Chapter 3.

`WinMain()` finally reaches the heart of the active part of the application — the main message loop. The main message loop is the only point where the earlier Win16 Windows did its task switching. Although this is not true of the Win32 operating systems except for Win32s on Win16 systems, Win32 systems do use this loop to yield task time when the task is idle. The main loop consists of a single while loop that invokes the windows API, `GetMessage()`. This function, from the application's point of view, simply tries to get a message from the interface. From the operating system's point of view, there is much more happening. On Win16 systems, this loop was the only way of getting messages and activating the callbacks (except for timer callbacks). It did this by getting the message through the `GetMessage()` call, massaging the message with `TranslateMessage()`, and finally activating the callback through the `DispatchMessage()` call. The functionality is similar in Win32 but the multitasking is no longer restricted to this loop. The Win32-based operating systems support multitasking through lightweight processes known as *threads*. This mechanism allows for task switches based on time slices and selecting processes based on priorities. With a true scheduler, the main loop is no longer as critical as it once was, although it is still quite necessary. The `Get-Message()` function still allows for the program to yield to other programs on the system, but we now know that task switching can occur at other times.

Earlier, I mentioned that there is a support function generated called `MyRegisterClass()`. This function has an explanation associated with it in the form of comments. It explains that this function is necessary for proper registration on systems prior to Windows 95 where the `RegisterClassEx` function was added. A closer look to this call sees that a data structure allocated as a local variable is initialized and then the call to `RegisterClassEx()` is made. From the comments, you would expect that a call to some other function be made instead, because we need to get this to work on other systems. The user is advised to test wizard-generated programs on all intended targets in case something like this occurs so that he or she can make the appropriate corrections in the program. In my case, I moved the program to a Digital Equipment Corporation 233MHz Multia running Windows NT v4.0 without fx!32 to test the program. The Alpha recognized it as a valid program, but it could not run it. Again, user beware.

We have now looked at all but two functions: `WndProc()` and `About()`. What is interesting about these two functions is that they are not directly called. Both are callbacks called on events. `WndProc()`, for example, is the main window procedure that the operating system calls to process events and requests from the operating system. The way to inform the operating system of its existence is by placing the address of `WndProc` into a structure that `RegisterClassEx()` uses. The underlying operating system then associates this callback with the process and uses it whenever it has a message for the process. `WndProc()` is invoked with a fixed set of parameters and uses one of them, `message`, as an index to identify which message is sent. The procedure then handles only those messages that it needs to and returns the rest to the operating system through a call to `DefWindowProc()`. `DefWindowProc()` is the default window procedure supplied by the operating system that provides default actions for the callback. This type of callback is typical for event-driven systems such as the Microsoft Windows operating systems and X Windows running on various UNIX operating systems.

The operating system also calls the other callback, About(). The call to DialogBox() in the WndProc() function informs the underlying operating system that we want to display a dialog box whose callback is the About() function. Because a dialog box is a special class of window, it also gets messages similar to the main window callback. It is through this mechanism that the About dialog box gets displayed when the user selects the About menu entry. Going back to WndProc(), you will see that the case of WM_COMMAND has an associated IDM_ABOUT identifier. This identifier is in the resource file where it is associated with the Help->About menu entry. When the user selects the appropriate entry, the operating system queues a message that contains the IDM_ABOUT value coded in one of the parameters. Understanding this mechanism sheds further light on the design of the WndProc() procedure.

What is missing from all of this is how the string is actually displayed. Our wizard created quite a bit of code to handle messages, but where is the string displayed in the window? It turns out that the string does not appear until the underlying operating system tells the main window callback that it *wants* it displayed. It does this by sending the WM_PAINT message requesting that the program draws what it needs to in the window. You may ask why it's a callback and the answer becomes apparent when you think about what is going on under the covers. When you first want to display the string, you need to coordinate with the graphical interface so that you do not start drawing the display before the window is ready for use. Additionally, the window may be hidden from view by other overlapping windows. When the window comes back into view, someone must redraw the window. For the Microsoft Windows model, it is the user's responsibility to refresh the window and the underlying operating system uses this message to indicate when. With all this code in place coordinating when we can draw the string or display the About box, we have a Microsoft Windows application to display our "Hello World!" string. The results of this work are in Figure 4.1. As you can see, there is a significant amount of work in displaying a simple string.

Figure 4.1 Graphical "Hello World" output.

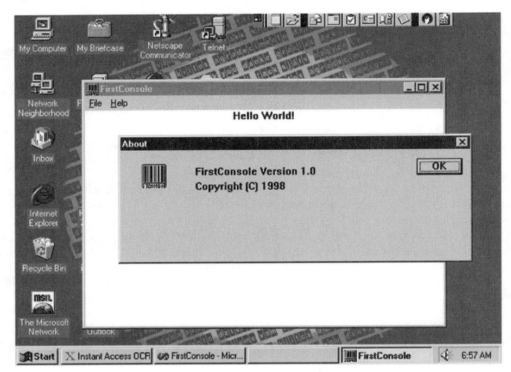

There is, however, another side to Windows and that is in the console mode. In this mode, data is displayed in character cell mode and Windows allows full control over placement of characters on the screen. This little known mode is an excellent mode for simple utilities and prototyping programs. It allows the developer the luxury to work on the heart of the application without concern for the graphical user interface.

Listing 4.2 A typical console "Hello World" program.

```
#include <stdio.h>

int main(int argc, char *argv[])
{
        char szBuf[10];

        printf("Hello world\n");
        printf("Enter a character to exit: ");
        scanf("%s", szBuf);

        return 0;
}
```

Listing 4.2 is an example of the console mode "Hello World" application. In comparison to Listing 4.1, it is amazingly smaller. In fact, it looks just like a non-Windows application. It uses `printf` to display the string and terminates very simply. However, it is not as "pretty" as its graphical sibling, as can be seen in Figure 4.2. It is utilitarian and that's the point. We can write the majority of our application and use a simple interface while developing the application. With proper design, the work can be split in two efforts and proceed in parallel.

Figure 4.2 Console "Hello World" output.

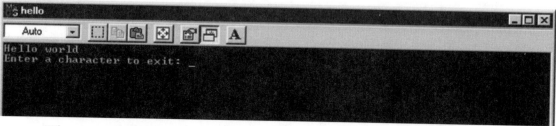

When you examine Figure 4.2, something jumps out at you. The icon in the upper left corner is an MS-DOS icon. Does this mean that console mode is really MS-DOS in disguise? One way to find out for sure is to take apart the application. My favorite method is to reverse engineer the application I generated. This is a simple way to see what your tools generated. Figure 4.3 shows the opening screen for the disassembler I use. You will note that the tool identifies this as a PE file. As you'll remember from Chapter 3, this file is the 32-bit file format for Win32 operating systems and MS-DOS cannot run this file by itself. The other question that arises is: what type of code does it contain? Figure 4.4 is the output from the disassembler and as you can readily see, it is a true 32-bit application.

Figure 4.3 Dissasembler opening screen for "Hello World" program.

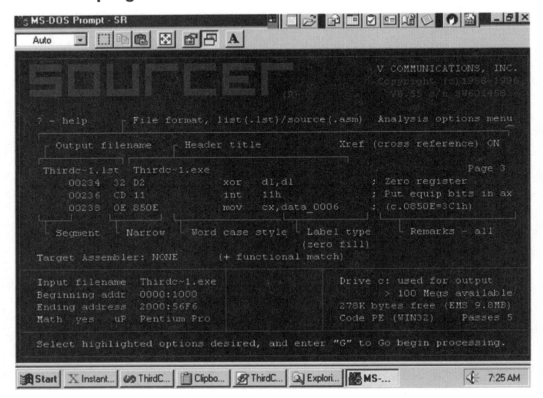

Examining Console Mode

Our somewhat unorthodox introduction to console mode highlights the simplicity of this mode. Unlike earlier Win16 systems, the Win32 API defines a set of calls for a character-based input and output to character-based applications. What the application receives is a window that acts like a terminal 0isplay. When you start a character mode application, the underlying operating system creates a window, referred to as a *console*, and assigns the application and its children to that window.

Figure 4.4   Disassembled "Hello World" output.

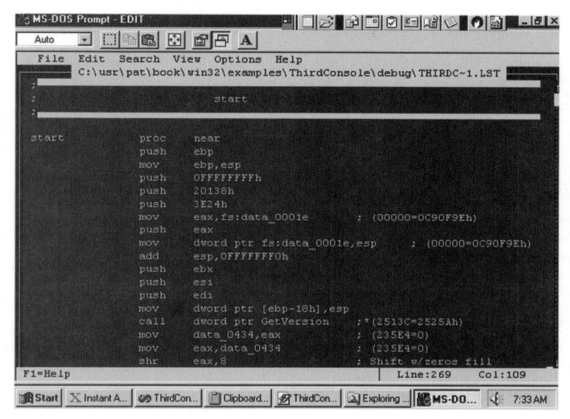

Consoles

Figure 4.5 illustrates the model for a console. The console appears to the application as an input buffer and multiple output buffers. Names CONIN$ and CONOUT$ are assigned to the input buffer and active output buffer. These names are used with file I/O-based console applications. These buffers are also available through file handles StdIn, StdOut, and StdErr. As you may imagine, the underlying operating system associates the StdIn handle with CONIN$ and associates StdOut and StdErr with CONOUT$. When an application is opened in console mode, it gets this set of buffers and sets up a console window to handle this output. It also associates the keyboard with this input whenever the window is selected. The application can now write to this StdOut or StdErr to display on this screen and read from StdIn to get keyboard input. Any child process that the application may later create then inherits this same window and set of handles with their associated buffers. This model is very similar to both MS-DOS and UNIX character cell applications. One difference that you should keep in mind is that the input buffer contains information about keyboard, mouse, and window resize events. This is true only when *not* using file I/O, so if you restrict your code to only file I/O, the MS-DOS comparison will hold true.

Figure 4.5 Console mode model.

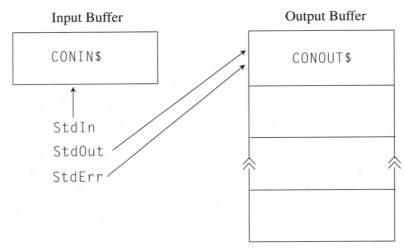

Input and Output Methods

File I/O

The Win32 API provides a set of file I/O functions for compatibility with other operating systems such as MS-DOS and UNIX. Although the calls are not identical to any of the APIs in these other operating systems, the Win32 calls function in a similar enough fashion to easily fit into any program. As mentioned earlier, the consoles have a set of handles in the form of StdIn, StdOut, and StdErr associated with them. You can easily create a simple application that uses ReadFile, with a handle to StdIn, to get keyboard input and WriteFile with a handle to a screen buffer to write from a character buffer. This write occurs to the screen buffer associated with the handle at the current cursor location for that buffer. It need not be StdOut or StdErr — it can be a handle to any handle created by other means. These handles may be obtained from other Win32 API calls such as DuplicateHandle and CloseHandle that can be used with either input or output handles. Handles may also be created through calls to CreateFile. For example, CreateFile can be used to open a handle to console input, CONIN$, or return a handle to the active screen buffer, CONOUT$, if the process has an open handle.

If you recall from our earlier discussion, canonical line processing modes exist for the Win32 API. This is similar to the UNIX raw/cooked modes. Depending on these settings, the behavior of the File API may differ. Also, only certain settings may be associated with a handle depending on whether it is an input or output handle.

The console input API has three modes associated with it: line input, processed input, and echo input. *Line mode* is used for handling input one line at a time. *Processed input* enables control character processing to take place. Finally, *echo mode* enables characters to be displayed on the console as each key is depressed.

Line Mode

When in line input mode, any application using `ReadFile` does not get any input until a full line is read. `ReadFile` does not return to the caller until the Enter key is pressed. What this implies is that editing keys, such as Backspace and Tab, is handled appropriately, and Ctrl-C is passed on to the appropriate handler routines. If line mode is disabled, `ReadFile` returns when one or more characters are available in the input buffer and the only key combination not passed on to the caller is Ctrl-Break.

Echo Mode

Echo can only be enabled in conjunction with line input mode. When enabled, characters are echoed to the screen as they are read by `ReadFile`. However, this can only occur if the `Read-File` caller has an open handle to the active screen buffer. Its primary intent is to toggle output when in line input mode to inhibit displaying characters for secure operations such as password entry.

Processed Mode

Processed input allows any system editing or control keys to be processed by the system and not passed on to the user. It works on the buffer returned by `ReadFile`. If echoing is enabled and you want the output to reflect the system editing, processed output must be enabled for the output handle. When line input is also enabled, Tab, Backspace, carriage returns, and bells are handled as follows:

- Tab characters cause the cursor to move to the next tab stop, which occurs every 8 characters.
- Backspace moves the cursor back one space without affecting the character at the cursor position.
- Bell sounds a short tone.
- Carriage returns are converted to carriage return, linefeed.
- Ctrl-C and Ctrl-Break will be passed on to the appropriate handler regardless of whether or not line input is enabled.

The output console API has two modes: wrap at EOL and processed output. A user application can use the File API to send output to the screen buffer by writing using `WriteFile` or when using `ReadFile` if echoing is enabled. The wrap at EOL mode performs exactly as the name implies. This mode determines whether long output lines will wrap to the beginning of the next line or be discarded beyond the end of the line. This is a convenience mode that emulates the functionality of video terminals. The other output mode, processed output mode, enables the output characters to be parsed for ASCII control sequences and then perform the correct action. An application using the processed output mode can, for example, specify the color attribute with which subsequent characters will be written.

Consider Listing 4.3 for a closer look at how this works. The program is a simple console mode program. Its function is to act the same way as the built-in echo command. Unlike its graphical equivalents, it starts at `main` as opposed to `WinMain`. This is the first departure we noted earlier. While it differs from the typical graphical program, it does give us the opportunity to access command line options via the `argc`, `argv` mechanism familiar to all MS-DOS and UNIX programs. However, the program does differ from one written for another operating system.

Listing 4.3 Simple file mode echo.

```
#include <windows.h>


int main(int argc, char* argv[])
{
        int nIdx;
        DWORD nChars, nWritten;
        HANDLE StdOut;

        /* First, let's create a handle for our win32 equivalent of stdout */
        StdOut = CreateFile("CONOUT$", GENERIC_WRITE, FILE_SHARE_WRITE, 0,
                CREATE_ALWAYS, FILE_ATTRIBUTE_NORMAL, NULL);

        /* Check for success */
        if(StdOut == INVALID_HANDLE_VALUE)
                return 1;

        /* Now let's loop through the passed in arguments and just output them */
        for(nIdx = 1; nIdx < argc; nIdx++)
        {
                char cSpace = ' ';
                WriteFile(StdOut, argv[nIdx], nChars = strlen(argv[nIdx]),
                    &nWritten, 0);
                if(nWritten != nChars)
                        return 1;
                if(!WriteFile(StdOut, &cSpace, 1, &nWritten, 0))
                {
                        return 1;
                }
        }

        /* Finished, now close the handle ... */
        CloseHandle(StdOut);

        /* ... and return success */
        return 0;
}
```

We previously saw that the console mode has equivalents to the stdin, stdout, and stderr mechanisms available on other operating systems. It differs, however, from other operating systems because these handles are not maintained by the operating system. In both MS-DOS and UNIX, stdin, stdout, and stderr are entries 0, 1, and 2 in a file table that maps this number into an internal file handle that the operating system then uses to access the file. When the process is created, these files are opened for us by the operating system. Nowhere within any of our programs — either within the compiler vendors' startup code and libraries, or our own application — do we open or close these files unless we are performing some special function, such as I/O redirection. The exception to the rule, under both MS-DOS and UNIX, is if our application is a daemon running on UNIX. Instead, Win32 gives us a special set of filenames that we must open ourselves. It makes sense, if you think about it. Again, most of the applications written for a Win32 operating system are graphical in nature. Therefore, adding this overhead to the operating system only serves a small population of expected applications. So, if you want a handle to a console, you must open the file yourself. That's what we have with our call to CreateFile(). It is special only in respect to the filename passed to the call. Because we are only going to output to our console window, our application only opens a single file, CONOUT$, and assigns this to the handle StdOut. Oddly enough, this call could potentially fail. As a result, we need to handle the potential error in some way. Our example exits and returns a failure return code of 1. Depending on the application, this may become some sort of message written to an error log somewhere or possibly a call to a graphical message element such as a MessageBox() if the CreateFile() call is part of a graphical program. Because our program is strictly a console mode program, a simple error return will suffice.

To output the arguments passed to the application, our application takes advantage of the argc, argv mechanisms. Our application simply falls into a for loop. We use nIdx as our pacer variable by terminating the loop through a comparison to argc and as our index into argv[]. This mechanism is trivial, but the methods used to write to the screen are not. Looking past the loop, we see two calls to WriteFile(). These calls are the Win32 equivalents to the write() call that is a UNIX system call. It is also similar to the write() call implemented by many MS-DOS libc runtime libraries. It differs from the UNIX and MS-DOS call in that the number of bytes written is not returned by the call. Instead, WriteFile() returns a type BOOL that is a zero on failure. The number of bytes written is actually written to a user memory location pointed to by the caller. This is an improvement over the UNIX version of this call in that the UNIX version returns a negative number which limits the range returned by the call. This was a typical problem in MS-DOS implementations. MS-DOS actually returned an unsigned 16-bit integer but the library limited the range by forcing the returned value into a signed integer. In our example, I chose to compare on the number written for the argument and the boolean return value for the space between arguments. This simple example shows you the basic form for a console program. However, if you look further down the program, you will notice that there is another Win32 call not normally associated with an MS-DOS or UNIX program. In this case, you see a call to CloseHandle(). In non-Win32 programs, we normally do not close the standard input and output files, but this is necessary for Win32 programs. Also, note the name of the function: CloseHandle(), not CloseFile(). The reason for this is thanks to the Windows NT architecture. When we discussed Windows NT, we noted that there is an object manager for all operating system objects. Each object may be a file and is referred to by a handle. This handle may refer to:

- communication devices,
- console input,
- console screen buffers,
- events,
- files,
- file mapping,
- jobs,
- mailslots,
- mutex,
- named pipes,
- processes,
- semaphores,
- sockets,
- threads, and
- access tokens.

Because this is the case, only a single system call is needed for all these objects, one of which is our file connected to a console. That call, `CloseHandle()`, is what we need to basically end our program before exiting through the following return.

Using the Console

Earlier, we saw some examples of how to use `ReadFile` and `WriteFile` to perform I/O with a console. While file I/O is one way of working with the console, the Win32 operating system has a Console API that enables us to work with a console window in a much simpler fashion.

Using the Console API, we can work directly with our input and output buffers. We can use `StdIn` to communicate directly with our input buffer and both `StdOut` and `StdErr` to work directly with our output buffers.

When working with console I/O, we have to keep in mind that console I/O is different than file I/O. We already know that the console input buffer consists of input records that contain information about mouse and window size events as well as keyboard input. This is true because the console API provides direct access to the input buffer, so that the application can receive mouse and window size events in addition to keyboard input. If we want to only receive keyboard input while using the console API, we can change console input mode so that the API will filter mouse and screen buffer size events. The console API also allows us to write input records to the input buffer, read input records without removing them from the input buffer, determine the number of pending events, or flush the input buffer. This gives us greater flexibility and control as compared to simple file I/O does.

Our console mode application can work with console output by manipulating the contents of one or more screen buffers. This is quite handy, because we can work with multiple buffers and then select which one that we want to be currently displayed. This is very useful, for example, in applications such as editors. We can display one buffer, make changes to another buffer and then simply select our alternate buffer to be displayed.

Let's look a little closer at our screen buffer. The screen buffer appears as a two dimensional array of character records. This array is typically known as TEXTMODE. Each element of the array may be either a Unicode or ASCII value of the character along with an attribute field to control the foreground and background colors for the character. This is actually rather convenient. It closely resembles the functionality of typical display cards in character cell mode. So, if you have any old MS-DOS programs that you wish to port to a Win32 operating system environment, you need only change the methods in which you wrote to the display card in order to perform the port. The logic remains the same.

The console API expands on the old display card access mode by providing functions that allows strings of characters, or character attributes, to be read from or written to any location in the screen buffer. It also provides for rectangular blocks of characters and attributes to be read from or written to any location, screen buffer, fill portion of the screen buffer, or copied blocks of the screen buffer within a console window (scroll section of the window).

The console API input is somewhat different from the file API we examined earlier. When we use a console API, we *always* receive raw character input, regardless of line input and processed input modes. The modes we spoke about earlier — echo input, raw/processed input, line wrap at EOL for output — are only valid for file I/O work. In addition, file I/O and console I/O are independent so that any settings that may affect input for applications using the console API have no effect on applications using the file API.

Simple Console I/O

Let's expand on this with some practical examples. We'll start off simple, then add to our knowledge by building on the initial examples. As you will see later, this code will become the foundation for much of the I/O work to be done in examples in later chapters.

As we saw earlier, a console application can get its input from the console and display characters on-screen through either the file I/O API or the console API. As the name implies, the file I/O API uses a streaming file model for its I/O. This model doesn't support either window resize or mouse events, and therefore, is somewhat restrictive. The console API, however, allows us direct access to the input buffer to read and write keyboard, mouse, and window size events. It also provides convenient functions that will move data, control display attributes, and scroll areas of the screen for our output buffers.

To take advantage of the console API calls, we must first provide the console API the ability to identify which buffers we want to use. For that purpose, the input buffer has been given the name CONIN$ and a handle used to refer to it, StdOut. In a similar manner, the output buffers are given the name CONOUT$, with handles StdOut and StdErr used to refer to the output buffers. The mnemonic is used primarily for file I/O.

In order to use any of the console API calls, you must have open handles to these buffers. We open handles by using the file I/O API call CreateFile, or the console API call GetStdHandle. We've already seen CreateFile in action and would now like to learn more about GetStdHandle. The arguments passed to GetStdHandle are: STD_INPUT_HANDLE, STD_OUTPUT_HANDLE, and STD_ERROR_HANDLE. The return value from GetStdHandle is then the correct handle for that console I/O stream. We need to use this call because unlike MS-DOS and UNIX, these handles do not correspond to 0, 1, and 2 respectively. Any code that makes such an assumption will immediately fail when you try to run it.

Once we have our handle, we can use it in very much the same way as we use any other handle in the Win32 operating system. For example, we can use a handle that comes from either `GetStdHandle` or `CreateFile` in file I/O through calls such as `ReadFile` and `WriteFile`, we can wait on events, such as input buffer not empty, through calls to `WaitForSingleObject` or `WaitForMultipleObjects`, etc. Waiting on events from handles is exceptionally handy when trying to do overlapped I/O. Conversely, a handle to an open console stream obtained from `CreateFile` can be used in any console I/O call.

Let's look at a fairly trivial example to better understand some of the concepts behind the Win32 operating system console I/O API. The ConsPut program in Listing 4.4 is very simple. It defines a single function, ConsPuts, which accepts a string and outputs it to the active output buffer. As you can see, all we do is make a call to `GetStdHandle` to get the handle to the console in use and make a call to `WriteConsole`, another console I/O call, whose parameters are very nearly identical to `WriteFile`. `WriteConsole` requires a parameter specifying the number of characters to output — we make a single call to `strlen` to get the length of the string so that we can pass the parameter to `WriteConsole`. Thanks to such a simple set of calls, `main` is simply a call to ConsPut to print the string. All in all, we couldn't have made the output string any easier and we'll see this function (or one similar to it) used in later chapters to simplify our code.

Listing 4.4 Console output example.

```
#include <windows.h>




//
// ConsPuts:
//     Print a string to StdOut on the console
//
int ConsPuts(char *pszString)
{
        DWORD nLen = strlen(pszString);
        DWORD nWritten;
        HANDLE hOutput = GetStdHandle(STD_OUTPUT_HANDLE);
        BOOL bRet;

        bRet = WriteConsole(hOutput, pszString, nLen, &nWritten, NULL);
        return (!bRet || (nWritten != nLen)) ? 0 : nLen;
}



int main(int argc, char *argv[])
{
        ConsPuts("Welcome to the your first console program.\r\n");
        return 0;
}
```

In our next example, we added a function to the program called ConGets. When you take a look at it, you see that it's very similar to the output function, ConsPuts. Like ConsPuts, ConsGets makes a simple call to GetsStdHandle to get the handle for StdIn. With that in hand, it makes a call to ReadConsole — analogous to WriteConsole. You'll find this program in Listing 4.5. Not much to tell here; if you understand ConsPuts, you'll understand ConsGets. As you can see, simple console I/O is indeed simple.

Listing 4.5 Console input example.

```
#include <windows.h>

#define MAXBUF4096

DWORD ConsPuts(char *pszString);
DWORD ConsGets(char *pszString, DWORD nLen);


//
// ConsPuts:
//     Print a string to StdOut on the console
//
DWORD ConsPuts(char *pszString)
{
    DWORD nLen = strlen(pszString);
    DWORD nWritten;
    HANDLE hOutput = GetStdHandle(STD_OUTPUT_HANDLE);
    BOOL bRet;

    bRet = WriteConsole(hOutput, pszString, nLen, &nWritten, NULL);
    return (!bRet || (nWritten != nLen)) ? 0 : nLen;
}



//
// ConsGets:
//    Get a string to StdIn on the console
//
DWORD ConsGets(char *pszString, DWORD nLen)
{
    DWORD nRead;
    HANDLE hInput = GetStdHandle(STD_INPUT_HANDLE);
    BOOL bRet;
```

```
        bRet = ReadConsole(hInput, pszString, nLen, &nRead, NULL);
        return (!bRet) ? 0 : nLen;
}



int main(int argc, char *argv[])
{
        char szBuffer[MAXBUF];
        DWORD nRead;

        ConsPuts("Welcome to the your second console program.\r\n");
        nRead = ConsGets(szBuffer, MAXBUF);
        szBuffer[nRead] = '\0';
        ConsPuts(szBuffer);
        return 0;
}
```

The previous two examples are relatively easy and somewhat trivial. However, I don't want you to think that the Win32 operating system console API is lacking in any way. On the contrary, it is quite rich. For example, in our last example we used ReadConsole, but the API also offers function calls to ReadConsoleInput, a variation on ReadConsole, and ReadConsoleOutput that reads both character and color attribute data from a rectangular block of character cells in a console screen buffer. It also offers calls such as WriteConsoleInput which allows you to write data directly to the console input buffer and WriteConsoleOutput, the corresponding function to ReadConsoleOutput, which writes character and color attribute data to a specified rectangle block of character cells in a console screen buffer.

We also have control functions that we can use to change parameters governing our input and output buffers. For example, we can flush or discard all data in the console input buffer through a call to FlushConsoleInputBuffer. Another useful control function is PeekConsoleInput that reads data from a specified console input buffer without removing it from the buffer. This is very handy for look-ahead scanning applications on the console input buffer. This is just a mere sample of the rich set of calls in the console I/O API. Review Table 4.1 (page 76) to see other control functions.

Writing Color Attributes to Consecutive Cells

What happens if you would like to write characters in a color other than white? The Win32 operating system console API has a solution for you. There are console function calls, two of which are WriteConsoleOutputAttribute and FillConsoleOutputAttribute, that can be used to attach color attributes to a block of characters. If we look at the example program in Listing 4.6, we see that it is similar to the program we used earlier to write a string to the screen. There are some changes between this program and that in Listing 4.4. The first is a new function, ClearConsole, that we use to clear the console window. It does this by setting the start coordinates to 0, 0, i.e., in the upper lefthand corner of the window, and making two calls, one to `FillConsoleOutputCharacter` followed by another to `FillConsoleOutputAttribute`. The first call fills a block of the window with space characters while the second call fills the attribute of the entire window to white on black. This effectively clears the screen.

Listing 4.6 Block write and attribute example.

```
#include <windows.h>

#define SCRSIZE 80*25

void ClearConsole(void);
int ConsCoordPuts(char *pszString, COORD dwWriteCoord);

//
// ClearConsole
//        Clears the console wind (SCRSIZE only)
//
void ClearConsole(void)
{
        HANDLE hOutput = GetStdHandle(STD_OUTPUT_HANDLE);
        DWORD dwWritten;
        COORD cCoordinate;

        cCoordinate.X = 0;
        cCoordinate.Y = 0;
        FillConsoleOutputCharacter(hOutput, ' ', SCRSIZE, cCoordinate, &dwWritten);
        FillConsoleOutputAttribute(hOutput,
           FOREGROUND_RED | FOREGROUND_GREEN | FOREGROUND_BLUE,
           SCRSIZE, cCoordinate, &dwWritten);
}


//
// ConsCoordPuts:
//        Print a string to StdOut at a given coordinate on the console
//
int ConsCoordPuts(char *pszString, COORD dwWriteCoord)
{
        DWORD nLen = strlen(pszString);
        DWORD nWritten;
        HANDLE hOutput = GetStdHandle(STD_OUTPUT_HANDLE);
        BOOL bRet;
```

```
        bRet = WriteConsoleOutputCharacter(hOutput,
                pszString, nLen, dwWriteCoord, &nWritten);
        return (!bRet || (nWritten != nLen)) ? 0 : nLen;
}


int main(int argc, char *argv[])
{
        WORD nAttribute = FOREGROUND_GREEN | BACKGROUND_RED
                        | BACKGROUND_GREEN | BACKGROUND_BLUE,
             nAttrArray[SCRSIZE],
             nIdx;
        HANDLE hOutput = GetStdHandle(STD_OUTPUT_HANDLE);
        char *pszString = "Welcome to the attribute console program.";
        DWORD dwWritten;
        DWORD nLen = strlen(pszString);
        COORD cCoordinate;

        // Clear the screen
        ClearConsole();

        // Print welcome message
        cCoordinate.X = 0;
        cCoordinate.Y = 10;
        ConsCoordPuts(pszString, cCoordinate);

        // Create an attribute array to write from then do it
        for(nIdx = 0; nIdx < SCRSIZE; nIdx++)
        {
                nAttrArray[nIdx] = nAttribute;
        }
        WriteConsoleOutputAttribute(hOutput,
          nAttrArray, nLen, cCoordinate, &dwWritten);

        return 0;
}
```

The second change comes in the form of a modified function, ConsCoordPuts, which works virtually identically to ConsPuts, except that it takes a coordinate as the starting point for its operation. This allows us to position the string to a known position in the window. With these two changes, we're ready to look at main.

The first thing our program does upon entry is call our new function, `ClearConsole`, to clear the screen. It then goes ahead and calls `ConsCoordPuts` to display our welcome string. Once the string is displayed, it changes the attributes of the displayed string by first initializing an attribute array and then writing the attribute to the block where we've just displayed our string. It does this through a call to `WriteConsoleOutputAttribute`. Simple.

I would like to point out that I wrote this program in this way so that I could illustrate the `WriteConsoleOutputAttribute` function call. I could have eliminated the `for` loop and the call to `WriteConsoleOutputAttribute`, and replaced that code with a single call to `FillConsoleOutputAttribute`. This would be much more efficient, but I would not have had the opportunity to illustrate the `WriteConsoleOutputAttribute` API call. If you do decide to write a similar piece of code in your next application, use `FillConsoleOutputAttribute`.

Reading and Writing Blocks of Characters and Attributes

The previous example did its work on the entire window. We could have restricted this to a small section of the window. We accomplish this by defining a new variable based on the type `SMALL_RECT` and defining a region to work on. The region allows us to specify the left, right, top, and bottom coordinates. You would then replace calls to such functions as `WriteConsoleOutputCharacter` with `WriteConsoleOutput`, passing it the new region parameter. The two functions work identically except that the latter works over a fixed region. You can find more of these functions in Table 4.1 (page 76).

Reading Input Buffer Events

What happens if you want handle Ctrl-C or Ctrl-Break? The Win32 operating system console API has a solution for this as well. It offers a function call, `SetConsoleCtrlHandler`, that allows you to register a handler for just that situation. The handler function takes a single argument that identifies which control character was input. When the function is invoked, it is up to the handler to do something and then return `TRUE` if the event is handled by the handler. It should return `FALSE` for any event other than `CTRL_C_EVENT` and `CTRL_BREAK_EVENT`.

Take a look at the example in Listing 4.7. We see that we have one of our favorite routines, `ConsPuts`, and a new one, `CtrlHandler`. `CtrlHandler` is very simple. It sets a flag identifying the event it intercepts. That's it. All the action is in `main`. In `main`, we start out by setting the control handler through a call to `SetConsoleCtrlHandler`. We then drop into a loop, spinning until either `bCtrlC` or `bCtrlBrk` is set by `CtrlHandler`. When that happens, it simply displays a message identifying which event occurred and exits. Again, very simple.

Listing 4.7 Event handler example.

```
#include <windows.h>

BOOL bCtrlC = FALSE, bCtrlBrk = FALSE;

BOOL CtrlHandler(ULONG CtrlType);
int ConsPuts(char *pszString);
```

```
//
// ConsPuts:
//      Print a string to StdOut on the console
//
int ConsPuts(char *pszString)
{
       DWORD nLen = strlen(pszString);
       DWORD nWritten;
       HANDLE hOutput = GetStdHandle(STD_OUTPUT_HANDLE);
       BOOL bRet;

       bRet = WriteConsole(hOutput, pszString, nLen, &nWritten, NULL);
       return (!bRet || (nWritten != nLen)) ? 0 : nLen;
}



//
// CtrlHandler
//      Handle ctrl-c and ctrl-break
//
BOOL CtrlHandler(ULONG CtrlType)
{
       switch(CtrlType)
       {
       case CTRL_C_EVENT:
               bCtrlC = TRUE;
               return TRUE;

       case CTRL_BREAK_EVENT:
               bCtrlBrk = TRUE;
               return TRUE;

       default:
               return FALSE;
       }
}
```

```
int main(int argc, char *argv[])
{
        ConsPuts("Welcome to the control handler program.\r\n");

        // Set the handler
        if(!SetConsoleCtrlHandler((PHANDLER_ROUTINE)&CtrlHandler, TRUE))
        {
                ConsPuts("Couldn't set handler!\r\n");
                ExitProcess(1);
        }

        // Spin waiting for an event
        while(!bCtrlC && !bCtrlBrk)
                ;

        // Identify the event an exit
        if(bCtrlC)
                ConsPuts("You hit ctrl-c.\r\n");
        if(bCtrlBrk)
                ConsPuts("You hit ctrl-break.\r\n");
        return 0;
}
```

Console Code Pages

Here's a riddle. What do you call an API that covers two operating systems, but differently for each one? The answer: a Microsoft Win32 API. Okay, that was a bit sarcastic but a good way to warn you about dangers that lie ahead. You see, one of the problems with the Win32 API is that features are often supported in the Windows NT/2000 stream that are *not* supported in the Windows 9X stream. Our first example falls within the console API, specifically with code pages.

Let's start out by defining a code page. Basically, a *code page* is the character set the Win32 operating system uses. It uses the code page as a method of interpreting input data, typically from a keyboard, and output data, typically on your display. Quite often, the code page is used for international applications. For example, the code page for U.S. English is different than the Cyrillic code page used in Russia. You'll typically see code pages grouped with locale. This is a switch available to C and C++ developers where they can set the locale — reflecting the local conventions and language for a particular geographical region.

This makes sense, but remember, I did start with a warning. The warning deals with Windows 9X vs. Windows NT/2000. All the code page functions — in general, any of the functions in which you set the code page, such as SetConsoleCP and SetConsoleOutputCP — are not supported by Windows 9X. So, any code you write must test for Window 9X in order to work properly.

Ready for Console Applications

We've examined console mode and wrote some small applications that illustrated how to do work with a Win32 console in a manner similar to the way we work with the BIOS and direct screen writes under MS-DOS. Armed with this knowledge, we can now proceed to dig deeper into the Win32 operating system because we can simplify communicating with our test programs (thanks to this mode). We no longer need to write complicated graphical programs to explore simple concepts. We will look at the way files are handled in the next chapter.

5

Chapter 5

Files

Introduction to Files

What is a file? This is actually a very good question. It seems as though many users think that it is simply a collection of bytes on a storage medium — the magnetic disk or optical CD-ROM style disk. Part of this confusion stems from Win32 operating system calls. For example, in a Win32 operating system, a file is created through the system call `CreateFile`. In almost every example of this system call, the call is used to create a disk file. However, we can get a better idea of what `CreateFile` actually does by looking at the definition of the system call.

The `CreateFile` function creates or opens an object and returns a handle that can be used to access the object. Note that our definition talks in generalities — about objects and not a specific type of object such as a file. `CreateFile` actually handles files, pipes, mailslots, communications resources, disk devices (for the Windows NT-based Win32 operating systems only), consoles, and directories. As you can see, the list of objects handled by `CreateFile` is actually quite long — much more than a simple disk file.

So let's try to generalize our definition of a file. For the sake of consistency, we will use the more generic "object" whenever we discuss the entity that `CreateFile` creates. This matches the definition as applied by Microsoft in its discussions of Win32 operating system calls. For the sake of our discussion in this chapter, a *file* is a collection of data that has certain attributes associated with it, stored on some form of secondary storage. This is the more traditional definition of a file.

Note that when we defined a file, we said that it is a collection of data that has attributes associated with it. This object-oriented-style definition is meant to expand our thinking so that we can begin to consider a file as more than the data itself. What do I mean by that? The data, or contents, of the file is what is important to us. However, the operating system requires more information than just the content of the file. For example, to the system, the file is merely a collection of bytes scattered about storage media such as a floppy disk or hard drive. To us, the file has a name and data important to us. We don't want to specify a set of numbers that represents the data's position on the storage media. We want to call it "file.txt" or "notepad.exe." In order to do that, the Win32 operating system must store additional information on the storage medium in order to understand what our desires are. So, at the very least, we see that the Win32 operating system must store our filename somewhere on the storage medium so that when we request our file through the CreateFile system call, the Win32 operating system knows what to do with it. This may seem like a trivial example, but is enough to expand our thinking.

Let's take a look at Figure 5.1 to get a better idea of what some of the attributes associated with the file may be. As mentioned earlier, the file houses a collection of data somewhere on the storage media. Associated with that, there is some additional storage allocated to the file attributes. For example, we spoke of a filename, i.e., how we prefer to reference the file. The Win32 operating system, however, doesn't care about the filename. It does care, however, where the file is located. Somehow, it has to associate our filename with that location. So, it groups together bytes of data that contain a string (the name we gave the file), along with information that refers to the position of the data on the disk. We also know that the Win32 operating system associates additional attributes such as read-only, read-write, etc., to a file. This is a convenience for us so that we can protect ourselves, for example, from an error that may destroy the contents of the file, by assigning a read-only attribute to it. That information is also stored along with our file position information and filename.

Figure 5.1   Conceptual file model.

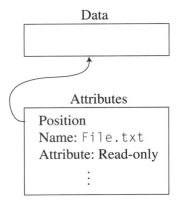

Data

Attributes

Position
Name: File.txt
Attribute: Read-only
⋮

As you can see from the previous discussion, we are talking in generalities. This is because the operating system, in general, is free to store that information in whatever way it sees fit. That is why we have different file system types such as FAT-12, FAT-16, NTFS, etc.

The differences among them are not the data contained on the file system, but *how* the attributes associated with the file are stored on the storage media. Sometimes, the file system type is fixed to the media.

For example, a CD-ROM may contain an ISO-9660 file system standardized by the International Standards Organization. This allows for easy interchange of the data contained on the CD-ROM between different computers running different operating systems. In this case, the operating system does not have a choice of how to store the information on the media. However, this is only true for interchangeable media. Another example is the FAT-12 file system typically used on a floppy disk. This file system, although not standardized by any organization, is the "de facto" standard thanks to the Win32 operating system's heritage, i.e., MS-DOS. Because Microsoft used this file system on floppy disks with MS-DOS and continued its use through to the Win32 operating systems, it became a standard. However, hard disks storage typically changed as disk size increased. Very early hard disk file systems were FAT-12. As disk size increased, the FAT-12 data structures that contained the disk attributes were too small to contain pointers large enough to address the entire disk, so FAT-16 was introduced. Later, Microsoft decided to increase the size of the name. At that time, the on disk data structures were changed again to allow for larger name sizes with the introduction of a new file type called VFAT. Disk size continued to increase, far outpacing FAT-16 and VFAT. That's when FAT-32 was introduced and I imagine that this will continue as long as we have secondary (disk) storage on our computers.

Although Figure 5.1 shows our attributes stored in one location, the Win32 operating system is free to store that information in more than one location. For example, in the FAT-style file systems, the position data is stored in what is known as the *FAT table*. This is the linked list where the position of the data on the storage media corresponds to the position of entry in the table. The content of the entry points to the position of the next block of data as well as next entry in the FAT table. All the other information is stored in the directory. We saw that when we closely examined the FAT file system in Chapter 3. From a programming perspective, we prefer to work at a level above this and simply think of the attributes of the file as some sort of hidden property of the file that we can manipulate through our Win32 system calls.

Creating a File

Earlier, we spoke of the primary method to create a Win32 file — the CreateFile system call. A bit of a misnomer, the CreateFile system call handles various types of objects, not just files. We can take a closer look at how this system call works by writing a simple program that creates a file. This program is shown in Listing 5.1. You can see from the simple example, the CreateFile system call takes quite a few parameters. It requires you to enter name and the mode you wish to open the file in, i.e., read-only, read-write, etc. It also requires a long list of other parameters, including:

- a flag indicating whether or not you wish to share the file with other processes,
- a pointer to a data structure that contains information regarding security,
- another flag telling the Win32 operating system how to create the file,
- yet another flag that contains the file attributes, and
- an interesting Win32 feature where you can give CreateFile a handle to a file whose attributes you wish to copy.

We're only using CreateFile in a very basic fashion so the parameters required for our call are simple. We desire to create a file, MyFile.txt, in the root directory. In order to do this, CreateFile is invoked by simply passing in the filename, and a number of flags indicating that we want to do a write with no security attributes associated with it and simple asynchronous I/O.

Listing 5.1 Simple CreateFile example.

```
#include <windows.h>

int main(int argc, char *argv[])
{
        HANDLE hFile;

        hFile = CreateFile("\\MyFile.txt",          // name of the file
                    GENERIC_WRITE,                    // open for writing
                    0,                                // do not share
                    NULL,                             // no security
                    CREATE_ALWAYS,                    // overwrite existing
                    FILE_ATTRIBUTE_NORMAL |           // normal file
                    FILE_FLAG_OVERLAPPED,             // asynchronous I/O
                    NULL);                            // no attr. template

        CloseHandle(hFile);
        return 0;
}
```

As you can see, main is very short. The program consists only of the call to CreateFile followed by a call to CloseHandle. You could have skipped the call to CloseHandle, but it is included for completeness. When you compile this file, and later execute it, it simply creates a zero length file. I've done this exercise and you can see the result in Figure 5.2.

Figure 5.2 Newly-created `MyFile.txt` **from** `CreateFile` **example**.

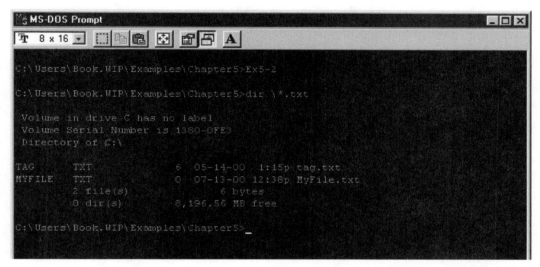

There are two exceptions to `CreateFile`. The first is when we use `CreateFile` on a directory. Only the Win32 operating system is allowed to write to a directory. Because we can only read from a directory, the `CreateFile` system call only opens a directory for read operations. There is another Win32 system call, `CreateDirectory`, that handles creating a new directory. It seems somewhat unusual that we use a system call that has the word "create" in it to open an existing object for reading, but that is the second exception. There is no system call within the Win32 operating systems that *only* opens a file for reading or writing. That is, there's no such call as "`OpenFile`" in the Win32 API specification. It only exists as a 16-bit compatibility call. For true Win32 applications, it is all done with the `CreateFile` system call.

Win32 File Functions

Now that we've had a taste of the Win32 file functions, let's take a closer look. Table 5.1 is a listing of these file functions. A quick scan of this table gives the reader the impression of a complete API. Unfortunately, that's not the case. The problem is that Win32 file functions, although attempting to give the programmer or developer an impressive set of system calls, actually fall far short of their goal. (Discourse continues on page 114.)

Table 5.1   Win32 file functions.

File Functions	
AreFileApisANSI	Determines whether a set of Win32 file functions is using the ANSI or OEM character set code page.
CancelIo	Cancels all pending I/O operations that were issued by the calling thread for the specified file handle.
CloseHandle	Closes handles to the following objects: • communications devices, • console input, • console screen buffers, • events, • files, • file mapping, • jobs, • mailslots, • mutex, • named pipes, • processes, • semaphores, • sockets, • threads, and • tokens.
CopyFile	Copies an existing file to a new file.
CopyFileEx	Copies an existing file to a new file while preserving extended attributes, OLE structured storage, NTFS alternate data streams, and file attributes.
CopyProgressRoutine	An application-defined callback function used with the CopyFileEx and MoveFileWithProgress functions, called when a portion of a copy operation is completed.
CreateDirectory	Creates a new directory.
CreateDirectoryEx	Creates a new directory with a specified path that retains the attributes of a specified template directory.
CreateFile	Creates or opens an object and returns a handle that can be used to access the object.

CreateIoCompletionPort	Either associates an instance of an opened file with a newly-created or an existing I/O completion port *or* creates an I/O completion port without associating it with a file.
DefineDosDevice	Allows an application to define, redefine, or delete MS-DOS device names.
DeleteFile	Deletes an existing file.
FileIOCompletionRoutine	An application-defined callback function used with the ReadFileEx or WriteFileEx function called when the asynchronous I/O operation is completed or canceled.
FindClose	Closes the specified search handle.
FindCloseChangeNotification	Stops change notification handle monitoring.
FindFirstChangeNotification	Creates a change notification handle and sets up initial change notification filter conditions.
FindFirstFile	Searches a directory for a file whose name and attributes match those specified.
FindFirstFileEx	Searches a directory for a file whose name matches the specified filename.
FindNextChangeNotification	Requests that the operating system signal a change notification handle the next time it detects an appropriate change.
FindNextFile	Continues a file search from a previous call to the FindFirstFile function.
FlushFileBuffers	Clears the buffers for the specified file and causes all buffered data to be written to the file.
GetBinaryType	Determines whether a file is executable, and if so, what type of executable file it is.
GetCurrentDirectory	Retrieves the current directory for the current process.
GetDiskFreeSpace	Retrieves information about the specified disk, including the amount of free space on the disk.
GetDiskFreeSpaceEx	Obtains information about the amount of space available on a disk volume.
GetDriveType	Determines whether a disk drive is a removable, fixed, CD-ROM, RAM disk, or network drive.
GetFileAttributes	Gets attributes for a specified file or directory.

GetFileAttributesEx	Gets attributes for a specified file or directory.
GetFileInformationByHandle	Retrieves information about a specified file identified by a handle.
GetFileSize	Retrieves the size, in bytes, of the specified file.
GetFileSizeEx	Retrieves the size, in bytes, of the specified file.
GetFileType	Returns the type of the specified file, i.e., disk file, character file, pipe, or unknown.
GetFullPathName	Returns the full path and filename of a specified file.
GetLogicalDrives	Returns a bitmask representing the currently available disk drives.
GetLogicalDriveStrings	Fills a buffer with strings that specify valid drives in the system.
GetLongPathName	Converts the specified path to its long form.
GetQueuedCompletionStatus	Dequeues an I/O completion packet from a specified input/output completion port.
GetShortPathName	Obtains the short path form of a specified input path.
GetTempFileName	Creates a name for a temporary file.
GetTempPath	Retrieves the path of the directory designated for temporary files.
LockFile	Locks a region in an open file.
LockFileEx	Locks a byte range within an open file for shared or exclusive access.
MoveFile	Renames an existing file or directory.
MoveFileEx	Renames an existing file or directory.
MoveFileWithProgress	Moves files while updating tracking information.
PostQueuedCompletionStatus	Allows you to post an I/O completion packet to an I/O completion port.
QueryDosDevice	Allows an application obtain information about MS-DOS device names.
ReadDirectoryChangesW	Returns information describing the changes occurring within a directory.

ReadFile	Reads data from a file, starting at the position indicated by the file pointer.
ReadFileEx	Reads data from a file asynchronously.
ReadFileScatter	Reads data from a file and stores the data into a set of buffers.
RemoveDirectory	Deletes an existing empty directory.
ReplaceFile	Replaces one file with another file and optionally creates a backup copy of the original file.
SearchPath	Searches for the specified file in the following directories: the directory from which the application loaded, current directory, Windows system directories, and directories listed in the PATH environment variable.
SetCurrentDirectory	Changes the current directory for the current process.
SetEndOfFile	Moves the end-of-file (EOF) position to the current position of the file pointer.
SetFileApisToANSI	Causes a set of Win32 file functions to use the ANSI character set code page.
SetFileApisToOEM	Causes a set of Win32 file functions to use the OEM character set code page.
SetFileAttributes	Sets a file's attributes.
SetFilePointer	Moves the file pointer of an open file.
SetFilePointerEx	Moves the file pointer of an open file.
SetFileSecurity	Sets the security of a file or directory object.
SetVolumeLabel	Sets the label of a file system volume.
UnlockFile	Unlocks a region in an open file.
UnlockFileEx	Unlocks a previously locked byte range in an open file.
WriteFile	Writes data to a file in both synchronous and asynchronous mode.
WriteFileEx	Writes data to a file in asynchronous mode only.
WriteFileGather	Gathers data from a set of buffers and writes the data to a file.

Obsolete Functions

_hread	Reads data from the specified file.
_hwrite	Writes data to the specified file.
_lclose	Closes the specified file.
_lcreat	Creates or opens a specified file.
_llseek	Repositions the file pointer in a previously opened file.
_lopen	Opens an existing file and sets the file pointer to the beginning of the file.
_lread	Reads data from the specified file.
_lwrite	Writes data to the specified file.
OpenFile	Creates, opens, re-opens, or deletes a file.
SetHandleCount	Sets the number of file handles available to a process.

From the 50,000-ft. view, the API seems impressive. There are system calls for dealing with files, directories, device drivers, and miscellaneous system calls for setting Win32 file function parameters. Upon closer inspection, we begin to see that these are somewhat incomplete. For example, we have multiple read and write functions tha deal with synchronous and asynchronous I/O, scatter-gather I/O, and very large memory (VLM). However, we'll see shortly that functionality available in some calls is lacking in others.

We will use the write family of system calls to study the limitations of the Win32 file functions. If we look at the definition of the WriteFile and WriteFileEx functions, we see that the WriteFile system call supports both synchronous and asynchronous I/O. When we look at WriteFileEx, we see that it supports asynchronous operation only. There is nothing really wrong with this. However, when we look further into the WriteFileEx description available from Microsoft in the MSDN library, we see that WriteFileEx cannot be used on communication ports for asynchronous I/O. Instead, Microsoft recommends using WriteFile. By the way, did I forget to mention that this is only true for Windows 95?

The situation gets worse when we consider WriteFileVlm. In this system call, we find that Microsoft needed to add very large memory support to their Win32 operating systems so they invented the VLM system calls. The limitations, however, are even more restrictive than those in the previous example. With the WriteFileVlm system call, you can only perform asynchronous I/O. To add insult to injury, this system call is only available to Windows 2000 and later operating systems. In Microsoft's defense, the system call was added at a later date, thereby missing inclusion in Windows 95. However, it is exactly these types of variations and conditions on the various system calls that make Win32 operating system programming potentially tedious and necessitates more thorough testing.

We can generalize the problems of the Win32 file functions by looking at the CreateFile and CloseHandle system calls. As discussed earlier, the CreateFile system call is a misnomer that would have been better named "CreateObject," because it actually works on a broad array of objects that include files. It returns a handle that is used in all subsequent system calls when referring to the open object, or file (for this discussion). We see that the Win32 operating system design starts out as an object-oriented operating system design. The handle is merely a token used by the Win32 operating system to identify the object. Because we only have a token at the creation of the object, destroying the object requires the Win32 operating system to be smart enough to identify the object from our token and "do the right thing." So, the Win32 operating system only provides a single system call, `CloseHandle`, to destroy the object.

Unfortunately, Microsoft does not follow through on this paradigm. We know that `CreateFile` can open a directory for read operations only. Microsoft supplies the `CreateDirectory` and `CreateDirectoryEx` calls to actually create a directory. Frankly, this could have been handled within the `CreateFile` system call — there is no real reason to separate the creation of a directory from `CreateFile`. Again referring to the MSDN library, we see that the `CreateDirectory` system call takes a subset of the parameters from the `CreateFile` system call, so there is nothing preventing the creation of the directory from an API definition. Adding the functionality of creating a directory would have been a trivial task given the broad range of objects, including directory objects, the `CreateFile` system call takes.

Now, I don't want you to get the wrong impression. All this negativity is not meant as an attack on Microsoft or the Win32 operating system. I am trying to alert you, the reader, to a potential pitfall in the Win32 operating system API. I want you to master this API and use it to its fullest. In order to do that, you must be aware of shortcomings that exist within the API. Now that you are aware of them, I suggest that you take the time to look into the Microsoft documentation, whether it is printed, online, or contained on the MSDN CD-ROMs. Studying the API will help improve your skills as a developer.

Character Sets

One of the features of the family of Win32 operating systems is their ability to work with multiple character sets, such as ANSI, Unicode, or other OEM character sets. The Win32 API provides three system calls to help the developer with this. The first call we wish to take a look at is `AreFileApisANSI`. This system call queries the underlying Win32 operating system and returns a nonzero or `TRUE` when the file functions are set to ANSI. It returns 0 or `FALSE` when the file functions are set to OEM. The question at this point is whether this is system-wide or unique to a particular process or window? The answer is that the character set function calls deal primarily with console windows.

The Win32 operating system supplies two system calls to switch between ANSI and OEM character sets: `SetFileApisToOEM` and `SetFileApisToANSI`. Both take no parameters and return nothing. So, you simply make the call and trust that the Win32 operating system was able to carry this through correctly.

WARNING: There may exist code page incompatibilities between the various OEM code pages. In order to avoid problems in this area, Microsoft recommends that you work in Unicode and then convert your text from Unicode to the appropriate OEM code page by using the relevant character to OEM function. An additional note: C programs that use `main` as their entry point will have the `argv` array passed to them in ANSI. You may want to access your command line through one of the process functions discussed later in Chapter 6 to avoid this problem.

Directories

The Win32 operating system provides a number of system calls suitable for use with directories. Earlier, we discussed creating and opening a directory through the use of CreateDirectory and CreateFile. Although only the Win32 operating system writes to a directory, we can use CreateFile to read from the directory. It is probably a better choice to use the FindFirstFile/FindNextFile/FindClose family of system calls instead. We can give the Win32 operating system a pattern to match when searching through a directory including a pattern to match all files. This gives us a simple way to search through the directory.

The model is very similar to the model used in the Win32 operating system for files, i.e., open followed by read operations, then finally close. In the case of a directory, you "open" a directory through a call to FindFirstFile. This call returns a handle as well as the first occurrence of a file matching the pattern given to the call. In essence, it is shortcut system call that performs both the open operation, as well as the first read. This could be a time saver depending on your application.

All subsequent directory read operations are performed through calls to FindNextFile. It uses the handle obtained from the FindFirstFile call and systematically moves through the directory returning one directory entry at a time matching the pattern passed to FindFirstFile. The function uses a Boolean return value to indicate success. A return of TRUE indicates success; FALSE indicates failure.

Unlike the MS-DOS equivalent of these calls, the Win32 operating system version requires that you close the handle to the directory. Although this may seem like a waste of resources to a developer coming from an MS-DOS background, in actually fits better in the Win32 model. All objects, regardless of how they were created, must be destroyed when no longer needed.

Let's take a look at a quick example of the Win32 directory functions. A quick, simple program is illustrated in Listing 5.2. It is a console-style program which starts at main. It has only three local variables:

- dmp — the WIN32_FIND_DATA structure,
- hDir — the handle to the directory returned by FindFirstFile and subsequently used by FindNextFile and FileClose, and
- szPattern — where we build our pattern for the FindFirstFile system call.

The structure of the program is very simple. First, we build our pattern using another system call, GetCurrentDirectory, that returns the current directory. We concatenate either "*.*" or "*.*" depending on whether or not the path returned by GetCurrentDirectory ends with a trailing '\' character. This is done by testing of szPattern, looking at the last character in the string. We need a little bit of testing here because, by nature, the root directory ends with a trailing '\' while all other paths end in characters *other* than '\'.

Listing 5.2 **Example of** `FindFirstFile`/`FindNextFile`/`FindClose`.

```
#include <windows.h>
#include <string.h>
#include <ctype.h>


BOOL main(INT argc, BYTE *argv[])
{
        WIN32_FIND_DATA  dmp;
        HANDLE hDir;
        BYTE szPattern[MAX_PATH];

        GetCurrentDirectory(MAX_PATH, szPattern);
        strcat(szPattern, szPattern[strlen(szPattern)-1] == '\\'
               ? "*.*" : "\\*.*");

        if((hDir = FindFirstFile((LPCTSTR)szPattern, (LPWIN32_FIND_DATA)&dmp))
          == INVALID_HANDLE_VALUE)
        {
                printf("Directory error\nPattern: \"%s\"\n", szPattern);
                return 1;
        }

        do
        {
                printf("\n%s", dmp.cFileName);
        }
        while(FindNextFile((HANDLE)hDir, (LPWIN32_FIND_DATA)&dmp));

        printf("\n\n");
        FindClose(hDir);
        return 0;
}
```

Once we have our pattern built, a simple call to `FindFirstFile` returns a handle and the first filename in the directory. Note that the structure following is a `do-while` loop. This is so we can properly handle the filename returned by the initial call to `FindFirstFile`. The loop continues until `FindNextFile` fails and returns a non-`TRUE` value. The loop then exits and the program terminates with a call to `FindClose` to free the handle. This basic structure is used in many programs that allow wild-card characters within a filename specification.

Although I criticized the Win32 operating system file functions, this family of system calls greatly simplifies searching a directory, as illustrated in the preceding example. Sometimes, it is better to take advantage of Win32 operating system peculiarities than try to use a more traditional approach. Microsoft may like to create special cases and take advantage of them, but that doesn't mean that we shouldn't take advantage of them as well.

The directory functions also include directory maintenance functions. These include `SetCurrentDirectory` that sets the current working directory, `RemoveDirectory` that will remove an empty directory, and `CreateDirectoryEx` that creates a directory similar to the `CreateDirectory` function.

File I/O

The file I/O portions of the Win32 operating system contain mainly the typical file I/O functions. That is, we have functions to read, write, open, and close files as well as functions to set file pointers, file attributes, etc. These functions include scatter-gather-type read and write operations. The scatter-gather functions transfer one or more blocks of memory to or from disk. These functions require a list of the address and number of bytes at each address memory to transfer in the read or write operation. These functions typically will replace multiple sequential file I/O, improving program performance.

We've already seen the functionality of `CreateFile`. We've also discussed the `ReadFile` and `WriteFile` operations and how they support both synchronous and asynchronous I/O. In synchronous I/O, the read or write operation blocks until the I/O is completed. In asynchronous I/O, the read or write function returns before the read or write operation completes. This allows for more efficient I/O operations. Often a particular piece of data may be written to a file while another operation, such as a read from another file, takes place. When such operations takes place, a method of synchronizing with the operation must exist so that an asynchronous read or write function call works correctly. In the Win32 operating system, we can achieve this through system calls such as `FileIOCompletionRoutine` — an application-defined callback function used in conjunction with `ReadFileEx` and `WriteFileEx`. For example, using `FileIOCompletionRoutine` allows a developer to begin a `ReadFileEx` operation in an asynchronous mode, and invoke the `FileIOCompletionRoutine` so that the program may use the data from the read operation, when the data is available. Other means of synchronizing with the asynchronous operation exist in the form of events that may be sent to a thread.

In the previous discussion, we spoke about synchronizing the asynchronous operation. This may sound odd at first, but realize that the Win32 operating system is a multithreaded environment where it is quite possible to start a thread, cause it to wait on an event, then go off and execute a `ReadFileEx` system call in the original thread. The main thread will be busy doing other chores and the waiting thread will "wake up" when data is ready, and proceed to do the work necessary with that data. This overlapped operation allows for increased efficiency. It is somewhat premature to discuss this now — we will be discussing processes and threads in a later chapter. For the moment, the reader may think of this as a way of letting the program do two things at once.

We can use the program in Listing 5.3 to better understand how some of the file I/O functions work. As you can see, the program is simple. It opens a file by a call to `CreateFile` using the string that was passed to it as a name as the argument to the program. `CreateFile` opens the file for a generic read operation and allows it to be shared with other processes. This is possible because there will be no modifications to the file and frankly, since the program simply reads the file and prints out, we don't care if another process changes it. The handle returned by `CreateFile` is compared against `INVALID_HANDLE_VALUE` to test for an error condition. If an error occurs when `CreateFile` attempts to open a file, it returns `INVALID_HANDLE_VALUE`.

Listing 5.3 Simple file I/O example.

```
#include <windows.h>

#define CTL_Z 0x1a

INT main(INT argc, BYTE *argv[])
{
        HANDLE hFile;
        DWORD nRead;
        BYTE c;

        if(argc != 2)
                return FALSE;

        if((hFile = CreateFile((LPCTSTR)argv[1], GENERIC_READ, FILE_SHARE_READ,
           NULL, OPEN_EXISTING, FILE_ATTRIBUTE_NORMAL, 0)) == INVALID_HANDLE_VALUE)
        {
                printf("Cannot find file \"%s\"\n", argv[1]);
                return 1;
        }
        while(ReadFile(hFile, (LPVOID)&c, (DWORD)1, &nRead, 0) && (nRead == 1))
        {
                if(c == CTL_Z)
                        break;
                printf("%c", c);
        }
        CloseHandle(hFile);
        printf("\n");
        return 0;
}
```

The body of the program is equally trivial. It simply reads a byte at a time by a call to `ReadFile` from within a `while` loop. `ReadFile` returns `TRUE` as long as no error conditions occur during the read operation. When an error does occur, such as attempting to read past the end of file, the loop terminates. The loop also terminates should a Ctrl-Z be encountered, keeping with MS-DOS conventions. Any byte read is written to the console by a call to `printf` inside the loop. When the program is finished, i.e., the end of the file is reached, it closes the handle through a call to `CloseHandle` and exits.

This is a somewhat trivial example, but it illustrates the basic file functions offered by the Win32 operating system. You can see that the concepts do not differ greatly from MS-DOS or UNIX. Only the system calls, and parameters to the system calls, change. Conceptually, the operations are identical.

There are, as mentioned earlier, some eccentricities in the Win32 file function system calls. In many other operating systems, if you desire to copy a file, you must do so by writing code similar to the example in Listing 5.3. However, Microsoft does seem to enjoy a shortcut or two. That's why we find an unusual system call that goes by the name of CopyFile (CopyFileEx). You can see the example in Listing 5.4. There isn't much to tell about this example. It simply takes two arguments, uses the first argument as source file, and the second argument as a destination file. With source and destination in hand, it invokes CopyFile to perform the file copy operation. As you can see, not much user code there. I did promise you a Microsoft shortcut, didn't I?

Listing 5.4 CopyFile **example.**

```
#include <windows.h>


BOOL main(INT argc, BYTE *argv[])
{
        if(argc != 3)
        {
                printf("syntax: copy <source> <destination>\n");
                return 1;
        }

        return !CopyFile(argv[1], argv[2], FALSE);
}
```

A Rich Set

We've only touched the surface of the file functions offered by the Win32 operating system. There are 64 file functions, not including 10 obsolete functions included for 16-bit Windows compatibility. Some of these calls are maintenance calls, while others are true I/O functions. Sprinkled in, we have a shortcut or two. With this many system calls, it is difficult to cover all them in this chapter. However, you should be ready to use these system calls in your next program.

Chapter 6

Processes and Threads

One basic operating system service is executing a program. There are many ways to do this. In the simplest of operating systems, such as early microprocessor systems like CP/M, the program is simply executed by a jump into the program entry point. In this operating system, an area of memory was reserved specifically for programs. This area, aptly named the TPA or Transient Program Area, had a fixed memory layout and all programs started at a fixed offset from the beginning of the program. The program was simply an image of this TPA and loaded by reading that image to memory. This model persisted into the 8086/8088 MS-DOS operating system as the .COM executable program. MS-DOS expanded on this model by allowing multiple memory areas to be allocated to a program. MS-DOS had a simple linked list memory management scheme that enabled multiple program images to reside in memory. To accompany this, Microsoft developed the .EXE file format that permitted relocation of the image anywhere in memory.

By no means do I want to imply that this little slice of operating system history is representative of how operating system programs are executed. Other operating systems, such as UNIX, take advantage of memory management hardware that typically provides address translation so that a program image loaded into a physical area of memory logically appears to be in a different memory location. It may be loaded in non-contiguous segments of memory that are made to appear as a contiguous memory area through the use of address translation mechanisms. In fact, the entire program may not be loaded in memory until the processor needs it. In other words, although the program *appears* to be entirely loaded, it is only loaded as necessary, a piece at a time. It also provides protection from inadvertent accesses from other programs. The question that you should now ask is: how do you model such a powerful set of concepts? The answer is through processes and threads. Let's begin by examining processes. We'll then see how these relate to threads in order to complete the picture.

Win32 Process and Threads

Win32 Process Overview

We will begin with how the Win32 operating system represents a program in memory. As you may recall, the program file, or .EXE file, contains the program image, information about what other files it may require, as well as the entry points of calls made to those files, and relocation information so that the loader may properly modify the program image as necessary to make it function properly. Naturally, the Win32 operating system kernel needs a way to accurately represent this program in memory. That is where the process comes in.

In a Win32 operating system, the *process* is an abstraction that is used by the kernel to represent the program in memory. This abstraction has certain attributes associated with it, e.g., information regarding the state of the program such as memory mapping, pages loaded, etc. It also has information about threads associated with the process. In fact, a process can be thought of as a container for threads, but we'll see more of that later.

In practice, the process represents a virtual image of the computer. It is a 4Gb virtual memory where the lower 2Gb of memory is private to the process, and 2Gb are dedicated to the Win32 kernel and shared with other processes in the system. All that is missing from this picture is information about the running state of the program. That is because the running state of the program is not contained within the process but in the thread. You see, a simple process that is not making thread calls to the Win32 operating system is still making use of threads. It is running a single thread *within* the process, so that a simple, non-multithreaded, Win32 program is really a threaded program running a single thread.

Win32 Thread Overview

Within Win32 operating systems, the most fundamental unit of execution is the thread. A *thread* is part of a program, loaded in memory, that is either executing or waiting to execute. In many ways, it is the equivalent of a task in other operating systems. One significant difference that sets threads apart from other execution models (such as tasks) is that they share memory space with other threads. This doesn't necessarily mean that an executing program must have multiple threads of execution, but it may.

So, what is a thread? In its simplest of forms, it is all the information that a processor needs in order to execute a program. For example, it is typically a program counter or instruction pointer, a stack pointer, and the register contents necessary for the program to execute. So, to relate this to a process, it is the dynamic information necessary for the process to run. As mentioned earlier, the process acts as a container for threads and contributes all the necessary information to define the program context, both executable and data memory. The Win32 operating system kernel supplies the mechanisms to make these abstractions reality for the computer's processor. In a multithreaded application, more than one of these threads are associated with a process. That means at any given instance, the processor may be executing one of many execution paths in the program.

In a multi-programming environment, the operating system switches between one of many programs or processes concurrently running on the computer. In a multithreaded environment, the operating system not only switches between processes, but between threads within the process as well. The benefits for the programmer are two-fold. First, there is much less overhead associated in switching threads because it only requires a change in processor context whereas the process switch requires the thread switch and the program environment switch. This may include swapping memory pages from memory to secondary storage for the old process, from secondary storage to memory for the new process, updating the processor translation look aside buffer contents, and updating all data structures associated with it. As you can see, thread switches are lighter weight than process switches, allowing for increased efficiency. Threads are also much more effective in a multiprocessor system because threads of single processes may be scheduled to run on more than one processor. As you are probably aware, the concurrent program operation in a uniprocessor system is an illusion played on us by time slicing. In a multiprocessor system, individual threads of the same program may run on different processors, so that the threads are truly running concurrently.

Aside from the operating system advantages of threads, there is a significant programming advantage as well, because all data within the program is available to all threads at all times. There is no overhead in accessing a piece of data. In fact, it is as simple as accessing a global variable in the program. This is both a blessing and a downfall in that it requires exceptional discipline to prevent problems associated with uncoordinated access of shared resources such as memory. We will take a closer look at that shortly.

I made the vague statement in an earlier discussion of processes that even though a process may not be executing a multithreaded application, it really is. With a better understanding of both processes and threads, we should now be able to see why. The process is all the information and associated computer resources required to run a program; the thread is all the information required by the computer's processors to run the program. By itself, the process is inert; it cannot execute the program because it does not have that information. The process requires at least one thread in order to run. Hence, the process contains a program's static information whereas a thread contains a program's dynamic information. These two abstractions, in combination with each other, make up a running Win32 program.

Win32 Thread and Process Mechanics

In the last section, we examined operating system abstractions that Win32 operating systems use to make programs run — looking at them from the program's point of view. What does it look like from the operating system's point of view? What does the operating system need to make these processes and threads work? That is where the Win32 operating system kernel comes in. The *kernel* implements data structures and code to perform the necessary actions to make it work — handling the task of selecting which thread to run, maintaining the virtual machine that is described by the processes, handle processor exceptions, etc.

Multitasking

Part of the goal of the Win32 operating system is to provide preemptive multitasking. That is, we want to have the illusion of multiple programs running concurrently. This requires a way to suspend a thread and resume another without any input from the thread itself. This is in contrast to the Microsoft-speak "cooperative multitasking" of the older Windows where a program had to give up processing time in order to allow other programs to run. In the Win32 operating system, an external force — the kernel itself — decides to suspend a thread in order to start another. It does this through time slicing.

Time Slicing

The Win32 operating systems are multitasking operating systems. Specifically, they implement a preemptive multitasking design that switches between threads utilizing *time slicing*. It allocates a processor time slice to each thread it executes. It picks one thread and executes it. When that thread executes, it does so until its time slice elapses. At that point, the Win32 operating system kernel swaps out the current thread for another thread stored on a queue, allowing that thread to run. As part of the thread switch, it stores the state of the preempted thread, usually called the *context*, and restores the saved context of the next thread in the queue.

According to Microsoft documentation, the length of the time slice depends on which Win32 operating system the program is running under and the processor running the program. These time slices are on the order of 20 milliseconds, giving the illusion of simultaneous operation. This time, commonly referred to as the *quantum*, is a tradeoff. Typically, operating system designers chose the quantum length to allow the greatest amount of thread execution time with respect to the operating system overhead. You see, there is some operating system code that runs in order to accomplish each context switch. The ratio of the quantum to this time plus the quantum represents an efficiency number commonly used to determine the quantum length. The decision of the length of the quantum becomes a tradeoff between this efficiency metric and response time to user I/O. For Microsoft Win32 operating systems, Microsoft chose 20 milliseconds.

There are other factors to consider in operating system efficiency and response time, such as the number of threads running concurrently. For one thing, each thread consumes a certain amount of operating system resources — from kernel memory space to swap file space — as well as running time. The more threads running at any given time, the more time spent by the kernel moving data around. In addition, the more threads running, the less time is given to any one thread. These combined factors slow down the system response time as well as program execution time. Therefore, as developers, we want to limit the number of threads in order not to slow down the application we're designing. We have to pay attention to the operating system scheduling as well in order to not produce a slow application. This is one of the complications of multithreaded program design. A proper design can really improve an application's performance, especially in multiprocessor systems. A poor design can make it run slower than molasses on a cold, winter day.

Scheduler

One important part of the Win32 operating system is the *scheduler*. It has the important task of searching through a list of threads ready to execute and setting up the necessary mechanisms to cause one to run. It assigns priorities to each thread as part of its selection criteria. It is, in essence, the "task master" that doles out each thread to run.

The Win32 operating system scheduler utilizes a priority scheme in order to allow certain threads and processes to run in favor of others. It works by maintaining a queue of executable threads for each priority level, referred to as *ready threads*. The queues are arranged in order of highest to lowest. The scheduler systematically traverses each queue, running threads as it goes along. The thread switch may involve a process switch as well, causing processes to be moved in and out of memory.

When a thread becomes available, the Win32 scheduler performs a context switch. The algorithm behind the Win32 scheduler context switch is simple. First, the kernel saves the context of the thread that just finished executing. Next, it places that thread at the end of the queue for its priority. It then proceeds to find the highest priority queue that contains ready threads. Finally, it removes the thread at the head of the queue, loads its context, and executes it.

Thread Affinity

In the Win32 operating systems, the scheduler can take advantage of the underlying hardware. Thanks to the thread design, the operating system can take advantage of multiprocessor systems. These computer designs employ more than one processor using architectures such as Symmetric Multi Processor (SMP) and Non-Uniform Memory Access (NUMA). The scheduler can assign any thread to run on any processor. Sometimes, however, it is detrimental for a thread to migrate from one processor to another. The Win32 operating system allows you to assign a preference to the processor(s) that a thread may run on. You can assign a thread to a subset of processors on which to run. This is known as *thread affinity* and is a very powerful tool.

Thread affinity allows you to guarantee certain threads to run with less overhead. If you recall our earlier discussion about threads and processes, you'll remember that we discussed some of the limitations that a thread incurs when running in an environment with many threads. This could be very detrimental for a thread that has a real-time constraint on it, for example a thread handling a communications port. Communications throughput could suffer greatly if the thread responsible for it is delayed by milliseconds. However, if you are running on a multiprocessor system, you can assign your communications threads to one processor while assigning all other threads to another processor. Now, your communications throughput increases, potentially improving your application's response time. This type of load balancing is one example of how thread affinity can help your system performance. I've used this in a server application and I'm sure you'll think of some potential uses in your applications as well.

Thread States

The scheduler only selects ready threads to run. It does this by allocating time to the thread. The scheduler does not allocate any processor time to threads that are suspended or blocked until they become ready to run, regardless of their priority. Typically, context switches result from a time slice that has elapsed, a higher priority thread becoming ready to run, or a running thread changing its state to wait.

An important efficiency note: when a running thread needs to wait, it relinquishes the remainder of its time slice.

If you kept up with the previous discussion and not fallen asleep, I have good news for you: the lesson on operating system theory ends here. Why? Well, most operating systems are very similar at this level. With only minor changes, I can make the previous description fit nearly any operating system. What makes one operating system different from another is in the implementation, so "the devil is in the detail." For example, the theory presented above could be applied to a real-time operating system by simply stating that the time it takes to perform a context switch is fixed and predictable.

We spoke about processes and threads, but never discussed how to create one. Here is another area where the details differentiate the operating system. For example, within the UNIX operating system environment you create a process by splitting the current thread of execution through a call to `fork` to create two identical processes, then execute the new process in the child process through a call to `exec`. This contrasts greatly from a Win32 operating system where a child process is created through a single call to `CreateProcess`. As you can see from these simple examples, we need to change our focus in order to better understand the Win32 operating systems.

Win32 Process and Thread API

After our introductory discussion of process and thread fundamentals, we looked at how these related to Win32 operating system. Well, now its time to see how we can make use of all this theory. In order to do that, we need to begin exploring the Win32 API for processes and threads. We can start by looking at the API in Table 6.1. (Discourse continues on page 129.)

Table 6.1 Win32 Process and Thread API.

`AttachThreadInput`	Attaches the input processing mechanism of one thread to that of another thread.
`CommandLineToArgvW`	Parses a wide-character Unicode command-line string and returns a pointer to a set of wide-character Unicode argument strings and a count of arguments, similar to the standard C run-time `argv` and `argc` values.
`CreateProcess`	Creates a new process and its primary thread that executes the specified executable file.
`CreateProcessAsUser`	Creates a new process and its primary thread. The new process then executes a specified executable file in the security context of the specified user.
`CreateProcessWithLogonW`	Creates a new process and its primary thread that runs the specified executable file in a given security context.
`CreateRemoteThread`	Creates a thread that runs in the address space of another process.
`CreateThread`	Creates a thread to execute within the address space of the calling process.

ExitProcess	Ends a process and all its threads.
ExitThread	Ends a single thread.
FreeEnvironmentStrings	Frees a block of environment strings.
GetCommandLine	Returns a pointer to the command-line string for the current process.
GetCurrentProcess	Returns a pseudo handle for the current process.
GetCurrentProcessId	Returns the process identifier of the calling process.
GetCurrentThread	Returns a pseudo handle for the current thread.
GetCurrentThreadId	Returns the thread identifier of the calling thread.
GetEnvironmentStrings	Returns the address of the environment block for the current process.
GetEnvironmentVariable	Retrieves a null-terminated string of characters of the specified variable from the environment block of the calling process.
GetExitCodeProcess	Retrieves the termination status of the specified process.
GetExitCodeThread	Retrieves the termination status of the specified thread.
GetGuiResources	Returns the count of handles to graphical user interface objects in use by the specified process.
GetPriorityClass	Returns the priority class for the specified process.
GetProcessAffinityMask	Returns a process affinity mask for the specified process and the system affinity mask for the system.
GetProcessIOCounters	Retrieves accounting information for all I/O operations performed by the specified process.
GetProcessShutdownParameters	Retrieves shutdown parameters for the currently calling process.
GetProcessPriorityBoost	Returns the priority boost control state of the specified process.
GetProcessTimes	Gets timing information about a specified process.
GetProcessVersion	Gets the major and minor version numbers of the Windows version on which a specified process expects to run.
GetProcessWorkingSetSize	Gets the minimum and maximum working set sizes of a specified process.

GetStartupInfo	Retrieves the contents of the STARTUPINFO structure that was specified when the calling process was created.
GetThreadPriority	Returns the priority value for the specified thread.
GetThreadPriorityBoost	Returns the priority boost control state of the specified thread.
GetThreadTimes	Gets timing information about a specified thread.
OpenProcess	Opens and returns a handle of an existing process object.
OpenThread	Opens and returns a handle of an existing thread object.
ResumeThread	Decrements a thread's suspend count, until it reaches zero where the execution of the thread is resumed.
SetEnvironmentVariable	Sets the value of an environment variable for the current process.
SetPriorityClass	Sets the priority class for the specified process.
SetProcessAffinityMask	Sets a processor affinity mask for the threads of a specified process.
SetProcessPriorityBoost	Disables the ability of the system to temporarily boost the priority of the threads of the specified process.
SetProcessShutdownParameters	Sets a shutdown order for a process relative to the other processes in the system.
SetProcessWorkingSetSize	Sets the minimum and maximum memory pages currently visible to the process in physical memory.
SetThreadAffinityMask	Sets a processor affinity mask for a specified thread.
SetThreadIdealProcessor	Specifies a preferred processor for a thread.
SetThreadPriority	Sets the priority value for the specified thread.
SetThreadPriorityBoost	Disables the ability to temporarily boost the priority of a thread (Windows NT/2000 only).
Sleep	Suspends the execution of the current thread for a specified interval.
SleepEx	The SleepEx function causes the current thread to enter a wait state until either an I/O completion callback function is called, an asynchronous procedure call (APC) is queued to the thread, or time-out interval elapses.
SuspendThread	Suspends the specified thread.

`SwitchToThread`	Causes the calling thread to yield execution to another thread that is ready to run on the current processor.
`TerminateProcess`	Terminates the specified process and all of its threads.
`TerminateThread`	Terminates a thread.
`ThreadProc`	Application-defined function that serves as the starting address for a thread.
`TlsAlloc`	Allocates a thread local storage (TLS) index.
`TlsFree`	Releases a thread local storage (TLS) index.
`TlsGetValue`	Gets the value in the calling thread"s thread local storage (TLS) slot for a specified TLS index.
`TlsSetValue`	Stores a value in the calling thread's thread local storage (TLS) slot for a specified TLS index.
`WaitForInputIdle`	Waits until the given process is waiting for user input with no input pending, or until the time-out interval has elapsed.

One of the first things you'll notice is that the API is split into four distinct sets — one for processes, another for threads, yet another for environment variables, and still another for "thread local storage." In the last group, the Win32 operating system provides a sort of "virtual array" in which you can assign and retrieve data by referencing it with an index. We will now examine each of the these four groups to better understand what the Win32 operating system offers us as developers for processor and thread management.

Process Management

Earlier, we looked at the Win32 operating system and found that there was an abstraction, known as a process, that defined the virtual machine that a program occupies when loaded by the operating system. This process is a container for threads that are the executing parts of the program. So, we need a way to make these processes happen and the Win32 operating system provides us with the API to do that.

Launching a Process

In previous versions of Windows, i.e., Windows 3.X and earlier, the primary mechanism for launching a program was `WinExec`. That is, the only operation we were allowed was to launch a program and once we launched it, it ran. Starting with Win32, `WinExec` became obsolete and was replaced with `CreateProcess`. This makes an excellent point to start our discussion. You see, in a Win32 environment, our program is the process once we create the process and attach a program name to it. We do this through the `CreateProcess` call where we ask the Win32 operating system to create a process to accommodate the program whose name we pass as an argument. We can also start a process in a given user or security context through calls to `CreateProcessAsUser` and `CreateProcessWithLogonW`, respectively.

We may pass arguments to a process in the form of a command line in order to allow the process to parse it, looking for command line arguments. The Win32 API provides the calls, `CommandLineToArgvW` and `GetCommandLine`, to manage command lines. In addition, environment variables are managed through the API calls `FreeEnvironmentStrings`, `GetEnvironmentStrings`, `GetEnvironmentVariable`, and `SetEnvironmentVariable`. These are two ways we can provide information to a new process while using the Win32 API.

Terminating a Process

There are times when we want to terminate a process. For example, we may start a program, such as Wordpad, to get information from the user. For example, we may want the user to modify a configuration file. When the user completes the modification, we will want to close the Wordpad process. This can be accomplished through a call to `TerminateProcess`.

There are times we may want to terminate our application. This may be the result of some unrecoverable error, or simply when exiting the application. This is accomplished through a call to `ExitProcess`. When the process is terminates, it may want to return an exit status to its parent. This exit status is the only parameter passed to `ExitProcess`. The parent can recover that exit status through a call to `GetExitCodeProcess`, by giving it the handle to the terminating process, or it can recover the extended error through a call to `GetLastError`. This covers both the birth and death of the process.

Working with Processes

The Win32 API has a number of calls that we can use for various purposes. For example, just as every kernel object has a handle, so does a process. We can get this by calling `GetCurrentProcess`. We can also get the identification of the process through a call to `GetCurrentProcessId`. These two calls allow us greater flexibility in the way we refer to a process.

In addition, we can control a process priority through calls to `GetPriorityClass` and `SetPriorityClass`, monitor its I/O activity with a call to `GetProcessIOCounters`, etc. The Win32 API is rich with process calls, and studying the API calls listed in Table 6.1 (on page 126) will definitely help you in your next project.

Thread Management

As we saw earlier, every process contains one or more threads. These threads are the actual running context for the process. Each thread has code associated with it that is common to other threads in the process. Typically, a thread will be a function within the application that has access to all global variables in the application. Coordination of access to these variables must be handled through the use of synchronization objects, which we will cover later. However, local variables are unique to each thread and are maintained on individual stacks unique to each thread. In addition, each thread can have locals storage known as *Thread Local Storage* (TLS) that it can request from the Win32 operating system. Let's take a closer look at this.

Launching a Thread

A thread can only exist inside of a process and typically is started by a thread within the process. However, we need to start somewhere. The Win32 operating system helps us by starting the first thread, so that each process runs with its initial thread. This is the thread that executes the "C" start code and eventually launches main(). However, many languages, such as C and C++, do not define grammar suitable for threads the way other languages, such as Ada, do. So the Win32 operating system provides calls such as CreateThread to create a thread in your process and CreateRemoteThread for a process other than the one your thread is running in. CreateThread is relatively straightforward. You create the thread by simply passing the call the address of the code you wish to execute, typically a pointer to a function, and other parameters such as initial stack size, as well as arguments, identifiers, etc. The same is almost true of CreateRemoteThread, but you cannot simply pass the address of a function in a remote process. In order to do this, the CreateRemoteThread call makes use of a mechanism known as ThreadProc. It is an application-defined function that corresponds to the start address of the remote thread.

Terminating a Thread

The Win32 API provides two methods to terminate a thread. The first is ExitThread. This function is called either explicitly or by returning from a thread procedure. It deallocates the current thread's stack and terminates. If the thread is the last thread in the process when this function is called, the thread's process is also terminated. Note that terminating a thread does not necessarily remove the thread object from the operating system. It persists until the last handle to the thread is closed.

You'll note that the ExitThread function is similar to the ExitProcess call we saw earlier. You may remember that the ExitProcess had a matching TerminateProcess call. Threads follow the same model with the TerminateThread call. If you have the handle of a thread, you can simply execute this call in order to terminate it. However, here's where the advantages of threads can also be a disadvantage. Because threads all operate from with the same global variables, a thread that is terminated using the TerminateThread call may be terminated at a very inconvenient time. For example, you may have some sort of synchronization mechanism open to lock a variable, and you asynchronously call TerminateThread before the thread releases the lock. That variable may become permanently locked and cause deadlocks in your application. You'll recognize this condition with unexplained freezing of your applications. Therefore, you must be very, very careful with this call and avoid it, if you can.

Managing Threads

The Win32 API provides a number of functions to manage threads. Threads can be suspended, resumed, sleep, etc. We'll take a closer look at these now, so that you can begin to understand how to use them.

You can suspend and resume the execution of a thread using the SuspendThread and ResumeThread functions. The SuspendThread function is asynchronous, in that it does not control the point in the code at which the thread's execution is suspended. Therefore, some of the same warnings applicable to TerminateThread are valid here. However, there are situations where you may want to simply suspend the thread. For example, you might want to suspend a thread when you are waiting for user input. When the input becomes available, you would call ResumeThread to have the thread continue from the point when it was suspended. Note that both calls are asynchronous with respect to the thread that they operate on, so you must carefully plan how to use these calls.

A thread can temporarily suspend itself for a specified interval by calling the `Sleep` or `SleepEx` functions. You would use this mechanism for a number of reasons. For example, you may be waiting for user input and want to give up the processor for a second to allow other processes and threads to run on the system. You may also want to start a thread as a "time out" thread that suspends for the time out period to monitor a second thread. If, when it resumes, the thread it monitors has not yet completed its task, you would then have a time out condition and execute code to deal with that condition.

I mentioned earlier that you may want to give up the processor while waiting for something to occur. The Win32 API has one other call, `SwitchToThread`, that allows you to simply give up the processor at a point in time. It behaves nearly identically to `Sleep` and `SleepEx`, except that there is no time period specified. You would use this call whenever you simply wanted to yield the processor and have no time constraints on when to restart the thread.

There are other thread management functions that allow you to get and set thread priorities, such as `GetThreadPriority` and `SetThreadPriority`, as well as which processor to execute on such as `SetProcessorAffinity` and `SetThreadIdealProcessor`. Also, you can get a handle to your processor with `GetCurrentThread`, execution times with `GetThreadTimes`, etc. — again, another rich Win32 API that, when used properly, can help the performance of your next application.

Thread Local Storage

Thread Local Storage (TLS) enables multiple threads of the same process to use an index allocated by the `TlsAlloc` function to store and retrieve a value that is local to the thread. To make use of TLS, an index is allocated when the process starts through a call to `TlsAlloc`. When each thread starts, it allocates a block of dynamic memory and stores a pointer to this memory through a call to `TlsSetValue`. Whenever a thread wants to use the local memory, it uses the TLS index in a call to `TlsGetValue`, which returns a pointer to local memory. Before each thread terminates, it must release its dynamic memory and return the index through a call to `TlsFree`.

So, what is this good for? You may recall that all threads of a process share the virtual address space and the global variables of that process and that the local variables of a thread function are local to each thread that runs the function. However, the static or global variables used by that function have the same value for all threads. Thread local storage is a layer of indirection that allows each thread to store its own virtual copy of global data. With TLS, you create a unique copy of a variable for each thread. Each thread then allocates an index that can be used by any thread of the process to retrieve its unique copy of global data, hence eliminating some of the problems of synchronization of access to global data. It is especially useful in DLLs where the DLL has no knowledge of the applications global data and hence cannot make use of other Win32 synchronization objects.

What's Next?

We now know more about a Win32 program. We know that it is a process, which is a container for one or more threads. We know that these run in a true multitasking environment and that we can control its execution through process and thread priority. However, our knowledge of processes and threads is not enough. We need to know how to share information between processes and how to synchronize them so that they don't trip over each other.

We'll cover that in the next chapters and get to see it in action when we tie it all together in the final chapter. This way, we'll build on each chapter in constructing an application. With that in mind, let's move on to interprocess communications.

7

Chapter 7

Interprocess Communications

When multiple threads communicate, they may do so by accessing common memory. This is easy to do, because the normal process data area is available to every thread within the process. In your C or C++ program, it's as easy as declaring a global variable and writing to it from one thread and reading from it in another. However, the beauty of this mechanism is also its downfall, because this is limited to a single process. There are times when multiple processes must exchange data as well. For example, when the command shell spawns multiple processes, their "standard input" or console input and "standard output" or console output are chained together to allow the output of one process to feed the input of another. This is based on the MS-DOS model, which is copied from the UNIX paradigm. This mechanism is known as a "pipe," also borrowing from the UNIX mechanism. The beauty is that it allows simple read and write operations to access data from another process. As an added bonus, the processes do not necessarily need to be on the same machine.

Another key method of communicating between processes makes use of memory-mapped files. Earlier, we covered reading and writing to files. We spoke about the advantages of memory-mapped files allowing us to access random locations in the file by simply reading and writing to an area of memory within the process. This way we eliminate the need to compute file offset before we perform the read or write operation. The memory-mapped file eliminates two system calls. It also shares a common, yet hidden, benefit — the use of automatic synchronization mechanisms built into the operating system. We will shortly see why this is important and how to make best use of it.

Pipes

Table 7.1   Win32 pipe API calls.

CallNamedPipe	Called by a client; it creates the client end of a named pipe, writes to and reads from it, and closes it.
ConnectNamedPipe	Called by the server; it waits for the client to connect to the pipe using CreateFile or CallNamedPipe.
CreateNamedPipe	Called by the server; it creates the named pipe.
CreatePipe	Creates an anonymous pipe, and returns handles to the read and write ends of the pipe.
DisconnectNamedPipe	Called by the server; it disconnects the named pipe (and, although it is not required, it should be called after the client has called CloseFile).
GetNamedPipeHandleState	Obtains information about the state of a named pipe handle.
GetNamedPipeInfo	Obtains information about a named pipe.
PeekNamedPipe	Reads from an anonymous or named pipe without removing data, and returns information about the remaining data.
SetNamedPipeHandleState	Sets the read and blocking modes of a named pipe.
TransactNamedPipe	Called by the client for a message mode named pipe; it combines WriteFile and ReadFile into one transaction, which may increase performance over a network.
WaitNamedPipe	Called by the client; it waits for an instance of a named pipe to become available.

By now, you should be asking, "Did I buy a book about programming or plumbing?" What the heck is all this about? Well, it is a simple mechanism to put data into and take data out of. In this fashion, it is a FIFO (First In First Out) mechanism. The reference to it as a pipe comes from UNIX days where the FIFO was thought of as a "data pipe" connecting processes together. This data pipe analogy is an accurate representation when one process writes to it and another reads from it. Thanks to the FIFO structure, data read from it by the reading process is read in the same order as it was written by the writing process. This supports the pipe metaphor.

With this concept under our belt, we will now take a closer look at what Win32 operating systems offer. Because pipes are designed to operate between processes, we need to look at what type of processes will be using them. First, we have a process that creates a child process. In this case, we simply need to create a pipe in the parent process and pass some sort of handle to the newly-created pipe to the child process. In contrast, we can have two processes that were created by one or more different processes. These two new processes will have nothing in common and you cannot pass a handle between independent processes. In fact, the processes may exist on different machines. In this case, you need some mechanism to open a common pipe between the two. Here, one of the two processes creates the pipe using a name, which was previously agreed to, between the two processes. This is commonly referred to as a *named pipe* as opposed to the one we discussed earlier, usually called an *anonymous pipe*. We will now take a closer look at each type.

Anonymous Pipes

Because anonymous and named pipes are similar in function, a lot of what we will discuss for anonymous pipes will also be valid for named pipes. However, the major differentiator between the two is that anonymous pipes are always local. They may be used for communication between a parent and child process, or between two children of the same process. They cannot be used across a network or by two processes that do not share a common ancestry.

So how do we make use of this mechanism? First, we create a pipe using `CreatePipe`, which returns two handles. Of these two handles, one handle is typically used for writing to the pipe, and the other for reading from the pipe. Note that this structure implies two simplex mechanisms, but that is not really the case because the pipe is full duplex. Because we have handles to the pipes, we can treat them in a manner similar to files. To read data from the pipe, you call `ReadFile` with the handle returned for reading from the `CreatePipe` call. Similarly, you write data to the pipe by calling `WriteFile` with the handle that `CreatePipe` returned for writing. After a little examination, we can readily see why there are process limitations on anonymous pipes. Because the handles are a result of a single call to `CreatePipe`, handle inheritance provides the only access to the pipe. So, only child processes of the process that created the pipe can access the pipe. That means that one way to use a pipe is parent/child communications if the parent creates the pipe and uses it to communicate with the child. Similarly, child/child communications are possible if the parent creates the pipe and hands it to two children who then use it to communicate with each other.

We can easily take a look at how anonymous pipes work with the simple example in Listing 7.1. As you may notice, there isn't much to it. This is intentional — we don't want to get caught up creating processes and dealing with inheritance. So, we start off with a simple call to `CreatePipe` to create the anonymous pipe that we will be using. We do a simple test of the return value to check for errors and continue if everything is OK. Now, we see exactly how easy it is to use the pipe. We do a `WriteFile` call in order to put data into the pipe and a `ReadFile` to get the data out of the pipe. If we compile and run it, we get a message that indicates how much data was written followed by a message that indicates how much data was read and the data read. The whole process is simple and straightforward. Our example seems somewhat useless because it only communicates to itself, but it demonstrates the FIFO nature of the pipe quite nicely. This lets us test the IPC mechanism from within a single process and avoids the complications of creating a child process.

Listing 7.1 Simple pipe example.

```
#include <stdio.h>
#include <windows.h>

#define PIPESIZE 1024

int main(int argc, char *argv[])
{
        HANDLE hReadPipe, hWritePipe;
        DWORD dwWritten, dwRead;
        char sBuffer[PIPESIZE];

        if(!CreatePipe(&hReadPipe, &hWritePipe, NULL, PIPESIZE))
        {
                printf("CreatePipe failed!\n");
                ExitProcess(1);
        }

        WriteFile(hWritePipe, "Hello", 5, &dwWritten, NULL);
        printf("%ld Bytes written\n", dwWritten);

        ReadFile(hReadPipe, &sBuffer, PIPESIZE, &dwRead, NULL);
        sBuffer[5] = 0;
        printf("%ld Bytes read, Data = \"%s\"\n", dwRead, sBuffer);

        CloseHandle(hReadPipe);
        CloseHandle(hWritePipe);
}
```

This was a simple example, but now we need to take a look at something somewhat more practical. A typical example is for a parent process to spawn a child process, then communicate data with it. The child process then goes ahead processing the data, then goes back into wait mode. One simple technique is for the child process to use its standard input and standard output for processing data and simply spawn the child process with pipes interconnecting the parent and the child. We will look at exactly such an example.

First, take a look at our child process in Listing 7.2. As you can see, it is not a very complicated program — a simple console mode program that reverses the case of characters on standard input and writes them to standard output. First, it starts by getting handles for standard input and standard output. Once in place, it proceeds to read from standard input into a buffer, reverse the upper- and lowercase characters, and write out the buffer to standard output. It repeats this process until all input is exhausted. You can test this program by simply running it and typing characters into it or pipe the output of another command such as dir into it. Such an example is in Figure 7.1. As you can see, all uppercase characters were converted to lowercase and vice versa.

Listing 7.2 Reversal child process.

```
#include <windows.h>
#include <ctype.h>

#define BUFSIZE 4096


int main(int argc, char *argv[])
{
        CHAR chBuf[BUFSIZE];
        DWORD dwRead, dwWritten, dwIdx;
        HANDLE hStdin, hStdout; BOOL fSuccess;

        // First, get handles to standard input and standard output so we
        // can use them later.
        hStdout = GetStdHandle(STD_OUTPUT_HANDLE);
        hStdin = GetStdHandle(STD_INPUT_HANDLE);
        if ((hStdout == INVALID_HANDLE_VALUE) ||
            (hStdin == INVALID_HANDLE_VALUE))
        {
                ExitProcess(1);
        }

        // Loop until either there's no input or a failure on the output,
        // converting characters in between.
        for (;;)
        {
                // Read from standard input.
                fSuccess = ReadFile(hStdin, chBuf, BUFSIZE, &dwRead, NULL);
                if (!fSuccess || dwRead == 0)
                {
                        break;
                }

                // Flip upper case to lower case and vice versa
                for( dwIdx = 0; dwIdx < dwRead; dwIdx++ )
                {
```

```
                        if(islower(chBuf[dwIdx]))
                                chBuf[dwIdx] = _toupper(chBuf[dwIdx]);
                        else if(isupper(chBuf[dwIdx]))
                                chBuf[dwIdx] = _tolower(chBuf[dwIdx]);
                }


                fSuccess = WriteFile(hStdout, chBuf, dwRead, &dwWritten, NULL);
                if (!fSuccess)
                {
                        break;
                }
        }
}
```

Figure 7.1   Test run of reverse.exe.

Given this example, we now need a driver. We need a program that will create a pipe, spawn the reverse program as a child process, and then drive data to it. This sounds simple and we said earlier that creating the pipe is easy. Well, I did not lie to you. Creating a pipe is very easy — but creating one that is inherited by a child process is not quite that simple.

In Listing 7.3, we have the listing of the driver for our example, parent.c. This program starts off by creating a child process, connecting program input either to standard input or to a file if one was specified on the command line. It then proceeds to read from the input file and write it to standard output. You can see this by following the sequence of function calls in main(). (Discourse continues on page 146.)

Listing 7.3 Anonymous pipe parent.

```c
#include <windows.h>

#define BUFSIZE 4096

#ifndef SUCCESS
# define SUCCESS 0
#endif
#ifndef FAILURE
# define FAILURE 1
#endif

HANDLE        hChildStdinRd,
         hChildStdinWr,
         hChildStdinWrDup,
         hChildStdoutRd,
         hChildStdoutWr,
         hChildStdoutRdDup,
         hInputFile,
         hSaveStdin,
         hSaveStdout;

BOOL SpawnChildProcess(CHAR *szChildName);
VOID WriteToPipe(VOID);
VOID ReadFromPipe(VOID);
VOID ErrorExit(LPTSTR);
VOID ErrMsg(LPTSTR, BOOL);

int main(int argc, char *argv[])
{
        SECURITY_ATTRIBUTES saAttr;
        BOOL fSuccess;

        // First, create the child process.
        if (!SpawnChildProcess("reverse"))
                ErrorExit("Create process failed");

        // Get a handle to the parent's input file.
        if (argc > 1)
```

```
                    hInputFile = CreateFile(argv[1], GENERIC_READ, 0, NULL,
                        OPEN_EXISTING, FILE_ATTRIBUTE_READONLY, NULL);
        else
            hInputFile = hSaveStdin;

        if (hInputFile == INVALID_HANDLE_VALUE)
            ErrorExit("no input file\n");

        // Write to pipe that is the standard input for a child process.
        WriteToPipe();

        // Read from pipe that is the standard output for child process.
        ReadFromPipe();

        return 0;
}


BOOL SpawnChildProcess(CHAR *szChildName)
{
        PROCESS_INFORMATION piProcInfo;
        STARTUPINFO siStartInfo;
        BOOL bRetVal;
        SECURITY_ATTRIBUTES saAttr;
        BOOL fSuccess;

        // Set the bInheritHandle flag so pipe handles are inherited.
        saAttr.nLength = sizeof(SECURITY_ATTRIBUTES);
        saAttr.bInheritHandle = TRUE;
        saAttr.lpSecurityDescriptor = NULL;

        // The steps for redirecting child process's STDOUT:
        //      1. Save current STDOUT, to be restored later.
        //      2. Create anonymous pipe to be STDOUT for child process.
        //      3. Set STDOUT of the parent process to be write handle of
        //          the pipe, so it is inherited by the child process.
        //      4. Create a noninheritable duplicate of the read handle and
        //          close the inheritable read handle.
        // Save the handle to the current STDOUT.
        hSaveStdout = GetStdHandle(STD_OUTPUT_HANDLE);
```

```
// Create a pipe for the child process's STDOUT.
if (!CreatePipe(&hChildStdoutRd, &hChildStdoutWr, &saAttr, 0))
    ErrorExit("Stdout pipe creation failed\n");

// Set a write handle to the pipe to be STDOUT.
if (!SetStdHandle(STD_OUTPUT_HANDLE, hChildStdoutWr))
    ErrorExit("Redirecting STDOUT failed");

// Create noninheritable read handle and close the inheritable read // han-
dle.
fSuccess = DuplicateHandle(GetCurrentProcess(), hChildStdoutRd,
            GetCurrentProcess(), &hChildStdoutRdDup, 0, FALSE,
                    DUPLICATE_SAME_ACCESS);
if (!fSuccess)
    ErrorExit("DuplicateHandle failed");

CloseHandle(hChildStdoutRd);

// The steps for redirecting child process's STDIN:
//      1.  Save current STDIN, to be restored later.
//      2.  Create anonymous pipe to be STDIN for child process.
//      3.  Set STDIN of the parent to be the read handle of the
//          pipe, so it is inherited by the child process.
//      4.  Create a noninheritable duplicate of the write handle,
//          and close the inheritable write handle.
// Save the handle to the current STDIN.
hSaveStdin = GetStdHandle(STD_INPUT_HANDLE);

// Create a pipe for the child process's STDIN.
if (!CreatePipe(&hChildStdinRd, &hChildStdinWr, &saAttr, 0))
    ErrorExit("Stdin pipe creation failed\n");

// Set a read handle to the pipe to be STDIN.
if (!SetStdHandle(STD_INPUT_HANDLE, hChildStdinRd))
    ErrorExit("Redirecting Stdin failed");

// Duplicate the write handle to the pipe so it is not inherited.
fSuccess = DuplicateHandle(GetCurrentProcess(), hChildStdinWr,
                    GetCurrentProcess(), &hChildStdinWrDup, 0,
                    FALSE,          // not inherited
                    DUPLICATE_SAME_ACCESS);
```

```
        if (!fSuccess)
                ErrorExit("DuplicateHandle failed");

        CloseHandle(hChildStdinWr);

        // Set up members of STARTUPINFO structure.
        ZeroMemory(&siStartInfo, sizeof(STARTUPINFO));
        siStartInfo.cb = sizeof(STARTUPINFO);          // Create the child process.
        bRetVal = CreateProcess(NULL,
                szChildName,        // command line
                NULL,               // process security attributes
                NULL,               // primary thread security attributes
                TRUE,               // handles are inherited
                0,                  // creation flags
                NULL,               // use parent's environment
                NULL,               // use parent's current directory
                &siStartInfo,       // STARTUPINFO pointer
                &piProcInfo);       // receives PROCESS_INFORMATION

        // After process creation, restore the saved STDIN and STDOUT.
        if (!SetStdHandle(STD_INPUT_HANDLE, hSaveStdin))
                ErrorExit("Re-redirecting Stdin failed\n");

        if (!SetStdHandle(STD_OUTPUT_HANDLE, hSaveStdout))
                ErrorExit("Re-redirecting Stdout failed\n");

        return bRetVal;
}


VOID WriteToPipe(VOID)
{
        DWORD dwRead, dwWritten;
        CHAR chBuf[BUFSIZE];

        // Read from a file and write its contents to a pipe.
        for (;;)
        {
                if (!ReadFile(hInputFile, chBuf, BUFSIZE, &dwRead, NULL) ||
                    dwRead == 0)
                        break;
```

```
                    if (!WriteFile(hChildStdinWrDup, chBuf, dwRead,
                        &dwWritten, NULL))
                            break;
        }


        // Close the pipe handle so the child process stops reading.
        if (!CloseHandle(hChildStdinWrDup))
                ErrorExit("Close pipe failed\n");
}


VOID ReadFromPipe(VOID)
{
        DWORD dwRead, dwWritten;
        CHAR chBuf[BUFSIZE];
        HANDLE hStdout = GetStdHandle(STD_OUTPUT_HANDLE);

        // Close the write end of the pipe before reading from the
        // read end of the pipe.
        if (!CloseHandle(hChildStdoutWr))
                ErrorExit("Closing handle failed");

        // Read output from the child process, and write to parent's STDOUT.
        for (;;)
        {
                if (!ReadFile(hChildStdoutRdDup, chBuf, BUFSIZE, &dwRead,
                  NULL) || dwRead == 0)
                        break;
                if (!WriteFile(hSaveStdout, chBuf, dwRead, &dwWritten, NULL))
                        break;
        }
}


// Print an error message and abort.
VOID ErrorExit(LPTSTR lpszMessage)
{
        DWORD dwCnt, dwWritten;
        CHAR szString[BUFSIZE];
        HANDLE hStderr = GetStdHandle(STD_ERROR_HANDLE);
```

```
        dwCnt = wsprintf(szString, "%s\n", lpszMessage);
        WriteFile(hStderr, szString, dwCnt, &dwWritten, NULL);
        ExitProcess(FAILURE);
}
```

While the sequence of steps in the program is relatively simple, all the action is in Spawn-ChildProcess(). The reason behind this is the set of rules behind creating a Win32 process. Because our pipe can only be passed to a child process as a handle, the handle must be "inheritable," that is, it must possess the correct attributes to allow it to be inherited by the child process. This requires that you to first save the current handle for either STDIN or STDOUT so that it can be restored later. Next, you must create the anonymous pipe to be inherited by the child process and set the handle of the parent process to be the corresponding read or write handle of the pipe, so that it will be inherited by the child process. You must also create a noninheritable duplicate of the original handle and discard the inheritable read handle. Otherwise, the child will inherit a handle not intended for it, that is, our original handle. With this in place, you create the child process and then restore the original handle. This is the only way to pass a handle to the child process. All this activity for both STDIN and STDOUT takes place in SpawnChildProcess().

The actual data transfer is quite simple. This code is contained in WriteToPipe() and ReadFromPipe(). As you can see, the data is transferred as a data stream by standard file read and write API calls. From the parent side, the pipes are the special handles set up earlier. From the child side, the pipes are the normal console handles — nothing special takes place. All the work happens on the parent process side.

Where would you use this? It could come in handy in a command line interpreter or shell. It also could be used as a driver for multiple pass programs such as compilers. It allows the child to be a simple program and concentrate the complexity in the parent process. Of course, this complexity is relative. We dedicate a few lines of code to create the pipe. It just isn't as simple as creating the pipe itself. It is, however, a great mechanism for connecting the parent process to the child process.

Named Pipes

Like anonymous pipes, named pipes allow two or more processes to communicate with each other. They differ, however, from anonymous pipes in the way a process acquires access to the pipe. As we saw earlier, any process that intends to use an anonymous pipe needs a set of handles to the pipe. With a named pipe, any process that knows the name of the named pipe can access it. This means that the processes accessing a pipe do not need to be related; they only need to know a single string. To use a named pipe, a process must create the pipe by calling the CreateNamedPipe function that returns a handle to the pipe similar to the anonymous pipe CreatePipe call. The first process to call this function creates the pipe. Successive calls create a new instance of that pipe and it inherits the attributes of the first instance of the pipe.

These pipes are very flexible, because a named pipe can be a network connection between two computers, as well as a simple buffering scheme on a single computer. Therefore, a named pipe may be used across a network on different machines, as a remote pipe, or it may be used locally, on a single machine. This is far more powerful than an anonymous pipe —

allowing for the creation of logging/monitoring tools, special debug ports for use in custom debuggers, etc.

Another difference between anonymous and named pipes is the way with which you may write to them. In the case of an anonymous pipe, the data is written to and read from as a stream of bytes. Named pipes come in two types: byte-mode and message mode pipes. Byte-mode pipes are similar to anonymous pipes and allow transfer of a stream of bytes. Reads and writes to byte-mode pipes do not have to be of equal size. With message mode pipes, data is written to and read from as a series of messages. This is consistent with traditional network protocols. It allows for an entire message to be transferred in an atomic fashion, guaranteeing no interleave of data from other competing processes.

In message mode, data transfers are performed to and from buffers. The number of bytes written is controlled by the write operation and is typically the size of the write buffer. The number of bytes read in the message matches the number written, thanks to the atomic operation of the message mode named pipe. Should the read buffer be larger than the incoming message size, only the number of bytes written are read. Again, each message is a single, atomic data transfer and only as much data written in a single write operation may be read in a single read operation.

A typical application of named pipes is in client/server applications. The named pipe is created by the server. The clients, knowing the name of the pipe before creating the pipe, attach to the pipe created by the server through a similar mechanism as the server. To be more specific, a named pipe is created with the `CreateNamedPipe` call. However, both client and server then use `ReadFile` and `WriteFile` to transfer data. Thanks to the generic handle model of Win32 operating systems, all work performed on a pipe does not differ greatly from the mechanisms used for files. In fact, even the `CreateNamedPipe` API call isn't very different from its `CreateFile` cousin.

As you can see, named pipes fit in client/server applications. However, this does not mean that named pipes are *only* used by client/server applications. Peer-to-peer applications also use named pipes. Because there is nothing special about a server, the program may assume either a server or peer role based on the design of the process. Should one program provide a service on a request from another program, the application is a client/server application. Should the programs be equally likely to both request services as well as provide them, the application is a peer-to-peer one. For the purposes of our discussion, we will discuss named pipes in the context of a client/server application.

Naming Convention

Because we are talking about named pipes, we need to know how to go about naming them. Maybe you'd like to name it Fred or George after your favorite uncle. Possibly, Rover suits you because you really love your Golden Retriever. Well, the good news is you can... sort of.

As we mentioned earlier, named pipes can be used either on a single machine or across a network. Naturally, we need some way of specifying whether we want a local or remote pipe. Microsoft could have accomplished this by adding some sort of argument to their API, but they chose a more flexible way of doing it. They came up with a naming convention that incorporates the name of the remote machine.

How did they do this? They decided to create a naming convention similar to their universal naming convention. The general form of their naming convention is:

```
\\machine_name\pipe\pipe_name.
```

The actual name of the pipe can be Rover, but it must be prefaced with proper information to make it a valid pipe. You will notice that the name is a fixed format with two variable components. The first variable component is machine_name. This is the host name assigned to the computer in the Control Panel network applet. For local pipes, there is a special machine name, '.' used as an abbreviation for the machine name. This is similar to the use of '.' to indicate the current or "self" directory in the Win32 file system convention. The second variable component is the name of the actual pipe itself. This convention allows you to specify the name of the pipe as well as the host in one string. This is quite useful for C programmers. For example, you could use a wsprintf call to build the pipe name. You could default the machine name to '.' and then replace it with the remote machine if one is specified.

A Simple Example

When we look at what it takes to create a client/server application, we could easily get lost. After all, many server applications go through great lengths to handle many requests concurrently. Although in practice this is exactly what we want, we want to look at something simple. For now, we want to study how named pipes are used in a client/server application.

Listing 7.4 is an example of a simple server. All it really does is send a simple message to any client that attaches to it. That message is a short "Hello" followed by a count of how many clients previously attached to it. If you take a look at it, you see that it is composed of a for loop that has no exit condition. This forces the server to remain active after we start it. Normally, we would take other steps to force it to remain active, but this server is structured in a way to allow us to simply examine pipes.

Listing 7.4 Simple named pipe server.

```
#include <stdio.h>
#include <windows.h>

#define PIPESIZE 512
#define PIPE        "\\\\.\\pipe\\mypipe"

int main(int argc, char *argv[])
{
      HANDLE hPipe;
      DWORD dwWritten, dwRead, dwLastError, dwCount;
      char sBuffer[PIPESIZE];
      BOOL fConnected;
```

```
for(dwCount = 0; ; ++dwCount)
{
      if((hPipe = CreateNamedPipe(PIPE,
            PIPE_ACCESS_DUPLEX,
              PIPE_TYPE_MESSAGE | PIPE_READMODE_MESSAGE |         PIPE_WAIT,
            PIPE_UNLIMITED_INSTANCES,
            PIPESIZE,
            PIPESIZE,
            0,
            NULL)) == INVALID_HANDLE_VALUE)
      {
            printf("CreateNamedPipe failed!\n");
            ExitProcess(1);
      }
      else
      {
            printf("CreateNamedPipe scceeded! Handle = %08lx\n", hPipe);
      }


      fConnected = ConnectNamedPipe(hPipe, NULL) ?
        TRUE : ((dwLastError = GetLastError()) == ERROR_PIPE_CONNECTED);
      if(dwLastError == ERROR_CALL_NOT_IMPLEMENTED)
      {
            printf("Are you using Windows 9X?\nNo named pipes here!\n");
            ExitProcess(1);
      }


      if(fConnected)
      {
            wsprintf(sBuffer, "Hello #%ld", dwCount);
            printf("Pipe connected #%d.\n", dwCount);
            WriteFile(hPipe, sBuffer, lstrlen(sBuffer), &dwWritten, NULL);
            printf("Iteration #%d: %ld Bytes written\n", dwCount, dwWritten);
                      FlushFileBuffers(hPipe);
            DisconnectNamedPipe(hPipe);
            CloseHandle(hPipe);
      }
}
}
```

Looking a little further into the server, we see that it creates the named pipe with a call to CreateNamedPipe. This is a simple call that returns a handle similar to CreateFile. This handle is used in all file calls that follow. Note that CreateNamedPipe returns INVALID_HANDLE_VALUE if any sort of error occurs during the creation of the named pipe. Once the pipe is created, we need to wait until a client connects to it. We do that through a call to ConnectNamedPipe. However, ConnectNamedPipe returns not only when a client connects, but it may return if some sort of error occurs. So, you need to perform a comparison on the error that occurs when ConnectNamedPipe returns. If the error is ERROR_PIPE_CONNECTED, then we've actually succeeded. We also have to look for another error, ERROR_CALL_NOT_IMPLEMENTED. The reason for this is simple — named pipes are not implemented in Windows 9X. As a result, we quit if we find that the underlying Win32 operating system doesn't support named pipe calls. Unfortunately, it would have been better if Create-NamedPipe returned some sort of indication that the call is unimplemented, but this is what Microsoft decided on.

If the server does have a client connected, it simply proceeds to format some data, pass it to the client, and proceed to close the pipe after flushing all data in the pipe. This procedure guarantees data integrity. Of course, any real server would actually remain in some sort of loop, responding to client requests until its function is complete, but we wanted a simple example. We also would not have committed the server to react to a single client at a time. In fact, we probably would want to dispatch a thread to service this client and return to wait for another client to connect. Again, simplicity in this example helps us focus on named pipes without having to worry about other complexities.

Listing 7.5 is our client. It starts out by looping on a CreateFile. This is how the client synchronizes with the server. Like our server loop, the client does not know that it connected to a pipe from the CreateFile return. Rather, it has to get the last error and specifically test for ERROR_PIPE_BUSY. However, it still needs to wait for data in the pipe. This is accomplished by the call to WaitNamedPipe. When it returns, we know that our pipe has data in it and can exit the loop to get data. Once a connection is established, getting data from the pipe is as simple as a call to ReadFile or WriteFile. Atomic operations result from a combination of the PIPE_TYPE_MESSAGE and PIPE_READMODE_MESSAGE specified in the CreateNamedPipe call and the call to ReadFile or WriteFile, as a block of data. Once the data is read, a simple call to DisconnectNamedPipe and CloseHandle terminates the connection to the pipe. As you can see, using named pipes can be very easy.

Listing 7.5 Named pipe client.

```
#include <stdio.h>
#include <windows.h>

#define PIPESIZE 1024
#define PIPE      "\\\\.\\pipe\\mypipe"

int main(int argc, char *argv[])
{
    HANDLE hPipe;
```

```
      DWORD dwWritten, dwRead, dwError;
      char sBuffer[PIPESIZE];
      BOOL fConnected;

      for(;;)
      {
            if((hPipe = CreateFile(PIPE,
                  GENERIC_READ | GENERIC_WRITE,
                  0,
                  NULL,
                  OPEN_EXISTING,
                  0,
                  NULL)) != INVALID_HANDLE_VALUE)
            {
                  break;
            }

            if((dwError = GetLastError()) != ERROR_PIPE_BUSY)      {
                  printf("Could not open pipe, hPipe = %08lx error = #%d.\n",
hPipe, dwError);
                  ExitProcess(1);
            }

            if(!WaitNamedPipe(PIPE, 20000))
            {
                  printf("Could not open pipe #2.\n");
                  ExitProcess(1);
            }
      }

   ReadFile(hPipe, &sBuffer, PIPESIZE, &dwRead, NULL);
   sBuffer[dwRead] = 0;
     printf("%ld Bytes read, Data = \"%s\"\n", dwRead, sBuffer);
   FlushFileBuffers(hPipe);
   DisconnectNamedPipe(hPipe);
   CloseHandle(hPipe);
}
```

A Closer Look at Data Flow

We know that the data can be either byte stream or fixed length messages. We also know that the pipe is full duplex and fully bidirectional. As a result, both the server and client can read from and write to the pipe. However, the server has a lot of control over the parameters of the pipe and can create the pipe to be used in only one direction. This fixes the pipe to half duplex operation, allowing for controlled access to the pipe. This is controlled by the PIPE_ACCESS_INBOUND, PIPE_ACCESS_OUTBOUND, and PIPE_ACCESS_DUPLEX flags.

A process can specify whether or not the pipe should be buffered. This is done when the pipe is first created. The process can also specify whether it should wait for the client to connect to the pipe or should return an error code, if the client has not already connected. These options help control physical data flow through the pipe.

A pipe can also be created with an overlapped flag, FILE_FLAG_OVERLAPPED, which causes read and write operations to signal an event when they are complete. This allows other functions to continue processing while the read or write operation is taking place. When the pipe is not operating in the overlapped mode, functions such as ReadFile and WriteFile will not return until they have finished processing. Overlapped support is useful in multithreaded applications because it allows one thread to service multiple named pipes.

Earlier, we mentioned atomic transfer of data. There may be more than one client hanging off a pipe at any one moment. This may occur as the result of more than one process accessing the pipe, or multiple threads within the same process accessing the pipe. This can be further aggravated when we consider that the processes may reside on different computers and that the pipes may be remote pipes allowing the communication over a network. We need to make certain that the data pumped through the pipe from one process doesn't become intertwined with data from another process. Utilizing message-based pipes helps, but we want to make certain that any request goes to the correct client. That is the developer's responsibility. You must structure messages on common pipes with some sort of machine/process id. Typically, you will have a common pipe for a new client to initiate contact, and then assign a unique name to that client for further communications.

There are a number of API calls that allow you to see the status of the named pipe in one way or another. For example, GetNamedPipeInfo returns information about the pipe such as input and output buffer sizes, number of instances allowed to the pipe, etc. You can get similar information from a call to GetNamedPipeHandleState. Complementing these calls, SetNamedPipeHandleState can set pipe parameters such as the maximum number of bytes collected from the client and the maximum time out period that can elapse before data is transmitted over the network.

Another factor to consider is efficiency. Again, these pipes may actually be network connections so there are many factors that affect performance. Here, we can improve performance by using TransactNamedPipe instead of ReadFile and WriteFile. When we use ReadFile and WriteFile, we place two requests across the network. By using TransactNamedPipe instead, we issue a single request for both the read and write operation, effectively cutting down on the overhead for the network operation. An even simpler way of making a transaction-based message is CallNamedPipe. It combines calls to CreateFile, WaitNamedPipe, TransactNamedPipe, and CloseFile in a single API call. Can't get any simpler than that. Note that this is only good for clients.

As you can see, both the anonymous and named pipe mechanisms are very powerful. Pipes allow independent processes to communicate with each other in a manner as simple as writing to a file. The common Win32 operating system method of utilizing a handle to use with the API calls such as ReadFile and WriteFile make working with pipes a piece of cake.

Even our simple examples, although small in size, are very powerful. They are truly valuable services provided by the Win32 operating systems.

Shared Memory

Win32 Operating System Memory Basics

Process memory is logical memory, managed by the Win32 kernel, be it NT-based or 9X-based. The kernel manages memory through the use of the processor Translation Lookaside Buffer (TLB) mechanism. This mechanism allows the processor to make fixed lengths of memory, referred to as *pages*, appear at logical addresses other than the physical addresses the pages of memory normally correspond to. It accomplishes this through an internal mapping mechanism that takes the internal address and translates it to a different address, so that the electrical signals coming out of the processor match the translated address. Because the TLB is under kernel control, the kernel can change this mapping at any time. The processor also has a mechanism in place so that whenever a program references a page that is not mapped, it generates an exception that the kernel intercepts. These two mechanisms provide the kernel with powerful mechanisms for our use.

The kernel takes advantage of these mechanisms on our behalf. For example, it gives each application the illusion of having all physical memory available to it by moving these pages to and from disk. During the execution of an application, the kernel intercepts the memory reference exception and allocates a page of memory on first encounter. Whenever the processor needs more memory, it scans its internal tables and may swap this page of memory to a swapping or paging file. Upon subsequent encounters of a page exception, it goes back to the swap file and places it in memory. This may not be the original location it was in, so the kernel makes use of the TLB to make the page of memory *appear* to be back in its original location. This is a powerful mechanism.

What does all this have to do with interprocess communications? Well, a natural extension of this mechanism is to make a page of memory appear in two process spaces. This results in a very fast interprocess communication mechanism. A process does not need to make an API call to transmit data, which entails switching from user to kernel mode, moving data around and then switching back to user mode. Here, all that a process needs to do is write to its own memory. When the process transitions from active to waiting, the data is transmitted to the receiving process when the normal kernel actions of making the process active takes place. This is the mechanism we now want to examine more closely.

Shared Memory

Whenever we need to make use of an object managed by the kernel, a handle usually references that object. Shared memory is no exception. The mechanism used to allow references to shared memory is the traditional file model. In order for a set of processes to make use of the mechanism, one of the processes creates a file mapping object, specifying a name that can be used by other processes to obtain a handle to the mapping object. From here on out, each process uses the mapping object to map a view of the file into its own address space. While each process maps the object into the same pages of physical storage, the virtual addresses of the mapped views can vary from one process to another.

Let's take a closer look at the individual API calls to make use of this. The process that initiates the use of shared memory calls `CreateFileMapping` to create a file mapping object. This does not, however, map the file. You need to specify a handle to an open file — typically one returned by `CreateFile` — to map the file. You can also use the swap file by using the handle `(HANDLE)0XFFFFFFFF` in the call to `CreateFileMapping`.

One advantage to using a named file instead of the swap or paging file is that it allows you to use data in an existing file or save the data generated by one or more of the processes. If you are strictly interested in sharing data, then you should use the paging file.

When you map a named file, open it for exclusive access. Keep the handle open until you are finished with the shared memory. This prevents other, non-related processes from accessing the file in any way. Forgetting to do this may lead to unpredictable results.

To get started, you make a call to `CreateFileMapping` to associate a name with the file-mapping object. The name for the mapped file may be composed of any character except for `NULL` and the path name separator character "\". In addition, its size is limited to `MAX_PATH` bytes for ASCII names and `MAX_PATHW` for Unicode names. Other processes open a handle to the same object using the `OpenFileMapping` call, passing it this name as a parameter. You don't have to worry about name collision with other objects, such as pipes, because the file mapping object names exist in their own flat name space.

Earlier, we implied a sequence of events necessary to establish a memory-mapped file for use in a shared memory application. The timing relationship is actually stronger than a simple sequence of events. You actually need synchronization to make sure that the process creating the mapping object creates the object before any of the other processes try to open it. By the way, if no object name is specified in the `CreateFileMapping` call, the handle can still be shared with other processes by the less convenient means of handle duplication or inheritance.

In some cases, it is important to map the file to the same address in all processes. This can be accomplished with a call to `MapViewOfFile`. This allocates shared, committed pages with read/write or read-only access. This access is controlled in the call to `MapViewOfFile` as either `FILE_MAP_READ` or `FILE_MAP_WRITE`. The access specified must be compatible with the one in `CreateFileMapping` or `OpenFileMapping` or, in the case of named files, the mode when the file was opened with `CreateFile`.

Unfortunately, access to shared memory-mapped files is uncoordinated. If more than one process has write access to the shared memory, a Mutex object should be used to prevent simultaneous writing. Otherwise, this can produce unpredictable results or corrupted data. This, or some other type of synchronization, must be used throughout the lifetime of the applications.

There are size limits associated with memory-mapped files. You can specify the maximum size by using the `CreateFileMapping` call to limit the size of the views that can be mapped. You can also map the entire file or any portion of it. The only restrictions on it is that the view may be any 64Kb aligned offset in the file starting at the beginning of the file.

There is a lifetime associated with memory-mapped files. For example, any pages committed by mapping a view will be released when the last process with a view on the mapping object terminates. A process can also "unmap" its view by calling `UnmapViewOfFile`. Once this happens, either the named file or the swap area associated with the mapping object will be updated. Finally, a process can also update a file by calling `FlushViewOfFile`.

Making the Connection

You now have enough tools in hand to start working with this software plumbing. OK, enough with the plumbing references, but you get the picture. You have a very powerful, streamlined mechanism to communicate with. You can make use of this in command interpreters, such as when you use the '|' separator, or to communicate between machines in a network. The use of pipes in your next application is sure to make IPC work simple.

If pipes are not enough, the shared memory is sure to fit the bill. Mapping named files or swap files and accessing them as memory will certainly make transfer of large structure information a snap. However, with this luxury comes the price of synchronizing access to the shared regions. We'll examine synchronization mechanisms in the next chapter, so that you can get a better idea of how to use them in shared memory applications.

Chapter 8

Synchronization Mechanisms

With a true multitasking operating system, there are no guarantees on execution time. Even with Microsoft's operating system, different schedulers, and scheduling algorithms that exist between them, cannot guarantee identical timing. The picture becomes much more complicated when you consider multiple processor systems such as Symmetric Multi Processor (SMP) and Non-Uniform Memory Access (NUMA). As a result, concurrent tasks require some way of synchronizing their operations. In this chapter, we will examine synchronization mechanisms and how these mechanisms relate to processes and threads. We will see how to make use of these objects and alert you to their potential pitfalls. Let's begin by examining what synchronization objects look like.

What Are Synchronization Objects?

There is no guarantee when a piece of code will run — especially on computers sporting multiple processors. When a piece of code we write shares some system resource, be it a device such as a printer or a single byte of RAM, we need to make sure that multiple threads or processes don't get in our way. For example, what happens if we decide to send something to a printer? Our Win32 operating system takes that file and places it on queue. From there, a print spooler takes over and prints our data. Now what happens if you were to send two files, `file1.doc` and `file2.doc`, to the printer at the same time? One of our requests would get to the system before the other. Let's say `file1.doc` did. Then `file1.doc` would be placed on the queue before `file2.doc` and they would be printed in sequence. Nice, orderly printing of two files.

Now let's dig a little deeper. There was a single program, a print spooler, that used something called a *queue* to organize how files were printed. Why do we need this? We need a spooler because if we didn't have such a program, the individual characters and printer commands would interlace as a function of the Win32 operating system scheduler. This would confuse our printer and we'd get a lot of wasted paper. So, it used a queue to organize requests and print them in an orderly fashion. So, our Win32 operating system handles the shared resource with a queue.

Let's go down a little further. The spooler has a data structure, a queue, that it uses to coordinate the files to be printed. As you may recall from your early computer education, a *queue* is a data structure that functions in a first-in, first-out manner. If we generalize on this structure, we see that we were able to synchronize the access to a shared resource (our printer) through the use of a data structure (the spooler's queue).

Now let's generalize this view and use this example as a way to begin understanding synchronization objects. As you'll remember, a synchronization object is a data structure. This data structure has some state associated with it that allows the proper operation of two or more processes or threads.

In a Win32 operating system, the definition of a synchronization object is very similar. A *synchronization object* is a data structure that has a state. That state, either Signaled or Not-Signaled, is used to coordinate the execution of two or more threads. Generally, a synchronization object is used to coordinate threads of execution — either a process or a thread within a process.

A thread of execution interacts with one of these objects by modifying the object's state or waiting for it to be in a Signaled state. The Win32 operating system (when a thread waits for an object) blocks the thread for the entire time that the state of the object is unchanged by setting the object state to Not-Signaled. In this manner, two or more threads of execution — be it process or threads within a process — can synchronize their access to a shared resource.

You may now ask, "what are these objects?" The Win32 operating system offers four types of synchronization objects: Mutex objects, Semaphore objects, Event objects, and Critical Section objects. These objects are either identical to those you learned in your early computer programming education or very similar to them. In a Win32 operating system, each type of synchronization object has its own meaning and typical use. A Mutex is similar to the Dykstra P and V operators and is used to prevent simultaneous use of a shared resource, such as a file, shared memory, or a peripheral device. A Semaphore object is a counting data structure that counts threads as they pass in and out of the the data structure. An Event object is similar to a signal used in other operating systems and is used to notify a waiting thread that an event has occurred. A Critical Section object is the same as a Mutex except that it can only be used by the threads of a single process, typically to guard against simultaneous access to critical memory areas (hence the name).

Synchronizing Processes

Of the four types of synchronization objects, three are interprocess synchronization objects and may be used by processes: Mutex, Semaphore, and Event. Each type has its own API calls for creating an object or modifying its state. However, they share the same functions, `Wait-ForSingleObject` and `WaitForMultipleObjects`, for wait operations allowing you to wait on any of the three synchronization processes with an optional time out. The wait ends when the object is signaled or alternately times out.

When you create an interprocess synchronization object, the kernel allocates space in system memory, initializes the object, and returns a handle to the creating process. Any child process may inherit this handle or it may be duplicated and passed to unrelated processes. Alternately, the object may be assigned a name by the creating process and other processes can access it by opening a handle to the object.

The lifetime of the object is dependent on its use. The system performs garbage collection and removes the space allocated to the object when all processes finish using it and the last handle to the object is closed. The Win32 kernel also closes the object handles when a process exits.

Mutex

In an application, you use a Mutex to prevent simultaneous use of a shared resource, such as a file, shared memory, or a peripheral device. A Mutex can be in one of two states: owned (Not-Signaled) or unowned (Signaled). In a way, it acts as a token, by allowing the process that "owns" the token to proceed while others are forced to wait. When a process or thread waits for a Mutex object, it is asking the Win32 kernel for ownership. If another process or thread currently owns the Mutex, the waiting process or thread blocks until the ownership is released.

An example of a typical use for a Mutex will help us better understand it. We will look at an application where two or more processes communicate through a shared memory segment as described in Chapter 7. During the course of our discussion, we spoke of how there is a need to synchronize access to the shared memory region. To help us coordinate this access, we could use a Mutex to avoid simultaneously writing to the memory. Before executing the sections of code in which the shared memory is accessed, each process calls a wait function, probably `WaitForSingleObject`, to request ownership of the Mutex. It receives ownership of the object and any other process requesting ownership of the Mutex blocks because the shared memory area is currently in use. When the owner process finishes using the shared memory area, the process releases its ownership of the Mutex. The process that owns the Mutex can make additional wait calls on the same Mutex without blocking. However, it must release ownership once for each time that a wait was satisfied. This functionality is identical to Dykstra's P and V operators.

Note that the use of a Mutex is not limited to a process. Because a process is a collection of threads, any thread within the process may also use a Mutex. The Mutex is particularly helpful for lock access to areas of memory within the process, although we'll see later that there are other mechanisms just as useful.

Semaphore

In many ways, a Semaphore object is similar to Mutex. Like a Mutex, it also maintains a count. However, it differs in the way it interprets the count. When you create a Semaphore, you specify a maximum count, and the state of the Semaphore is Signaled as long as its count is greater than zero. Each time that a wait operation is completed, the Semaphore's count is decremented. When a process releases the object, the Semaphore's count is incremented.

You would use a Semaphore in an application where you need to limit the number of threads or processes actively using a shared resource. For example, suppose you were designing a traditional Bulletin Board System (BBS) and you wanted to create a process per port. You would want to limit the number of processes created to the number of serial ports available in the system. You would design your application to initialize the Semaphore to the number of serial ports available, and assign each process a port. Before creating a child process, the parent process calls a wait function to see if the Semaphore is Signaled. As each child process is started, the count is decremented and the child is given a handle to the Semaphore. When the maximum number of child processes are executing, the count is zero and the Semaphore state is Not-Signaled. At this point, the wait function blocks, and no more processes are launched. As each child terminates, it releases the Semaphore. This action causes the Win32 operating system to increment the count, in turn allowing the parent to continue, scan for unused ports, and create new processes to service them. This simple mechanism simplifies the design of the parent process because you need only create a loop that scans for free ports, starts a process, and waits. The Semaphore object then throttles the parent, allowing the child process to act as a simple program whose only concern is servicing the port. The child need not even know about the parent or deal with the Semaphore because the handle is closed when the child exits.

Event

An Event object provides a signaling mechanism to notify one or more processes or threads that an event has occurred — similar to the UNIX signal. The major difference between the two is that a UNIX signal is part of a fixed signal associated with the processes, whereas a Win32 Event is created by the Win32 kernel and is independent of the process. With an Event object, you can set the Event's state to set (Signaled) or reset (Not-Signaled state). Additionally, you can "pulse" an Event, which sets the Event briefly and then automatically resets it.

There are two types of Event objects. Let us now take a closer look at each.

Manual Reset   A Manual Reset is a broadcast mechanism. When a Manual Reset Event is set (Signaled), all waiting threads are released until the Event is explicitly reset (Not-Signaled). In this way, its operation is "manual," requiring the user to explicitly change the state of the Event. You use a Manual Reset Event to create or write data by a single process or thread that will be read by a number of other processes or threads. In this way, all the subscribers to the writing process or thread are blocked, while the data is updated and allowed to freely access the data when needed. The Manual Reset Event essentially broadcasts a pause and a resume from the creator to the subscribers.

Auto Reset   Unlike the Manual Reset Event, the Auto Reset Event acts in an automatic fashion. That is, when an Auto Reset Event is set (Signaled), a single waiting process or thread is released and then the Event is automatically reset (Not-Signaled). All other blocked processes or threads continue to wait until the Auto Reset Event is again set, when the process repeats. The Auto Reset Event is used to throttle processes or threads waiting on the Event, allowing only one at a time to proceed. Which process or thread starts next is a function of the Win32 kernel scheduler.

Synchronizing Threads

Threads can utilize all three of the synchronization objects we spoke about. In addition, there is another object, the Critical Section object, that can only be used by threads.

This object is similar in scope and functionality to the Mutex. For example, a Critical Section object can only be "owned" by one thread at a time and a thread can repeatedly enter a Critical Section object without blocking. As is the case with a Mutex, it must leave once for each time it entered. They differ in that they exist in memory allocated by the process, and are garbage-collected when the process terminates or may be deleted when it is no longer needed to release the system resources allocated for it.

Finishing Up

Now we've covered all the facets involved in making multithreaded programs. We've covered how to create them, how to manipulate files for them, set up ways for multiple processes to communicate, and how to synchronize the execution of multiple processes and threads. We've also dug down into the Win32 operating system itself in order to better understand how all this works. Let's now move on to a real application where we can finally see it in action.

Chapter 9

cmd32.exe — **A Sample Application**

Until now, we've concerned ourselves primarily with the Win32 API. We've looked at the system call mechanisms, file system functions, memory management, and process management functions. Now it's time to look at how to put together a console mode Win32 application. There are lots of potential applications we can use. I considered quite a few. For example, we could create an HTTP server. However, this type of application typically runs in the background and affords us little opportunity to examine the console interface we discussed earlier. I also thought of creating a computer language. This type of application, while giving us plenty of examples of console I/O, doesn't really deal with process management and I/O redirection. In addition, the typical GUI integrated development environment (IDE) is a significant improvement over the older interactive languages such as GWBASIC. There is, however, a piece missing from all the Microsoft Win32 operating systems, and that is an open source Win32 version of the MS-DOS cmd32.exe. So I created one.

Why is this a program you want to run? Frankly, there are times when it is much easier to type a command in a command shell than navigate through the explorer interface built into the Win32 operating system. Many times, folks who consider themselves power users, drop into the MS-DOS window in order to do this. Using cmd32.exe, you can do this without dropping into MS-DOS. Also, this is an open source project — you get the source code to boot so you can tailor it to do what you want. So, let's look at the design of this command line interpreter and see how the Win32 API fits in.

Starting the Command Line Interpreter

In a typical operating system, the command line interpreter is pretty much the last program started. In UNIX, for example, a boot loader of some sort, e.g., milo, netboot, osfboot, etc., loads the kernel, which in turn loads init. For non-X-Window System start-up sequences, init starts a process to monitor tty ports, looking for a login, and starts the shell when the user logs in. For X Window System start-up sequences, init starts X which in turn starts a graphical login process. The shell is then started at the user's request. On the opposite end of the spectrum, MS-DOS starts command.com or any other interpreter program specified in the CONFIG.SYS file as the last step of the start-up sequence. This program is the first program to run in an MS-DOS environment and establishes the environment for all subsequent programs. The process is similar in Windows 9X when an AUTOEXEC.BAT file is present because the Windows 9X family follows a hybrid model somewhere between the non-graphical UNIX and X Window System UNIX models. Even the Windows NT family follows a process similar to the X Window model where the graphical user interface brings up a login process and the shell is invoked at the user's request. From this, we see that we have a broad range of start-up processes for our shell to fit into the Win32 operating system environment.

This is all great theory, but how does this relate to our Win32 operating system? Well, the model used for MS-DOS is very similar to the one used in most Win32 operating systems. We could, for example, start our command interpreter instead of starting the graphics environment, but I do not recommend this. Why? I think the response to this is the question, "what is my computer?" It is *more* than the hardware and programs that run in order to get a prompt on your screen. It is a collection of applications that you use on your computer to make it useful. In essence, the operating system is only the vehicle between your hardware and your applications. The two reasons for theWin32 operating system's phenomenal success is that it can run on almost any commercially available hardware designed to a certain standard and runs a plethora of applications. Because they are virtually all graphical in nature, defeating the graphics in the Win32 operating system would severely diminish your computer's value.

There are two methods I would recommend for starting our interpreter — via the normal task bar "Start" button, or starting a window on start-up. You can accomplish this by creating a shortcut to cmd32.exe and placing it in C:\WINDOWS\Start Menu\Programs\StartUp. You can see this in Figure 9.1 — my start-up directory shows the collection of programs that start on my notebook. I created a shortcut in the development directory, cut the shortcut from that directory, and pasted it into this directory. This starts one copy of the command line interpreter every time I boot up my computer (Figure 9.2). It is convenient for me, for example, to have a command line interpreter running to avoid having to exercise Explorer to navigate to a directory just to see what files are there when all I have to do is type a "dir" command instead. It is also faster and much more convenient for me to build applications in a command line window than bring up a large and powerful integrated development environment. Too many windows and graphics often complicate a task. For all these reasons, I keep a command line interpreter window open at all times.

Figure 9.1 Start-up folder showing the cmd32.exe **icon.**

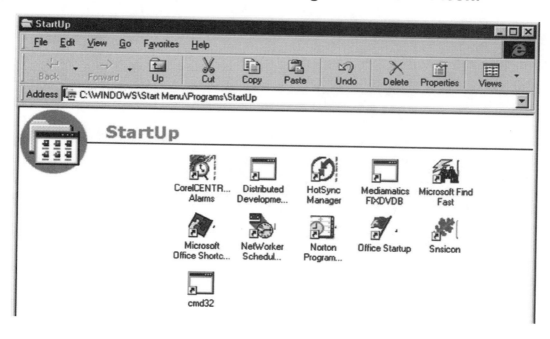

Figure 9.2 cmd32.exe **window.**

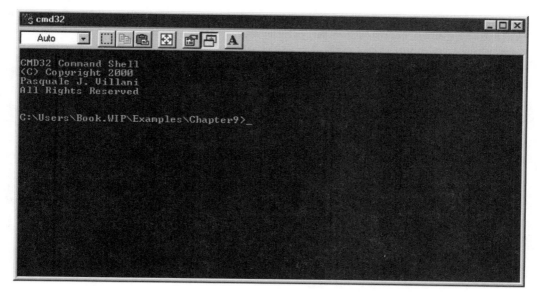

Do you need to follow these recommendations? No, not at all. You are free to experiment with it in any way you desire and use it however you'd like. That's the beauty behind having the source. To use a popular open source community paraphrase, "Use the source, Luke."

cmd32.exe

In the Win32 operating systems, the MS-DOS prompt is an MS-DOS environment usually in an Intel x86 virtual machine. It is a 16-bit program. Our version of `cmd32.exe` is written in C. There are no special coding tricks or foolery associated with it. It is a simple program designed to accept user input, parse them and execute the parsed command. It has a number of built-in commands identical to the MS-DOS version. This version does not allow the grouping of commands into a batch file, but that may be easily added. It also maintains the global environment block so that programs have access to the global environment variables.

Accessing Environment Variables

Part of the requirements on our shell program is the need to maintain the environment variables. We need to be able to access them so that we can use them within the program and set them so that we can modify them. For example, we need to get the PATH variable so that we can parse it and search for a command in each component of the path. We also need to set the PATH because the user can change the PATH as needed. This is only one example of an environment variable needed. Some applications also require environment variables to be set or changed and the shell is the only way a user may change these variables.

This need is not unique to Win32 operating systems. We see this in MS-DOS as well where the environment is kept within a global segment. Its roots can be traced back to UNIX where, in many cases, the environment is written to the user stack and accessed through the user program. In UNIX, there are two ways to access these variables. The first is as a pointer through the main invocation. In many UNIX programs, main is invoked with the third argument as a pointer to the environment variables. The second is a more portable method, utilizing library calls getenv() and putenv(). Win32 offers two similar calls through GetEnvironmentVariable() and SetEnvironmentVariable().

Listing 9.1 is a simple test program that gets the PATH variable from the environment and then modifies it. Both GetEnvironmentVariable and SetEnvironmentVariable require a string that is the variable name and the address of a buffer to contain the environment string. GetEnvironmentVariable also requires a DWORD value specifying the maximum length of the string to be copied into the buffer. Another interesting item to note is that they work with both ASCII and Unicode character sets, allowing internationalization. However, remember that the Unicode character set is only valid for Windows NT and Windows 2000.

Listing 9.1 `GetEnvironmentVariable`/`SetEnvironmentVariable` **example.**

```
/*
 * Environment example env_ex.c
 *
 * Get an environment variable, modify it and set it. Demonstrates the fundamental
 * methods of manipulating Win32 environment variables.
 */


#include <stdio.h>
#include <windows.h>

#define MAXBUF         4096


int main(int argc, char* argv[])
{
      char szBuffer[MAXBUF];

      printf("Hello world\n");
      if(0 == GetEnvironmentVariable("PATH", (LPTSTR)szBuffer, MAXBUF))
      {
            printf("PATH variable is not defined\n");
      }
      else
      {
            printf("old PATH = \"%s\"\n", szBuffer);
            strcat(szBuffer, ";C:\\SOME_DIR");
            SetEnvironmentVariable("PATH", szBuffer);
            GetEnvironmentVariable("PATH", (LPTSTR)szBuffer, MAXBUF);
            printf("new PATH = \"%s\"\n", szBuffer);
      }

      return 0;
}
```

So far, we have proven that we can get and set an environment variable within a program. This is great, but we need to pass the modified environment variable to a child program, otherwise our shell program is nearly useless. Too many programs depend on environment variables to ignore this. The question at hand is this, "how do we prove or disprove that our modified environment is passed to a child process?" Examining `CreateProcess()` indicates two ways of passing an environment to a child process. You could pass the address of an environment block or allow the child process to inherit your environment. We will now take a closer look at `CreateProcess()` to better understand how to launch a child process and what we can pass to it.

Architecture

The architecture for `cmd32.exe` is simple. `cmd32.exe` is organized as a table-driven executive that uses a collection of standalone functions to implement the internal commands. This executive performs a linear search through the table in order to find the function that corresponds to the command. If there is a match, the executive executes the corresponding function; otherwise it defaults to the terminating entry. This process is repeated forever, repeating the prompt-command cycle for every user command.

Let's take a closer look at how `cmd32.exe` does its work. `cmd32.exe` is very much a standard C program. Like all conventional C programs, execution starts at `main` (Listing 9.2).

Listing 9.2 `cmd32.exe main()` **function.**

```
INT
main(INT argc, BYTE *argv[])
{
        BYTE szPath[SIZE] = "";
        DWORD nRead;
        BYTE *cmd_tail;

        /* First, establish stdin and stdout */
        hStdout = GetStdHandle(STD_OUTPUT_HANDLE);
        hStdin  = GetStdHandle(STD_INPUT_HANDLE);
        hStderr = GetStdHandle(STD_ERROR_HANDLE);
        if(hStdin  == INVALID_HANDLE_VALUE
        || hStdout == INVALID_HANDLE_VALUE
        || hStderr == INVALID_HANDLE_VALUE)
                return 0;

        /* Initialize our program */
        hInput = hStdin;
        hOutput = hStdout;
        bCFlag = FALSE;
        echo_FLAG = FALSE;
        batch_FLAG = FALSE;
        strcpy(szDfltPrompt, "$p$g ");
        strcpy(szDfltPath, "");
        hHeap = GetProcessHeap();
```

```
if(!hHeap)
{
        return 1;
}
cmd_tail = GetCommandLine();

/* Check what PROMPT is set in env to over ride default */
nRead = GetEnvironmentVariable("PROMPT", szPrompt, sizeof(szPrompt));
if(!nRead)
{
        strcpy(szPrompt, szDfltPrompt);
}


/* Check what PATH is set in env to over ride default */
pszPath = HeapAlloc(hHeap, HEAP_ZERO_MEMORY, SIZE);
nRead = GetEnvironmentVariable("PATH", szPath, SIZE);
if(nRead)
{
        strcpy(pszPath, szPath);
}
else
{
        strcpy(pszPath, szDfltPath);
}

/* Main body for code.   Either read from Stdin and execute  */
/* commands or simply execute just once if -c specified. */
if(!cflag)
{
        /* Announce our version */
        printf(ANNOUNCE, copyright);
        printf("\n\n");

        FOREVER
        {
                default_drive = GetDrive();
                put_prompt(szPrompt);
                if(!ReadFile(hStdin, szCmdLine, MAX_CMDLINE, &nRead, 0))
                        continue;
                do_command(nRead);
```

```
                   }
        }
        else
        {
                BYTE FAR *p;

                default_drive = GetDrive();
                for(p = cmd_tail; *p != '\r'; p++)
                {
                        if(*p == '/' && (*(p + 1) == 'c' || *(p + 1) == 'C'))
                                break;
                }
                p += 2;
                strncpy(szCmdLine, p, 0x7f);
                for(nRead = 0; *p != '\r'; nRead++, p++)
                        ;
                ++nRead;
                do_command(nRead);
        }
        return 0;
}
```

cmd32.exe starts by initializing a number of internal variables, including the standard input, output, and error. Unlike the traditional UNIX model, we know that our Win32 operating system requires that you fetch these from the operating system for each console window. It then examines the command tail searching for options passed when the Win32 operating system invoked cmd32.exe. These options modify the execution of the interpreter. For example, cmd32.exe may also be invoked to execute a single command with the /c option, so it must modify its internal code path to comply with the user's single command execution. In the future, other options will modify cmd32.exe buffer space for environment and stacks. For these reasons, the parsing of command line variables occurs very early in main.

With command line options parsed, main continues initializing cmd32.exe environment variables affected such as PROMPT and PATH. Once completed, it examines whether or not it is in the single command mode or the iterative command interpreter mode. If it is in the single command mode, the remainder of the command line is copied into a local buffer and main invokes do_command() to execute the single command. If it is not executing a single command, cmd32.exe assumes it is in the interpreter mode.

Once cmd32.exe completes all this preliminary setup, it falls into the command loop. This loop is an infinite loop that outputs the prompt and then reads from standard input. Once the user enters the command, the buffer that received the keyboard input is passed to do_command(), allowing the command to be executed. Because this loop never exits, the sequence repeats for as long as the interpreter is active. cmd32.exe *can* exit — but we'll examine this mechanism later.

Both code paths, the single command code path and iterative command loop, share the function do_command() (Listing 9.3). This function actually carries out the execution of individual commands and is responsible for input and output redirection. It also parses the command tail into an argument list for use by internal commands.

Listing 9.3 The do_command() function.

```
VOID do_command(INT nRead)
{
        BYTE *pszLine;
        struct table *pTable;
        INT nIndex = 0;
        BOOL IORedirected = FALSE;
        BYTE szInput[MAX_CMDLINE], szOutput[MAX_CMDLINE];
        BOOL bAppendMode;

        // If nothing to do, just return
        if(nRead <= 0)
                return;

        // Initialize local variables
        szCmdLine[nRead] = '\0';
        bAppendMode = FALSE;

        // Parse for command line redirection.
        Redirect(szCmdLine, szInput, szOutput, &bAppendMode);
        IORedirected = (*szInput != '\0' || *szOutput != '\0');

        // Now parse for local command arguments.
        for(argc = 0; argc < 16; argc++)
        {
                argv[argc] = (BYTE *)0;
                args[argc][0] = '\0';
        }
        pszLine = scanspl(szCmdLine, args[0], '/');

        if(args[0][0] == '@')
        {
                at_FLAG = TRUE;
                nIndex++;
        }
```

```
        else
                at_FLAG = FALSE;

        // If preceeded by a @, swallow it, it was taken care of
        // elsewhere.  Also, change case so that our command verb is
        // case insensitive.
        while(args[0][nIndex] != '\0')
        {

                if(at_FLAG)
                        args[0][nIndex-1] = tolower(args[0][nIndex]);
                else
                        args[0][nIndex] = tolower(args[0][nIndex]);
                nIndex++;
        }
        if(at_FLAG)
                args[0][nIndex-1] = '\0';


        argv[0] = args[0];
        // this kludge is for a win32 wart emulation (see ExecCmd)
        tail = skipwh(pszLine);


        for(argc = 1; argc < NPARAMS; argc++)
        {
                pszLine = scan(pszLine, args[argc]);
                if(*args[argc] == '\0')
                        break;
                else
                        argv[argc] = args[argc];
        }


        if(*argv[0] != '\0')
        {
                /* Look for just a drive change command, and execute  */
                /* it if found.   */
                if(argv[0][1] == ':' && argv[0][2] == '\0')
                {
                        BYTE c = argv[0][0];

                        if(c >= 'a' && c <= 'z')
                                c = c - 'a' + 'A';
```

```
                        if(c >= 'A' && c <= 'Z')
                                default_drive = (c - 'A');
                }


                /* It may be a help command request. */
                else if( (argc > 1) &&
                        (argv[1][0] == switchchar) &&
                        (argv[1][1] == '?'))
                {

                        strcpy(tail, " ");
                        strcat(tail, argv[0]);
                        strcat(tail, "\r\n");
                        argc = 2;
                        argv[1] = argv[0];
                        argv[0] = "help";
                        argv[2] = 0;
                        ExecCmd(argc, argv);
                        if(IORedirected)
                                RestoreIO(hStdin, hStdout);
                }
                /* do a normal command execution   */
                else
                {
#ifdef DEBUG
                        printf("Looking up %s\n", argv[0]);
#endif

                        pTable = lookup(commands, argv[0]);
                        (*(pTable -> func))(argc, argv);
                        if(IORedirected)
                                RestoreIO(hStdin, hStdout);
                }
        }
}
```

Both the single command mode and the iterative command interpreter share a single algorithm. This algorithm is encompassed by do_command(). When initially invoked, do_command() pre-scans the command line for redirection. This is done through the invocation of Redirect() (Listing 9.4). We will take a closer look at this function because there are several key points that enable the redirection. (Discourse continues on page 176.)

Listing 9.4 The `Redirect()` function.

```
VOID Redirect(BYTE *pszCmdLine,
       BYTE *pszInput, BYTE *pszOutput,
       BOOL *pbAppendMode)
{
       BYTE
              szLocalBuffer[MAX_CMDLINE],
              *pszLine, *pszDest = pszCmdLine;
       SECURITY_ATTRIBUTES saAttr;

       // First - create an image, since we'll be copying back into
       // the original buffer.
       strcpy(szLocalBuffer, pszCmdLine);

       // Initialize the destination names for later use.
       *pszInput = *pszOutput = '\0';

       // Next, start looking for redirect symbols.
       pszLine = skipwh(szLocalBuffer);
       while(*pszLine != '\0')
       {
              switch(*pszLine)
              {
              case '<':
                     pszLine = scan(++pszLine, pszInput);
                     break;

              case '>':
                     if(*(pszLine + 1) == '>')
                     {
                            ++pszLine;
                            *pbAppendMode = TRUE;
                     }
                     else
                     {
                            *pbAppendMode = FALSE;
                     }
                     pszLine = scan(++pszLine, pszOutput);
                     break;
```

```
                default:
                        *pszDest++ = *pszLine++;
                        break;
                }
        }
        *pszDest = '\0';


        // Set the bInheritHandle flag so file handles are inherited.
        saAttr.nLength = sizeof(SECURITY_ATTRIBUTES);
        saAttr.bInheritHandle = TRUE;
        saAttr.lpSecurityDescriptor = NULL;


        // Now that we have the requested redirection, time
        // to perform it on the users behalh.
        if(*pszInput)
        {
                hInput = CreateFile(
                        pszInput, // pointer to name of the file
                        GENERIC_READ, // access (read-write) mode
                        FILE_SHARE_READ, // share mode
                        &saAttr, // pointer to security attributes
                        OPEN_EXISTING, // how to open
                        FILE_ATTRIBUTE_NORMAL, // file attributes
                        0);  // handle to file with attributes to copy
                if(hInput == INVALID_HANDLE_VALUE)
                {
                        hInput = hStdin;
                }
                else
                {
                        SetStdHandle(STD_INPUT_HANDLE, hInput);
                }
        }
        if(*pszOutput)
        {
                hOutput = CreateFile(
                        pszOutput,              // create output file
                        GENERIC_WRITE,          // open for writing
                        0,                      // do not share
                        NULL,                   // no security
                        CREATE_ALWAYS,          // overwrite existing
```

```
                        FILE_ATTRIBUTE_NORMAL |        // normal file
                        FILE_FLAG_OVERLAPPED,          // asynchronous I/O
                        NULL);                         // no attr. template
        if(hOutput == INVALID_HANDLE_VALUE)
        {
                hOutput = hStdout;
        }
        else
        {
                SetStdHandle(STD_OUTPUT_HANDLE, hOutput);
        }
    }
}
```

Besides command line redirection, `Redirect()` also has the desired side effect of removing the redirection lexical elements from the command line. This is necessary for virtually all programs because they perform their own command line processing and don't know what to do with our redirect symbols. `Redirect()` scans the command line looking for all entries that are preceded by the '<' or '>' symbols conventionally used for I/O redirection. It creates a temporary copy of the line and copies back only those parts that are not associated with redirection. `Redirect()` proceeds to change the standard input and output file descriptors by calls to Win32 calls that save the original file descriptor so we can recover it later and redirect the input or output stream. This is done once for the input stream and again for the output stream.

A key element makes redirection possible. From what we saw earlier, creating a process requires considerable work on our part because the Win32 operating system offers a lot of choices. For example, a child process may or may not inherit many attributes and objects from its parent. In our case, we want to make certain that any child process we may be creating receives our handles for input and output. We do this in `Redirect()` by taking advantage of the security attribute structure. This structure has a member, `bInheritHandle`, that when set to "true" (non-zero), allows handles to be inherited from parent to child. Because `Redirect()` is responsible for redirection, it makes sense that it should handle this detail as well. Once accomplished, `Redirect()` proceeds to open an input file or create an output file and set the appropriate standard handle so that they are inherited, if need be.

With I/O redirection out of the way, `do_command()` moves on to parsing the command line for possible use by internal commands. The internal commands use an internal representation of `argc` and `argv` similar to what `main()` sees in any conventional C program. Once the argument list is built, `do_command()` moves on to execute the command. It does this by first looking for the special case of a simple drive change. This is identifiable as a two character string pointed to by `argv[0]` where the second character is the ':' character. Should this be the case, the current drive is changed by saving the drive to an internal variable used throughout `cmd32.exe` and `do_command()` exits. If it isn't a drive change, `do_command()` checks for a special request to the help subsystem. If it identifies it as being such a request, `do_command()` builds a help command line, invokes `HELP.EXE`, and exits.

Finally, if the command is neither a drive change or a call to the help subsystem, do_command() attempts to invoke either an internal or external command to satisfy the user request. It does this through a call to lookup() (Listing 9.5) which performs the actual command lookup. The internal command's corresponding function is then executed by invoking the returned pointer to the internal function. Once the command completes, do_command() restores the I/O back to what it was originally through a call to RestoreIO() and exits.

Listing 9.5 The lookup() function.

```
struct table *lookup(p, token)
struct table *p;
BYTE *token;
{
        while(*(p -> entry) != '\0')
        {
                if(strcmp(p -> entry, token) == 0)
                        break;
                else
                        ++p;
        }
        return p;
}
```

When the default entry is invoked, it attempts to take the command parsed from the command line and locate an external program to fulfill the user's request. It follows a predetermined sequence of searches based on filename extensions. This is conventionally *.COM, *.EXE, and *.BAT, in that order. It spawns the external program, if found, and the external command returns to this point when it terminates.

Internal Commands

There are two internal commands we'll look at: cd and exit. These two functions are representative of internal commands in cmd32.exe. In the case of cd, the design is virtually identical to all other internal commands. Exit, however, is a special case that's used to quit the interpreter. Because of this, exit needs to do some special housekeeping prior to exiting. Let's start by examining cd (Listing 9.6).

Listing 9.6 Built-in cd command.

```
BOOL cd(INT argc, BYTE *argv[])
{
        /* Do command line sanity checks */
        if(argc > 2)
        {
```

```
            error_message(INV_NUM_PARAMS);
            return FALSE;
    }


    if(argc == 1)
    {
            BYTE szCurrentDir[MAX_CMDLINE];

            GetCurrentDirectory(MAX_CMDLINE, &szCurrentDir);
            printf("%s\n\n", szCurrentDir);
            return TRUE;
    }
    else if(argc == 2)
    {
            SetCurrentDirectory(argv[1]);
            return TRUE;
    }
    else
    {
            return FALSE;
    }
}
```

Cd starts out doing a sanity check as a simple method of checking the syntax. This sanity check is to make certain that the user only enters commands of the form "cd" or "cd direc-tory." Should a syntax error occur, an error is returned to the main command loop.

With the syntax check out of the way, it's time to parse the command line for options. In the case of cd, we are looking for an optional directory parameter. If no directory is present in the second argument, cd simply echoes the current directory through a call to the Win32 API call GetCurrentDirectory(). If one is present, cd proceeds to change the directory through a call to SetCurrentDirectory(), completing the cd operation.

Cd illustrates the general design of every internal command. First, the command performs a syntax check. Next, it proceeds to extract the information it needs by parsing the arguments that were passed upon invocation. Finally, the command is implemented typically using Win32 calls. Error checks are performed at each step and a means of recovery is designed into each step. When the command exits, due to an error or otherwise, it returns an exit code that indicates either success (TRUE) or failure (FALSE). In the event of a failure, the function calls an error routine to emit an error message. All commands within cmd32.exe follow this design.

CmdExit() handles the built-in exit command (Listing 9.7). The design of this function deviates significantly from other built-in commands because of the special nature of the command. One feature of cmd32.exe is that it can return a value that can convey information such as error codes back to the program that invoked the command. The return code information, by convention, is an error code of zero meaning success. cmd32.exe returns success unless otherwise told by an argument to the exit command. CmdExit() does this by a simple examination of argc. If there's only a single argument, it exits with a success code. Otherwise, it converts the first argument to a numeric value and returns that number as the return code.

Listing 9.7 Built-in exit command.

```
BOOL CmdExit(INT argc, BYTE FAR *argv[])
{
#ifdef DEBUG
        printf("Entered CmdExit\n");
#endif
        /* If no values passed, return errorvalue = 0  */
        if(argc == 1)
                ExitProcess(0);

        /* otherwise return what the user asked for   */
        else
        {
                INT nRetVal;
                static BYTE szNums[] = "0123456789";
                BYTE *pszNum;

                for(nRetVal = 0, pszNum = argv[1]; isdigit(*pszNum); pszNum++)
                {
                        INT j;

                        for(j = 0; j < 10; j++)
                                if(szNums[j] == *pszNum)
                                        break;
                        nRetVal += j;
                }
                ExitProcess(nRetVal);
        }
        return TRUE;
}
```

External Commands

ExecCmd() is the central point where cmd32.exe invokes external commands. This is an important function because all applications are invoked through this interface. Listing 9.8 illustrates the function ExecCmd() and the function seems excessive at a first glance. You shouldn't jump to conclusions too early in the game, however, because starting a program and accurately keeping track of its environment can consume significant resources. (Discourse continues on page 183.)

Listing 9.8 ExecCmd() **external command interface.**

```
BOOL ExecCmd(INT argc, BYTE *argv[])
{
        PROCESS_INFORMATION piProcInfo;
        SECURITY_ATTRIBUTES saAttr;
        BOOL bRetVal, bFound = FALSE, bBatch = FALSE;
        STARTUPINFO siStartInfo;
        WORD nIdx;
        BYTE szChildCmdLine[MAX_CMDLINE];
        BYTE szPath[SIZE] = "", *pszPath, *pszTerm;
        DWORD nRead;

        // See if there's a PATH spec out there somewhere. If not, use the default.
        nRead = GetEnvironmentVariable("PATH", szPath, SIZE);
        if(!nRead)
        {
                strcpy(szPath, szDfltPath);
        }

        // Go through and search the path.  Loop through the path looking
        // for the command.  Look in the current directory
        // first. If it matches a local file, copy in actual file name.
        if(MatchCommand(argv[0], szChildCmdLine, &bBatch))
        {
                bFound = TRUE;
        }
        else
        {
                for(pszPath = szPath, pszTerm = szPath; *pszTerm ; pszPath = pszTerm)
                {
                        // Isolate a path component to search
                        while(*pszTerm && (*pszTerm != ';'))
                        {
                                ++pszTerm;
                        }
                        if(*pszTerm == ';')
                        {
                                *pszTerm = '\0';
                                ++pszTerm;
                        }
```

```
                strcpy(szChildCmdLine, pszPath);
                strcat(szChildCmdLine, "\\");
                strcat(szChildCmdLine, argv[0]);
                if(MatchCommand(szChildCmdLine, 0, &bBatch))
                {
                        bFound = TRUE;
                        break;
                }
        }
}


// Did we find it?  If not, report an error and return
if(!bFound)
{
        error_message(FILE_NOT_FOUND);
        return FALSE;
}


// Build a command line to execute
for(nIdx = 1; nIdx < argc; ++nIdx)
{
        strcat(szChildCmdLine, " ");
        strcat(szChildCmdLine, argv[nIdx]);
}


// Set the bInheritHandle flag so file handles are inherited.
saAttr.nLength = sizeof(SECURITY_ATTRIBUTES);
saAttr.bInheritHandle = TRUE;
saAttr.lpSecurityDescriptor = NULL;


// Set up members of STARTUPINFO structure.
ZeroMemory(&siStartInfo, sizeof(STARTUPINFO));
siStartInfo.cb = sizeof(STARTUPINFO);           // Create the child process.

// The following is somewhat inetersting.  We don't specify a module
// name because of NT stream operating systems.  These require a
// null as the module in order to execute 16-bit programs.
// Yet another Microsoft "design feature."
bRetVal = CreateProcess(NULL,
        szChildCmdLine,         // command line
```

```
                &saAttr,                // process security attributes
                NULL,                   // primary thread security attributes
                TRUE,                   // handles are inherited
                0,                      // creation flags
                NULL,                   // use parent's environment
                NULL,                   // use parent's current directory
                &siStartInfo,           // STARTUPINFO pointer
                &piProcInfo);           // receives PROCESS_INFORMATION

        // Wait for the process to exit, if we didn't have an error
        if(bRetVal)
        {
                WaitForSingleObject(piProcInfo.hProcess, INFINITE);
        }
        else
        {
                error_message(EXEC_ERR);
        }

        return bRetVal;
}


BOOL CmdExit(INT argc, BYTE FAR *argv[])
{
#ifdef DEBUG
        printf("Entered CmdExit\n");
#endif
        /* If no values passed, return errorvalue = 0  */
        if(argc == 1)
                ExitProcess(0);

        /* otherwise return what the user asked for  */
        else
        {
                INT nRetVal;
                static BYTE szNums[] = "0123456789";
                BYTE *pszNum;

                for(nRetVal = 0, pszNum = argv[1]; isdigit(*pszNum); pszNum++)
```

```
        {
                INT j;

                for(j = 0; j < 10; j++)
                        if(szNums[j] == *pszNum)
                                break;
                nRetVal += j;
        }
        ExitProcess(nRetVal);
    }
    return TRUE;
}
```

Let's start by looking at the overall design. All commands are entered through the command line interface we examined earlier. This function parses the command line and breaks it into an internal argc/argv structure similar to the C calling convention for main. It then takes the first argument and attempts to match it against the internal dispatch table. The algorithm used for the match stops when a terminating null string entry is encountered. The function entry for the terminating null string entry is ExecCmd(). This makes ExecCmd() the default function invoked when the command entered does *not* match one of the internal commands. With this algorithm, an external command is treated no differently than an internal command. By making it the terminating entry in the search, we've guaranteed that cmd32.exe searches the internal commands prior to loading an external command.

Once ExecCmd() is invoked, it initializes and searches for the command in a fixed manner that includes searching for the .BAT, .COM, and .EXE forms of the command. This search is performed along fixed directories as specified in the PATH environment variable. Once Exec-Cmd() finds the command, it creates the proper environment before executing the external command. When the external command returns, ExecCmd() checks for errors prior to exiting to the interpreter's main loop, adding to the robustness of the design.

Let's take a closer look at the algorithm behind ExecCmd(). ExecCmd() starts by initializing the internal execution path variable. It builds the path string and creates a path that begins ".\" so that the current directory is searched first. Next, ExecCmd() uses a C do-while construct to repeat the search along each directory contained within the string constructed earlier. For each iteration, ExecCmd() tries to load a binary executable. It does so by attempting to find the first occurrence of the executable file through a call to FindFirstFile.

To execute a binary file (.COM or .EXE file), ExecCmd() first builds a command line to pass to the command. We need to do this because we had additional characters, thanks to command line redirection, that many Win32 programs would not understand. Once done, we need to set up our process so that our child process will inherit redirected input and output. This is done through the use of a SECURITY_ATTRIBUTES structure, saAttr, and setting the bInheritHandle field to TRUE.

We actually start our program with a call to CreateProcess. The call is somewhat interesting, because we can't specify a module name. The Windows NT/2000 stream of Win32 operating systems, however, is somewhat different. These require a null as the module in order to execute 16-bit programs — yet another one of Microsoft's Win32 nuances. Programmer beware.

Upon return from the `CreateProcess` API call, `ExecCmd()` waits for the child process to end by waiting for an event through a call to `WaitForSingleObject`. This is done only if `CreateProcess` succeeded. If there was an error, `ExecCmd()` makes a call to `error_message` to translate the error code into useful user feedback in the form of error messages — an absolute necessity for the user. Without them, `cmd32.exe` would be nearly useless.

Wrapping Up `cmd32.exe`

There are many more files to `cmd32.exe` than are described here. What I've done is discuss a few commands that are representative of the other commands in the set. Feel free to make changes and redistribute this code. It is released under the terms of the GNU Public License (GPL) that guarantees you the availability of the source in any distribution of this code. Combine the availability of the source with the explanations in this book and I'm sure you'll have fun making additions to it.

Closing Thoughts

This chapter demonstrates the fundamentals of operating system command line interpreters, and how to create one for the Win32 operating system in particular. In general, these techniques are similar to those used in command line interpreters in other operating systems. Although the system calls may be different, the general principles are the same.

Our version of `cmd32.exe` is not a full implementation. There are two features that are noticeably missing. First, we do not handle batch files. This can be easily handled, but I felt that it would clutter our example if I included it here. The second feature missing is pipes. Again, we can easily add this, as we did all the work necessary in Chapter 7. It was a design choice I made in order to create a simple parser for the command line.

What's important is that we have now seen a small project for the Win32 operating systems. We have worked with a set of fundamental calls and learned the nuances of the Win32 API. I hope that this helps you in your future projects. Remember, these are powerful operating systems capable of much more than what was previously available for IA-32 platforms. Above all, have fun as you go on to master the Win32 operating system APIs.

Windows 95
`kernel32.dll` **Exports**

Ordinal Number		Offset	Function Name
50	0	0002D8B0	AddAtomA
102	1	00034C49	AddAtomW
103	2	0002F3FB	AllocConsole
104	3	00021AF6	AllocLSCallback
105	4	00021B29	AllocSLCallback
106	5	0002E70B	AreFileApisANSI
107	6	00034CD0	BackupRead
108	7	00034CBE	BackupSeek
109	8	00034CD0	BackupWrite

Ordinal Number		Offset	Function Name
110	9	0002B59F	Beep
111	A	00034C64	BeginUpdateResourceA
112	B	00034C64	BeginUpdateResourceW
113	C	0002DDB8	BuildCommDCBA
114	D	0002DDE3	BuildCommDCBAndTimeoutsA
115	E	00034C7F	BuildCommDCBAndTimeoutsW
116	F	00034C64	BuildCommDCBW
117	10	0002DCD1	CallNamedPipeA
118	11	00034CD0	CallNamedPipeW
119	12	00021959	Callback12
120	13	00021966	Callback16
121	14	00021973	Callback20
122	15	00021980	Callback24
123	16	0002198D	Callback28
124	17	0002199A	Callback32
125	18	000219A7	Callback36
129	19	00021940	Callback4
126	1A	000219B4	Callback40
127	1B	000219C1	Callback44
128	1C	000219CE	Callback48
130	1D	000219DB	Callback52
131	1E	000219E8	Callback56
132	1F	000219F5	Callback60
133	20	00021A02	Callback64
134	21	0002194C	Callback8

Ordinal Number	Offset		Function Name
135	22	00033CA6	ClearCommBreak
136	23	0002D00F	ClearCommError
137	24	0000BC72	CloseHandle
138	25	00034C40	CloseProfileUserMapping
139	26	0002688D	CloseSystemHandle
140	27	000347E0	CommConfigDialogA
141	28	00034C7F	CommConfigDialogW
142	29	0000705C	CompareFileTime
143	2A	0002DEA8	CompareStringA
144	2B	00034CBE	CompareStringW
145	2C	00034C64	ConnectNamedPipe
146	2D	00022C10	ContinueDebugEvent
147	2E	0003EBBE	ConvertDefaultLocale
148	2F	00012354	ConvertToGlobalHandle
149	30	0002DC81	CopyFileA
150	31	00034C7F	CopyFileW
151	32	0002EB4F	CreateConsoleScreenBuffer
152	33	00007CA9	CreateDirectoryA
153	34	0002DBCA	CreateDirectoryExA
154	35	00034C7F	CreateDirectoryExW
155	36	00034C64	CreateDirectoryW
156	37	00007375	CreateEventA
157	38	00034C9A	CreateEventW
158	39	00007817	CreateFileA
159	3A	000073FD	CreateFileMappingA

Ordinal Number	Offset		Function Name
160	3B	00034CBE	CreateFileMappingW
161	3C	00034CD0	CreateFileW
162	3D	00034C9A	CreateIoCompletionPort
163	3E	0002CDA1	CreateKernelThread
164	3F	000070FA	CreateMailslotA
165	40	00034C9A	CreateMailslotW
166	41	0000733F	CreateMutexA
167	42	00034C7F	CreateMutexW
168	43	00034CD9	CreateNamedPipeA
169	44	00034CD9	CreateNamedPipeW
170	45	0002D24C	CreatePipe
171	46	000074A4	CreateProcessA
172	47	00034CE2	CreateProcessW
173	48	00034CD0	CreateRemoteThread
174	49	000073D2	CreateSemaphoreA
175	4A	00034C9A	CreateSemaphoreW
176	4B	00032448	CreateSocketHandle
177	4C	00034CA3	CreateTapePartition
178	4D	00006DD6	CreateThread
179	4E	00036FB2	CreateToolhelp32Snapshot
180	4F	00022CB0	DebugActiveProcess
181	50	00006693	DebugBreak
182	51	00034C7F	DefineDosDeviceA
183	52	00034C7F	DefineDosDeviceW
184	53	00027E9B	DeleteAtom

Ordinal Number	Offset		Function Name
185	54	00018636	DeleteCriticalSection
186	55	0002DC5A	DeleteFileA
187	56	00034C49	DeleteFileW
188	57	00006F24	DeviceIoControl
189	58	00023F9B	DisableThreadLibraryCalls
190	59	00034C49	DisconnectNamedPipe
191	5A	0002D229	DosDateTimeToFileTime
192	5B	0002CF97	DuplicateHandle
193	5C	00034C64	EndUpdateResourceA
194	5D	00034C64	EndUpdateResourceW
195	5E	00009883	EnterCriticalSection
196	5F	000411E2	EnumCalendarInfoA
197	60	00034C9A	EnumCalendarInfoW
198	61	000417AC	EnumDateFormatsA
199	62	00034C7F	EnumDateFormatsW
200	63	0002D718	EnumResourceLanguagesA
201	64	0002D812	EnumResourceLanguagesW
202	65	0002D6E9	EnumResourceNamesA
203	66	0002D7E2	EnumResourceNamesW
204	67	0002BD60	EnumResourceTypesA
205	68	0002C465	EnumResourceTypesW
206	69	00041030	EnumSystemCodePagesA
207	6A	00034C64	EnumSystemCodePagesW
208	6B	00040F78	EnumSystemLocalesA
209	6C	00034C64	EnumSystemLocalesW

Ordinal Number		Offset	Function Name
210	6D	000416C0	EnumTimeFormatsA
211	6E	00034C7F	EnumTimeFormatsW
212	6F	00034C91	EraseTape
213	70	00033D00	EscapeCommFunction
214	71	0001AFB0	ExitProcess
215	72	0001795F	ExitThread
216	73	0002D64E	ExpandEnvironmentStringsA
217	74	00034C7F	ExpandEnvironmentStringsW
218	75	00002C2D	FT_Exit0
219	76	00002C73	FT_Exit12
220	77	00002C8B	FT_Exit16
221	78	00002CA3	FT_Exit20
222	79	00002CBB	FT_Exit24
223	7A	00002CD3	FT_Exit28
224	7B	00002CEB	FT_Exit32
225	7C	00002D03	FT_Exit36
226	7D	00002C43	FT_Exit4
227	7E	00002D1B	FT_Exit40
228	7F	00002D33	FT_Exit44
229	80	00002D4B	FT_Exit48
230	81	00002D63	FT_Exit52
231	82	00002D7B	FT_Exit56
232	83	00002C5B	FT_Exit8
233	84	00002791	FT_Prolog
234	85	00002A57	FT_Thunk

Ordinal Number	Offset		Function Name
235	86	0002D5B3	FatalAppExitA
236	87	00034C64	FatalAppExitW
237	88	000232F7	FatalExit
238	89	00007086	FileTimeToDosDateTime
239	8A	00007BE3	FileTimeToLocalFileTime
240	8B	00007C3B	FileTimeToSystemTime
241	8C	0002EF4D	FillConsoleOutputAttribute
242	8D	0002EEAD	FillConsoleOutputCharacterA
243	8E	00034CAC	FillConsoleOutputCharacterW
244	8F	0002D8DF	FindAtomA
245	90	00034C49	FindAtomW
246	91	0000632F	FindClose
247	92	0000BC72	FindCloseChangeNotification
248	93	000079EB	FindFirstChangeNotificationA
249	94	00034C7F	FindFirstChangeNotificationW
250	95	00007893	FindFirstFileA
251	96	00034C76	FindFirstFileW
252	97	0001893B	FindNextChangeNotification
253	98	000078CB	FindNextFileA
254	99	00034C64	FindNextFileW
255	9A	00007C67	FindResourceA
256	9B	0002D6A7	FindResourceExA
257	9C	0002D79E	FindResourceExW
258	9D	0002D75A	FindResourceW
259	9E	0002EFEE	FlushConsoleInputBuffer

Ordinal Number		Offset	Function Name
260	9F	000291D6	FlushFileBuffers
261	A0	0002336C	FlushInstructionCache
262	A1	0002751C	FlushViewOfFile
263	A2	00034CAC	FoldStringA
264	A3	00034CAC	FoldStringW
265	A4	000070B7	FormatMessageA
266	A5	00034CD0	FormatMessageW
267	A6	0002F491	FreeConsole
268	A7	000242EB	FreeEnvironmentStringsA
269	A8	00034C49	FreeEnvironmentStringsW
270	A9	00021D72	FreeLSCallback
271	AA	0001BB98	FreeLibrary
272	AB	00023F86	FreeLibraryAndExitThread
273	AC	000213ED	FreeResource
274	AD	00021DAD	FreeSLCallback
275	AE	0002E64B	GenerateConsoleCtrlEvent
276	AF	0001BC1F	GetACP
277	B0	0002D90E	GetAtomNameA
278	B1	00034C7F	GetAtomNameW
279	B2	00034C64	GetBinaryType
280	B3	00034C64	GetBinaryTypeA
281	B4	00034C64	GetBinaryTypeW
282	B5	00007B1E	GetCPInfo
283	B6	00034A26	GetCommConfig
284	B7	0002D03B	GetCommMask

Ordinal Number		Offset	Function Name
285	B8	0002D07D	GetCommModemStatus
286	B9	0002D05A	GetCommProperties
287	BA	0002D09C	GetCommState
288	BB	0002D0BF	GetCommTimeouts
289	BC	0001A047	GetCommandLineA
290	BD	00024287	GetCommandLineW
291	BE	00034C76	GetCompressedFileSizeA
292	BF	00034C76	GetCompressedFileSizeW
293	C0	00007A0B	GetComputerNameA
294	C1	00034C64	GetComputerNameW
295	C2	00032260	GetConsoleCP
296	C3	0002F1B5	GetConsoleCursorInfo
297	C4	0002E84C	GetConsoleMode
298	C5	00032281	GetConsoleOutputCP
299	C6	0002E973	GetConsoleScreenBufferInfo
300	C7	0002E9BD	GetConsoleTitleA
301	C8	00034C64	GetConsoleTitleW
302	C9	0002DEF3	GetCurrencyFormatA
303	CA	00034CBE	GetCurrencyFormatW
304	CB	00007744	GetCurrentDirectoryA
305	CC	00034C64	GetCurrentDirectoryW
306	CD	00024633	GetCurrentProcess
307	CE	00012347	GetCurrentProcessId
308	CF	00023ED8	GetCurrentThread
309	D0	0000EEED	GetCurrentThreadId

Ordinal Number		Offset	Function Name
310	D1	00007CDB	GetDateFormatA
311	D2	00034CBE	GetDateFormatW
312	D3	0002ADB5	GetDaylightFlag
313	D4	000348A2	GetDefaultCommConfigA
314	D5	00034C7F	GetDefaultCommConfigW
315	D6	00007781	GetDiskFreeSpaceA
316	D7	00034CAC	GetDiskFreeSpaceW
317	D8	00007680	GetDriveTypeA
318	D9	00034C49	GetDriveTypeW
319	DA	000185F8	GetEnvironmentStrings
320	DB	000185F8	GetEnvironmentStringsA
321	DC	00034C40	GetEnvironmentStringsW
322	DD	0002D5DE	GetEnvironmentVariableA
323	DE	00034C7F	GetEnvironmentVariableW
324	DF	00027DEC	GetErrorMode
325	E0	0002CD3E	GetExitCodeProcess
326	E1	0002CDCB	GetExitCodeThread
327	E2	0000786C	GetFileAttributesA
328	E3	00034C5B	GetFileAttributesW
329	E4	00029262	GetFileInformationByHandle
330	E5	00006E60	GetFileSize
331	E6	00006FC1	GetFileTime
332	E7	00005761	GetFileType
333	E8	000077C1	GetFullPathNameA
334 ·	E9	00034C9A	GetFullPathNameW

Ordinal Number	Offset		Function Name
335	EA	000325DB	GetHandleContext
336	EB	00034C64	GetHandleInformation
337	EC	00021CC9	GetLSCallbackTarget
338	ED	00021CA2	GetLSCallbackTemplate
339	EE	0002F34F	GetLargestConsoleWindowSize
340	EF	00012A1F	GetLastError
341	F0	00007039	GetLocalTime
342	F1	0000FC11	GetLocaleInfoA
343	F2	00034C9A	GetLocaleInfoW
344	F3	0002D549	GetLogicalDriveStringsA
345	F4	00034C64	GetLogicalDriveStringsW
346	F5	00004B9C	GetLogicalDrives
347	F6	0002D3C3	GetMailslotInfo
348	F7	0000745A	GetModuleFileNameA
349	F8	00034C7F	GetModuleFileNameW
350	F9	00007479	GetModuleHandleA
351	FA	00034C49	GetModuleHandleW
352	FB	0003288F	GetNamedPipeHandleStateA
353	FC	00034CD0	GetNamedPipeHandleStateW
354	FD	0002D2AD	GetNamedPipeInfo
355	FE	00007B41	GetNumberFormatA
356	FF	00034CBE	GetNumberFormatW
357	100	0002F043	GetNumberOfConsoleInputEvents
358	101	0002F203	GetNumberOfConsoleMouseButtons
359	102	0001E576	GetOEMCP

Ordinal Number		Offset	Function Name
360	103	0002CE0D	GetOverlappedResult
361	104	0002AA65	GetPriorityClass
362	105	0002CB38	GetPrivateProfileIntA
363	106	00034C9A	GetPrivateProfileIntW
364	107	0002D9C7	GetPrivateProfileSectionA
365	108	0002DB15	GetPrivateProfileSection-NamesA
366	109	00034C7F	GetPrivateProfileSection-NamesW
367	10A	00034C9A	GetPrivateProfileSectionW
368	10B	000075AA	GetPrivateProfileStringA
369	10C	00034CBE	GetPrivateProfileStringW
370	10D	0002DA60	GetPrivateProfileStructA
371	10E	00034CAC	GetPrivateProfileStructW
372	10F	00006C18	GetProcAddress
373	110	0002DE5C	GetProcessAffinityMask
374	111	0001E422	GetProcessFlags
375	112	0001A590	GetProcessHeap
376	113	00034C64	GetProcessHeaps
377	114	00034C64	GetProcessShutdownParameters
378	115	00034CAC	GetProcessTimes
379	116	00024639	GetProcessVersion
380	117	00034C7F	GetProcessWorkingSetSize
381	118	00027DC3	GetProductName
382	119	0002CB06	GetProfileIntA
383	11A	00034C7F	GetProfileIntW
384	11B	0002D94D	GetProfileSectionA

Ordinal Number	Offset		Function Name
385	11C	00034C7F	GetProfileSectionW
386	11D	00007533	GetProfileStringA
387	11E	00034CAC	GetProfileStringW
388	11F	0002B881	GetQueuedCompletionStatus
389	120	00021D14	GetSLCallbackTarget
390	121	00021CEC	GetSLCallbackTemplate
391	122	0002CF2C	GetShortPathNameA
392	123	00034C7F	GetShortPathNameW
393	124	00007510	GetStartupInfoA
394	125	00034C49	GetStartupInfoW
395	126	00005650	GetStdHandle
396	127	00007A8D	GetStringTypeA
397	128	0002DE82	GetStringTypeExA
398	129	00034CAC	GetStringTypeExW
399	12A	00034C9A	GetStringTypeW
400	12B	0003EC32	GetSystemDefaultLCID
401	12C	0003EC17	GetSystemDefaultLangID
402	12D	000076AB	GetSystemDirectoryA
403	12E	00034C64	GetSystemDirectoryW
404	12F	000246F8	GetSystemInfo
405	130	0002B63F	GetSystemPowerStatus
406	131	0002D14E	GetSystemTime
407	132	00034C7F	GetSystemTimeAdjustment
408	133	0002CF74	GetSystemTimeAsFileTime
409	134	00034CA3	GetTapeParameters

Ordinal Number	Offset		Function Name
410	135	00034CB5	GetTapePosition
411	136	00034C52	GetTapeStatus
412	137	0002DB91	GetTempFileNameA
413	138	00034C9A	GetTempFileNameW
414	139	0002DB54	GetTempPathA
415	13A	00034C64	GetTempPathW
416	13B	0002CEBF	GetThreadContext
417	13C	0002B599	GetThreadLocale
418	13D	0002AA2C	GetThreadPriority
419	13E	0002CDEA	GetThreadSelectorEntry
420	13F	00034CAC	GetThreadTimes
421	140	0000683C	GetTickCount
422	141	00007A57	GetTimeFormatA
423	142	00034CBE	GetTimeFormatW
424	143	0002D1B3	GetTimeZoneInformation
425	144	00009AB0	GetUserDefaultLCID
426	145	0003EC1E	GetUserDefaultLangID
427	146	000213D3	GetVersion
428	147	0001EFAF	GetVersionExA
429	148	00034C49	GetVersionExW
430	149	0000795B	GetVolumeInformationA
431	14A	00034CD9	GetVolumeInformationW
432	14B	000076E4	GetWindowsDirectoryA
433	14C	00034C64	GetWindowsDirectoryW
434	14D	00007288	GlobalAddAtomA

Ordinal Number		Offset	Function Name
435	14E	00034C49	GlobalAddAtomW
436	14F	00004904	GlobalAlloc
437	150	00004937	GlobalCompact
438	151	00027EB7	GlobalDeleteAtom
439	152	0002D856	GlobalFindAtomA
440	153	00034C49	GlobalFindAtomW
441	154	0002CC24	GlobalFix
442	155	0002CC02	GlobalFlags
443	156	00006CAD	GlobalFree
444	157	0002D885	GlobalGetAtomNameA
445	158	00034C7F	GlobalGetAtomNameW
446	159	00006C69	GlobalHandle
447	15A	00006C47	GlobalLock
448	15B	0002CC72	GlobalMemoryStatus
449	15C	0002CBBE	GlobalReAlloc
450	15D	0002CBE0	GlobalSize
451	15E	00004918	GlobalUnWire
452	15F	0002CC4B	GlobalUnfix
453	160	00006C8B	GlobalUnlock
454	161	00004913	GlobalWire
455	162	000376B4	Heap32First
456	163	000375C7	Heap32ListFirst
457	164	00037632	Heap32ListNext
458	165	00037746	Heap32Next
459	166	00006D34	HeapAlloc

Ordinal Number	Offset		Function Name
460	167	00034C64	HeapCompact
461	168	000165D7	HeapCreate
462	169	00006D13	HeapDestroy
463	16A	00006D80	HeapFree
464	16B	00034C49	HeapLock
465	16C	00006D55	HeapReAlloc
466	16D	00034C76	HeapSetFlags
467	16E	00006DAB	HeapSize
468	16F	00034C49	HeapUnlock
469	170	00034C88	HeapValidate
470	171	00034C64	HeapWalk
471	172	00027F06	InitAtomTable
472	173	00011CD2	InitializeCriticalSection
473	174	00011B89	InterlockedDecrement
474	175	0002662A	InterlockedExchange
475	176	0001A506	InterlockedIncrement
476	177	0003EC38	InvalidateNLSCache
477	178	0000ADAF	IsBadCodePtr
478	179	000098C1	IsBadHugeReadPtr
479	17A	000084F0	IsBadHugeWritePtr
480	17B	000098C1	IsBadReadPtr
481	17C	00009A35	IsBadStringPtrA
482	17D	0002A00E	IsBadStringPtrW
483	17E	000084F0	IsBadWritePtr
484	17F	00018988	IsDBCSLeadByte

Ordinal Number	Offset		Function Name
485	180	00041C17	IsDBCSLeadByteEx
486	181	00021C35	IsLSCallback
487	182	00021C69	IsSLCallback
488	183	00041BEE	IsValidCodePage
489	184	0003EA50	IsValidLocale
490	185	00001907	K32Thk1632Epilog
491	186	000018E2	K32Thk1632Prolog
492	187	00007AB3	LCMapStringA
493	188	00034CBE	LCMapStringW
494	189	000098A9	LeaveCriticalSection
495	18A	00007433	LoadLibraryA
496	18B	0001EAE9	LoadLibraryExA
497	18C	00034C7F	LoadLibraryExW
498	18D	00034C49	LoadLibraryW
499	18E	0002CFB8	LoadModule
500	18F	0000E620	LoadResource
501	190	00004904	LocalAlloc
502	191	00026BA6	LocalCompact
503	192	00007C0F	LocalFileTimeToFileTime
504	193	00026BBA	LocalFlags
505	194	00004A20	LocalFree
506	195	0002CC95	LocalHandle
507	196	0002CAE4	LocalLock
508	197	00006CCF	LocalReAlloc
509	198	0002CCD9	LocalShrink

Ordinal Number	Offset		Function Name
510	199	00006CF1	LocalSize
511	19A	0002CCB7	LocalUnlock
512	19B	00028F54	LockFile
513	19C	00034CBE	LockFileEx
514	19D	000213F2	LockResource
515	19E	000169F9	MakeCriticalSectionGlobal
516	19F	00001ADC	MapHInstLS
517	1A0	00001AD7	MapHInstLS_PN
518	1A1	00001B08	MapHInstSL
519	1A2	00001B01	MapHInstSL_PN
520	1A3	00001B59	MapHModuleLS
521	1A4	00001B68	MapHModuleSL
522	1A5	00001FDF	MapLS
523	1A6	00001BC1	MapSL
524	1A7	00001B78	MapSLFix
525	1A8	0000FBF4	MapViewOfFile
526	1A9	0000F9B1	MapViewOfFileEx
527	1AA	0003797D	Module32First
528	1AB	000379F1	Module32Next
529	1AC	0002DCA9	MoveFileA
530	1AD	00034C7F	MoveFileExA
531	1AE	00034C7F	MoveFileExW
532	1AF	00034C64	MoveFileW
533	1B0	00021857	MulDiv
534	1B1	00007AD1	MultiByteToWideChar

Ordinal Number	Offset		Function Name
535	1B2	00042C5D	NotifyNLSUserCache
536	1B3	000073AB	OpenEventA
537	1B4	00034C7F	OpenEventW
538	1B5	0002D3FF	OpenFile
539	1B6	0002D522	OpenFileMappingA
540	1B7	00034C7F	OpenFileMappingW
541	1B8	0002D4D7	OpenMutexA
542	1B9	00034C7F	OpenMutexW
543	1BA	0002404C	OpenProcess
544	1BB	00034C40	OpenProfileUserMapping
545	1BC	0002D502	OpenSemaphoreA
546	1BD	00034C7F	OpenSemaphoreW
547	1BE	000268FC	OpenVxDHandle
548	1BF	0002D67C	OutputDebugStringA
549	1C0	00034C49	OutputDebugStringW
550	1C1	0002EA90	PeekConsoleInputA
551	1C2	00034C9A	PeekConsoleInputW
552	1C3	0002D2E9	PeekNamedPipe
553	1C4	00034C9A	PostQueuedCompletionStatus
554	1C5	00034C91	PrepareTape
555	1C6	00037752	Process32First
556	1C7	000377DD	Process32Next
557	1C8	00020EEC	PulseEvent
558	1C9	00033E86	PurgeComm
559	1CA	000028D0	QT_Thunk

Ordinal Number		Offset	Function Name
560	1CB	0002DC27	QueryDosDeviceA
561	1CC	00034C7F	QueryDosDeviceW
562	1CD	00034C64	QueryNumberOfEventLogRecords
563	1CE	00034C64	QueryOldestEventLogRecord
564	1CF	0002DD72	QueryPerformanceCounter
565	1D0	0002DD95	QueryPerformanceFrequency
566	1D1	00024AE8	QueueUserAPC
567	1D2	0002CD5E	RaiseException
568	1D3	0002E794	ReadConsoleA
569	1D4	0002EADC	ReadConsoleInputA
570	1D5	00034C9A	ReadConsoleInputW
571	1D6	0002F23B	ReadConsoleOutputA
572	1D7	0002EE11	ReadConsoleOutputAttribute
573	1D8	0002ED75	ReadConsoleOutputCharacterA
574	1D9	00034CAC	ReadConsoleOutputCharacterW
575	1DA	00034CAC	ReadConsoleOutputW
576	1DB	00034CAC	ReadConsoleW
577	1DC	00005806	ReadFile
578	1DD	000285C0	ReadFileEx
579	1DE	00022E3E	ReadProcessMemory
580	1DF	0001BFC2	RegisterServiceProcess
581	1E0	000128FD	ReinitializeCriticalSection
582	1E1	00020F5C	ReleaseMutex
583	1E2	00006E00	ReleaseSemaphore
584	1E3	0002DC07	RemoveDirectoryA

Ordinal Number	Offset		Function Name
585	1E4	00034C49	RemoveDirectoryW
586	1E5	00020F24	ResetEvent
587	1E6	0001E510	ResumeThread
588	1E7	0002CA39	RtlFillMemory
589	1E8	00007B6A	RtlMoveMemory
590	1E9	00015D79	RtlUnwind
591	1EA	00007BA7	RtlZeroMemory
592	1EB	00001EC8	SMapLS
593	1EC	00001F7E	SMapLS_IP_EBP_12
594	1ED	00001F79	SMapLS_IP_EBP_16
595	1EE	00001F74	SMapLS_IP_EBP_20
596	1EF	00001F6F	SMapLS_IP_EBP_24
597	1F0	00001F6A	SMapLS_IP_EBP_28
598	1F1	00001F65	SMapLS_IP_EBP_32
599	1F2	00001F60	SMapLS_IP_EBP_36
600	1F3	00001F5B	SMapLS_IP_EBP_40
601	1F4	00001F83	SMapLS_IP_EBP_8
602	1F5	00001F46	SUnMapLS
603	1F6	00001F3C	SUnMapLS_IP_EBP_12
604	1F7	00001F37	SUnMapLS_IP_EBP_16
605	1F8	00001F32	SUnMapLS_IP_EBP_20
606	1F9	00001F2D	SUnMapLS_IP_EBP_24
607	1FA	00001F28	SUnMapLS_IP_EBP_28
608	1FB	00001F23	SUnMapLS_IP_EBP_32
609	1FC	00001F1E	SUnMapLS_IP_EBP_36

Ordinal Number	Offset		Function Name
610	1FD	00001F19	SUnMapLS_IP_EBP_40
611	1FE	00001F41	SUnMapLS_IP_EBP_8
612	1FF	0002F291	ScrollConsoleScreenBufferA
613	200	00034CAC	ScrollConsoleScreenBufferW
614	201	000078F1	SearchPathA
615	202	00034CBE	SearchPathW
616	203	00033ECE	SetCommBreak
617	204	00034A67	SetCommConfig
618	205	00033EDC	SetCommMask
619	206	0002D0E2	SetCommState
620	207	0002D103	SetCommTimeouts
621	208	0002DE19	SetComputerNameA
622	209	00034C49	SetComputerNameW
623	20A	0002EC11	SetConsoleActiveScreenBuffer
624	20B	00034C49	SetConsoleCP
625	20C	0002EC41	SetConsoleCtrlHandler
626	20D	0002E8C5	SetConsoleCursorInfo
627	20E	0002E926	SetConsoleCursorPosition
628	20F	0002E7C8	SetConsoleMode
629	210	00034C49	SetConsoleOutputCP
630	211	0002F2E9	SetConsoleScreenBufferSize
631	212	0002F085	SetConsoleTextAttribute
632	213	0002EA0C	SetConsoleTitleA
633	214	00034C49	SetConsoleTitleW
634	215	0002F3AA	SetConsoleWindowInfo

Ordinal Number	Offset		Function Name
635	216	0000771D	SetCurrentDirectoryA
636	217	00034C49	SetCurrentDirectoryW
637	218	0002ADC5	SetDaylightFlag
638	219	00034964	SetDefaultCommConfigA
639	21A	00034C7F	SetDefaultCommConfigW
640	21B	000290FE	SetEndOfFile
641	21C	0002D626	SetEnvironmentVariableA
642	21D	00034C64	SetEnvironmentVariableW
643	21E	00012434	SetErrorMode
644	21F	00020EB4	SetEvent
645	220	0002E6F3	SetFileApisToANSI
646	221	0002E6FF	SetFileApisToOEM
647	222	0000784C	SetFileAttributesA
648	223	00034C64	SetFileAttributesW
649	224	00006FA0	SetFilePointer
650	225	00007000	SetFileTime
651	226	000325A7	SetHandleContext
652	227	00028F3C	SetHandleCount
653	228	00034C7F	SetHandleInformation
654	229	0000DACA	SetLastError
655	22A	0002D192	SetLocalTime
656	22B	0003EC48	SetLocaleInfoA
657	22C	00034C7F	SetLocaleInfoW
658	22D	00032E27	SetMailslotInfo
659	22E	0002D27D	SetNamedPipeHandleState

Ordinal Number	Offset		Function Name
660	22F	0001CFFE	SetPriorityClass
661	230	00034C64	SetProcessShutdownParameters
662	231	00034C7F	SetProcessWorkingSetSize
663	232	00005694	SetStdHandle
664	233	0002B6CD	SetSystemPowerState
665	234	0002D171	SetSystemTime
666	235	00034C64	SetSystemTimeAdjustment
667	236	00034C91	SetTapeParameters
668	237	00034CC7	SetTapePosition
669	238	000247AC	SetThreadAffinityMask
670	239	0002CEE5	SetThreadContext
671	23A	00034C49	SetThreadLocale
672	23B	0001CF81	SetThreadPriority
673	23C	0002D1D9	SetTimeZoneInformation
674	23D	0002A17D	SetUnhandledExceptionFilter
675	23E	0002DD4A	SetVolumeLabelA
676	23F	00034C64	SetVolumeLabelW
677	240	00033C5A	SetupComm
678	241	0002BCD9	SizeofResource
679	242	00021059	Sleep
680	243	0001657E	SleepEx
681	244	00023F2D	SuspendThread
682	245	0002D1FD	SystemTimeToFileTime
683	246	00034C7F	SystemTimeToTzSpecificLocalTime
684	247	000240B6	TerminateProcess

Ordinal Number	Offset		Function Name
685	248	00023EDE	TerminateThread
686	249	0003788A	Thread32First
687	24A	000378F8	Thread32Next
688	24B	00002DFF	ThunkConnect32
689	24C	0001A05F	TlsAlloc
690	24D	0001A05F	TlsAllocInternal
691	24E	0002A97B	TlsFree
692	24F	0002A97B	TlsFreeInternal
693	250	00022B0D	TlsGetValue
694	251	00022ADF	TlsSetValue
695	252	00036F75	Toolhelp32ReadProcessMemory
696	253	0002D347	TransactNamedPipe
697	254	00033F6C	TransmitCommChar
698	255	00021EF9	UTRegister
699	256	00021F24	UTUnRegister
700	257	00001FEB	UnMapLS
701	258	00001C4E	UnMapSLFixArray
702	259	0002A25F	UnhandledExceptionFilter
703	25A	0001E0ED	UninitializeCriticalSection
704	25B	00028FF3	UnlockFile
705	25C	00034CAC	UnlockFileEx
706	25D	00011750	UnmapViewOfFile
707	25E	00034CBE	UpdateResourceA
708	25F	00034CBE	UpdateResourceW
709	260	00021766	VerLanguageNameA

Ordinal Number	Offset		Function Name
710	261	00034C7F	VerLanguageNameW
711	262	0000DAE8	VirtualAlloc
712	263	00011BEF	VirtualFree
713	264	00034C6D	VirtualLock
714	265	0002CCFB	VirtualProtect
715	266	000269C3	VirtualProtectEx
716	267	0002CD1B	VirtualQuery
717	268	00012B69	VirtualQueryEx
718	269	00034C6D	VirtualUnlock
719	26A	0002D124	WaitCommEvent
720	26B	0002CF0B	WaitForDebugEvent
721	26C	00006E21	WaitForMultipleObjects
722	26D	0000731F	WaitForMultipleObjectsEx
723	26E	0000A83D	WaitForSingleObject
724	26F	00020FD4	WaitForSingleObjectEx
725	270	0003263A	WaitNamedPipeA
726	271	00034C64	WaitNamedPipeW
727	272	00007AEF	WideCharToMultiByte
728	273	0002CFE8	WinExec
729	274	0002E74E	WriteConsoleA
730	275	0002F0D5	WriteConsoleInputA
731	276	00034C9A	WriteConsoleInputW
732	277	0002EC7D	WriteConsoleOutputA
733	278	0002F122	WriteConsoleOutputAttribute
734	279	0002ECD6	WriteConsoleOutputCharacterA

Ordinal Number		Offset	Function Name
735	27A	00034CAC	WriteConsoleOutputCharacterW
736	27B	00034CAC	WriteConsoleOutputW
737	27C	00034CAC	WriteConsoleW
738	27D	0000580D	WriteFile
739	27E	000285DD	WriteFileEx
740	27F	0002DA17	WritePrivateProfileSectionA
741	280	00034C7F	WritePrivateProfileSectionW
742	281	0000762C	WritePrivateProfileStringA
743	282	00034C9A	WritePrivateProfileStringW
744	283	0002DABF	WritePrivateProfileStructA
745	284	00034CAC	WritePrivateProfileStructW
746	285	00022F34	WriteProcessMemory
747	286	0002D98D	WriteProfileSectionA
748	287	00034C64	WriteProfileSectionW
749	288	0002CB75	WriteProfileStringA
750	289	00034C7F	WriteProfileStringW
751	28A	00034CA3	WriteTapemark
752	28B	0003E99A	_DebugOut
753	28C	0003EA4D	_DebugPrintf
754	28D	000072E1	_hread
755	28E	0002CAA0	_hwrite
756	28F	000280CF	_lclose
757	290	0002CA76	_lcreat
758	291	000280E0	_llseek
759	292	000072B7	_lopen

Ordinal Number		Offset	Function Name
760	293	000072E1	_lread
761	294	0002CAA0	_lwrite
762	295	0003EA4D	dprintf
763	296	00007217	lstrcat
764	297	00007217	lstrcatA
765	298	00034C64	lstrcatW
766	299	0000712C	lstrcmp
767	29A	0000712C	lstrcmpA
768	29B	00034C64	lstrcmpW
769	29C	00007166	lstrcmpi
770	29D	00007166	lstrcmpiA
771	29E	00034C64	lstrcmpiW
772	29F	000071A0	lstrcpy
773	2A0	000071A0	lstrcpyA
774	2A1	00034C64	lstrcpyW
775	2A2	000071DA	lstrcpyn
776	2A3	000071DA	lstrcpynA
777	2A4	00034C7F	lstrcpynW
778	2A5	00007251	lstrlen
779	2A6	00007251	lstrlenA
780	2A7	0002B7EC	lstrlenW
1		000013D4	[NONAME]
2		000013D4	[NONAME]
3		000013D4	[NONAME]
4		000013D4	[NONAME]

Ordinal Number	Offset	Function Name
5	000013D4	[NONAME]
6	000013D4	[NONAME]
7	000013D4	[NONAME]
8	000013D4	[NONAME]
9	000013D4	[NONAME]
10	00011C6E	[NONAME]
11	0001F146	[NONAME]
12	0000F3AB	[NONAME]
13	0001D164	[NONAME]
14	0000E6DB	[NONAME]
15	0000A48B	[NONAME]
16	000366EE	[NONAME]
17	00001319	[NONAME]
18	0000C132	[NONAME]
19	0002B73E	[NONAME]
20	000297CC	[NONAME]
21	00029827	[NONAME]
22	00029804	[NONAME]
23	00020E8B	[NONAME]
24	00027B6C	[NONAME]
25	00027E4A	[NONAME]
26	00027F0A	[NONAME]
27	00027A5B	[NONAME]
28	00027A5F	[NONAME]
29	00027A63	[NONAME]

Ordinal Number	Offset	Function Name
30	00027A67	[NONAME]
31	00027EAB	[NONAME]
32	00027BAE	[NONAME]
33	00004966	[NONAME]
34	00026573	[NONAME]
35	00027E6E	[NONAME]
36	00027A57	[NONAME]
37	00027A7E	[NONAME]
38	0000203D	[NONAME]
39	00002074	[NONAME]
40	000017A1	[NONAME]
41	00001677	[NONAME]
42	0000179E	[NONAME]
43	0000165A	[NONAME]
44	0000179B	[NONAME]
45	00001511	[NONAME]
46	00001736	[NONAME]
47	00001798	[NONAME]
48	000022CB	[NONAME]
49	000022F4	[NONAME]
51	000023D8	[NONAME]
52	00037A94	[NONAME]
53	00037ACD	[NONAME]
54	00021E49	[NONAME]
55	00021E7B	[NONAME]

Ordinal Number	Offset	Function Name
56	00003747	[NONAME]
57	0002B76F	[NONAME]
58	0002B7B6	[NONAME]
59	000278B4	[NONAME]
60	000278E5	[NONAME]
61	00027E32	[NONAME]
62	000278CE	[NONAME]
63	00027903	[NONAME]
64	0002792F	[NONAME]
65	00027945	[NONAME]
66	00027FC9	[NONAME]
67	00028010	[NONAME]
68	00002326	[NONAME]
69	00002382	[NONAME]
70	000037BD	[NONAME]
71	00023FCB	[NONAME]
72	00006850	[NONAME]
73	00006864	[NONAME]
74	0002B47C	[NONAME]
75	0002B488	[NONAME]
76	0002B4A8	[NONAME]
77	00006870	[NONAME]
78	00006900	[NONAME]
79	0002B4F8	[NONAME]
80	0002B520	[NONAME]

Ordinal Number	Offset	Function Name
81	0002B548	[NONAME]
82	0002B574	[NONAME]
83	00006958	[NONAME]
84	0002B588	[NONAME]
85	0002B590	[NONAME]
86	00004320	[NONAME]
87	0002A7A8	[NONAME]
88	0002A7E8	[NONAME]
89	000026F4	[NONAME]
90	00002843	[NONAME]
91	00027FE6	[NONAME]
92	0001EBB1	[NONAME]
93	0001C000	[NONAME]
94	0003E98B	[NONAME]
95	0003E965	[NONAME]
96	0003E968	[NONAME]
97	00004230	[NONAME]
98	0000426D	[NONAME]
99	0001BCD0	[NONAME]
100	000204C6	[NONAME]
101	0002930A	[NONAME]

B

The Companion CD-ROM

The CD-ROM contains the examples — along with the compilers and editors necessary to build the examples — for the book *Programming Win32 Under the API* by Pat Villani, ISBN 1-57820-067-9. The compiler is the Free Software Foundation gcc compiler suite, ported to Win32. This compiler is absolutely free and redistributable under the provisions of the GNU Public License (GPL). You can also find this code at `http://www.opensourcedepot.com/`, along with other open source projects, news, links, etc.

When you examine the CD-ROM, you'll note the following directories:

dsassm02	— a Win32 disassembler
Examples	— example files for this book
gcc	— gcc ported to Win32 (this directory is meant to run gcc from CD-ROM)
mingw32	— the Win32 gcc port, installable on your hard drive
Utilities	— a host of convenient utilities
WinVi32	— a vi clone for Win32

You'll also find the README file that contains the ASCII contents of what you are currently reading.

The first directory you should explore is Examples. This directory contains all the example code from the book. The examples are organized into subdirectories that are named after the chapters that the code example comes from, i.e., Chapter1, Chapter4, etc. In each of these subdirectories, you'll find subdirectories that correspond to the code listing, i.e., 4-1, 4-2, etc. So, if you want to play with the code in Listing 4.2 and your CD-ROM is the D: drive, you look at D:\Examples\Chapter4\4-2.

I'm also including a set of tools on this CD-ROM. This way, you don't have to go out and spend hundreds of dollars for a commercial C development package. This is the Free Software Foundation "GNU Compiler Collection" and contains C, C++, Fortran 77, and Objective C compilers for the CRTDLL and MSVCRT environments. You'll find these and instructions on how to install them in the mingw32 directory. Basically, there are two versions: one for each runtime library option, either crtdll.dll or msvcrt.dll. You'll need one of these on a system in order to run a program. Crtdll is on all Win32 systems, but is no longer updated. It is available on platforms such as Windows 3.11/Windows NT 3.5 and platforms that use Win32s. Msvcrt is not guaranteed to be on Windows operating systems, but it is more up-to-date and may offer more features. It handles threading better than crtdll and supplies functions not normally found in crtdll. You'll have to decide which one to use.

If you don't want to install this on your system, you can run the compiler directly from the CD-ROM. Assuming your CD-ROM is your D: drive, you would set your path to point to the CD-ROM with the command C:\> PATH=D:\GCC\BIN;%PATH% in an MS-DOS window. You can then compile any example and any other Win32 code in this window. Depending on your CD-ROM drive speed, this may be slower than running from your hard drive, but it is a quick and easy way to develop C code for Win32.

As you may have noticed while reading the book, I'm an old UNIX hacker. Hence, I grew up with vi and continue to use it. Please, no spam about emacs being better than vi. I have had too many people argue that point with me for over a decade now. I just like vi. Period. Anyway, I've included a version in the directory WinVi32. You can also run this from the CD-ROM environment described earlier.

Finally, the various utilities to dump PE files, disassemble PE files, etc., mentioned in the book are in the Utilities directory. Each of these programs comes with its own installation instructions and you'll find that in the associated zip file.

If you want to keep up on the development of my command shell, go to http://www.opensourcedepot.com/. You can also contact me via email at patv@opensourcedepot.com

---

Index

F

FAT
  areas 43, 49
  attribute bits 54
  directory structure 53
  entry values and meanings 50
  file format 43
  file system 40, 43, 45, 52
  read example 49
  table 107
  write example 50
FAT-12 40, 106–107
FAT-16 106–107
FAT-32 56, 107
  disk format 56
FIFO (First In First Out) 136–137, 158
File Allocation Table
  See FAT
file formats
  COM 57
  EXE 57
  executable 57
  PE 58
file I/O 89–90, 118
  example 119
file systems 40
  overview 37
filenames 106
files 38, 105
  batch 184
  conceptual model 106
  creating 107
  definition 105
  executable 61
  memory-mapped 135, 154
FindFirstFile 116
floppy disk 40, 43–44, 50
  architecture 43
  drives 40

G

gdb 18–19, 21
GetCurrentProcess 130

H

HAL 29–30
handles 90–91, 93, 95, 110, 138, 146
  inheritable 146
hard disk 44
  architecture 44
  partition layout 44
Hardware Abstraction Layer
  See HAL
head movement 43
"Hello World" program 78

I

I/O 94–98, 118
  cancelling operations 110
  console vs. file 94
  synchronous and asynchronous 114, 118
IAT 70
.idata 72
input
  processed 90
Integrated Development Environment (IDE) 163
Intel IA-32 37
interlace 42
International Standards Organization 107
internationalization 166
interprocess communications
  See Chapter 7
ISO-9660 107

J

JCL 1

K

kernel32.dll 4, 6, 34–35, 43
  exports
    See Appendix A
kernels 123–124, 153

GNU 8–10
  compiler 9
GNU gcc compiler 8
GNU Public License (GPL) 184

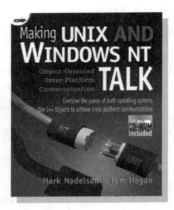

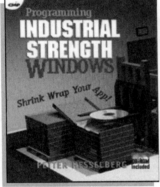

What's on the CD-ROM?

The CD-ROM contains the examples — along with the compilers and editors necessary to build the examples — for the book **Programming Win32 Under the API**. The compiler is the Free Software Foundation gcc compiler suite, ported to Win32. This compiler is absolutely free and redistributable under the provisions of the GNU Public License (GPL). You can also find this code at http://www.opensourcedepot.com/, along with other open source projects, news, links, etc.

When you examine the CD-ROM, you'll note the following directories:

dsassm02	— a Win32 disassembler
Examples	— example files for this book
gcc	— gcc ported to Win32 (this directory is meant to run gcc from CD-ROM)
mingw32	— the Win32 gcc port, installable on your hard drive
Utilities	— a host of convenient utilities
WinVi32	— a vi clone for Win32

For more information on the CD-ROM contents, directory structure, installation, and so forth, see Appendix B (page 217) in the book or the README file on the CD itself. The files were formatted using the Joliet filenaming system.